WOVEN TEXTILE DESIGN

JAN SHENTON

LAURENCE KING

Published in 2014 by
Laurence King Publishing Ltd
361-373 City Road
London EC1V 1LR
Tel: +44 20 7841 6900
Fax: +44 20 7841 6910
e-mail: enquiries@laurenceking.com
www.laurenceking.com

ISBN: 978 1 78067 337 0

A catalogue record for this book is available from the British Library.

Design by Eleanor Ridsdale
Senior editor: Sophie Wise
Printed in China

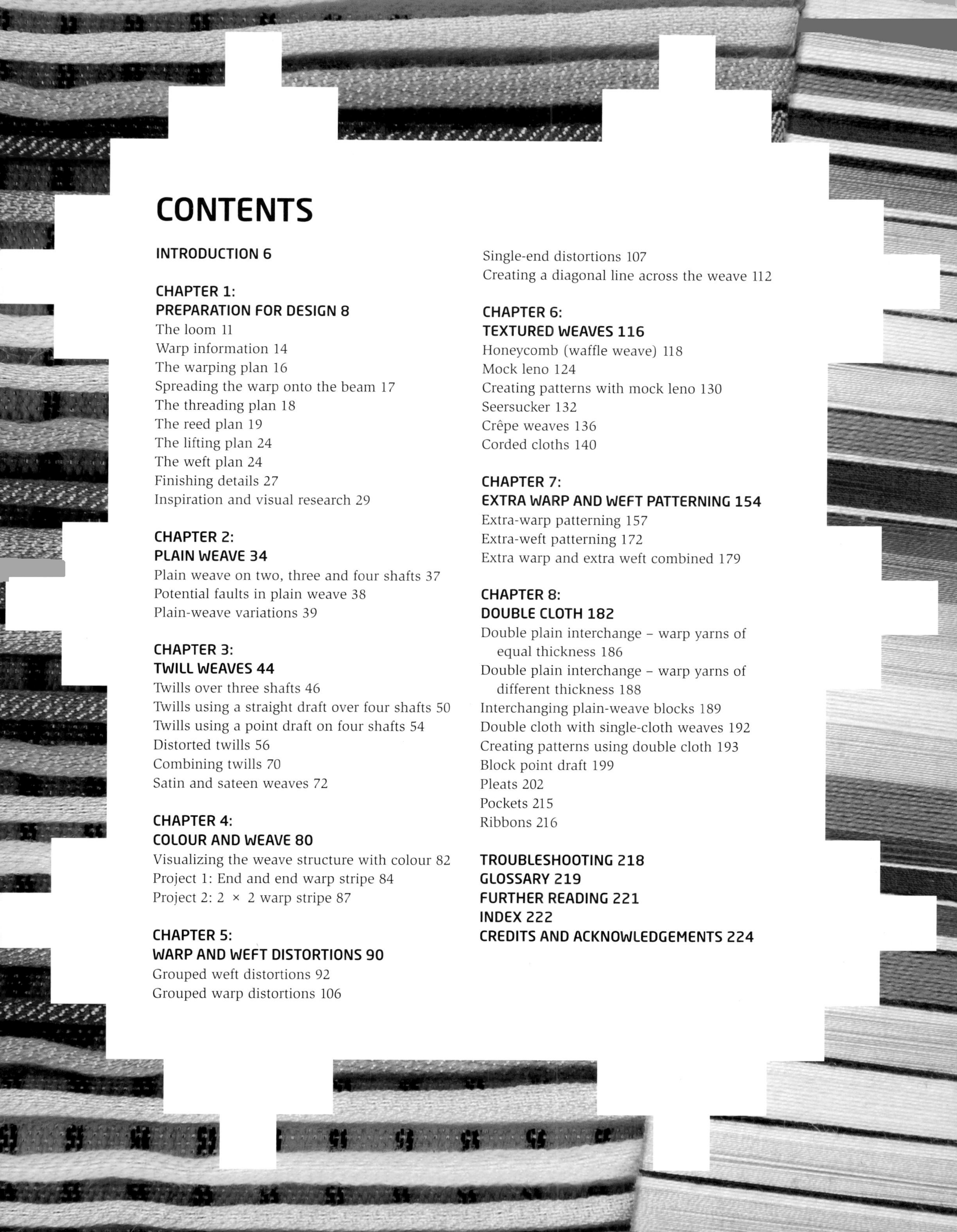

CONTENTS

INTRODUCTION

The purpose of this book is to introduce weavers to basic weave structures and inspire them to use their creative talent so they can develop their own designs and produce beautiful, original fabrics. It encourages experimentation and pushing the boundaries of what is possible. It is often while learning the craft that weavers question those boundaries, take chances and try out different yarns and colour combinations.

There is a natural tendency in novice weavers to experiment broadly, and the more knowledge and experience they have, the easier it will be for them to adapt their weaves for manufacture in the textile industry. The unconventional can be developed and translated for manufacture while still retaining some of its originality.

In these pages, there are tips for identifying mistakes made in the setting-up process and during weaving, as well as simple solutions to these common problems and advice on how to make the job easier. There are definitions of the different terms used in weaving and explanations on how to plan and work through the more complex design processes on point paper.

The woven designs used as examples in this book have been chosen to show the designer what fantastic possibilities there are. The technical specifications accompanying them should help weavers translate their own ideas using their own colour palette and combinations of yarn. The woven examples will not match any of the technical details included exactly, but do show the variety available when experimenting with different yarns and structures. As a weave designer you will want to plan and produce your own original designs. Only by being the originator of an idea can you take complete ownership and have full control of the development of a project.

The mixing of colour when weaving is magical. Even with the simplest of structures, weaving is a unique way of blending colour. The use of very fine yarns with contrasting colours in the warp and weft means the fabric will change colour when the light catches it – sometimes the warp colour is more obvious, sometimes the weft colour is, and sometimes there is an even mix of the two. If thicker yarns in contrasting colours are used, the individual threads and colours are more visible, and if producing a single-coloured cloth, the structure used will add surface interest.

Technical knowledge and hands-on experience of setting up the loom, and of how different structures are created by actually making them, will help those going into the industry understand the manufacturing process. Some weavers will continue to produce their own collections as bespoke pieces; others will create sample designs for sale to the industry; some will work in the industry, and others will teach. The actual practice of weaving by hand is the best way to understand and to discover how to develop new ideas. Whatever your future is as a weaver, the information included in this book will help you to develop independently and creatively.

Example of reverse twill using nylon cord in warp and weft.

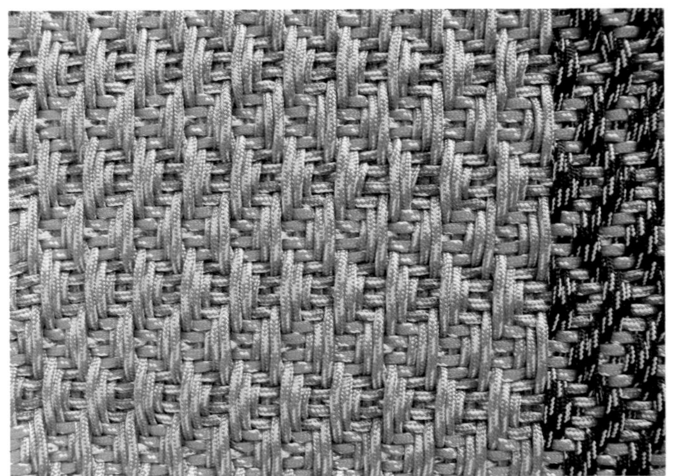

Plain weave examples using nylon monofilament and nylon cord.

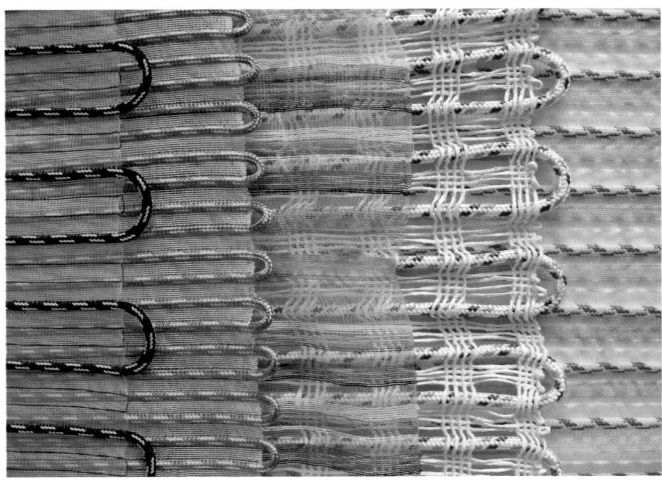

Skirt constructed in twill weave using leather strips from Jonathan Saunders's AW2012 collection.

Fluro tangerine and black weave from Willow's AW2012 collection 'Monarch Movement'.

1
PREPARATION FOR DESIGN

PREPARATION FOR DESIGN

Woven fabric is a constructed cloth typically made from two sets of yarn – the **warp**, which goes through the loom vertically, and the **weft**, which passes between the warp threads horizontally.

All information concerning the making of a woven cloth must be recorded on a specification, or work, sheet before the preparation of yarn, setting up the loom and actual weaving can take place. The cloth construction, sequence of threading and the order of shaft movement are recorded in diagrammatic form to enable easy translation.

It is more natural for a designer to follow visual instructions in a graphic form, than to read through a script, so information is normally recorded on point paper (graph paper). The specification sheet can then be consulted at a later date for a variety of situations:

- To reproduce an identical cloth.
- As a requirement as part of a competition entry.
- To accompany a design that is sold to industry.

It is fatal to rely on memory, so you need to record full details while you are planning, and then add any additional information while you are weaving, such as new lifting plans or weft yarn combinations.

The information recorded on the specification sheet includes the **warping plan**, **threading plan**, **reed plan**, **lifting plan** and **weft plan**. The sheet may also include such additional information as dyeing calculations, finishing details and the weight of the cloth.

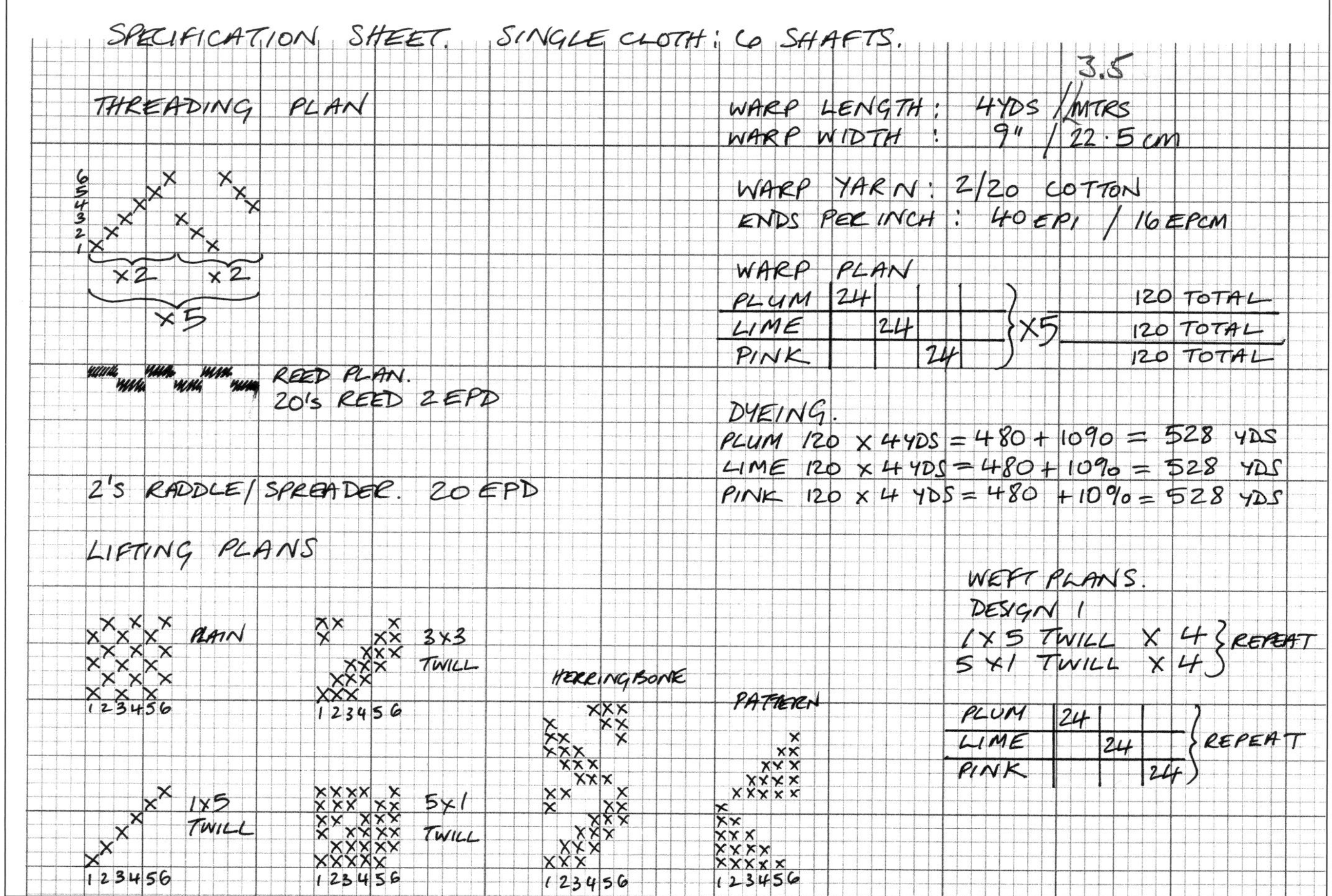

Example of a specification sheet including all the details and information needed to produce the woven fabric.

THE LOOM

There are several types of hand loom, with different methods and mechanisms for raising the shafts, either with your hands or your feet. Hand-operated looms can have as few as two shafts and as many as 24 or more. When using table looms, you use your hands to raise the shafts using levers or pulleys, as well as to insert the weft yarn. Some designers prefer this method as it allows time for reflection and consideration of the design. With treadle looms, several pedals are used to raise, and in some cases lower, the shafts, leaving the hands free to deal with the weft threads. A dobby loom has only one pedal, with a peg plan being used to control which shafts are lifted.

There are also different ways of making the warp, transferring it onto the loom and 'dressing' the loom. You will have been shown a particular system in preparing the loom. No set of instructions will be exactly the same, and each method works beautifully. Rather than confuse matters by giving alternating advice, this book will provide tips throughout each chapter that will be appropriate to all systems, and will hopefully help to solve the minor problems that can arise during the setting up of the loom.

An eight-shaft table loom. This example has two warp beams at the back. The shafts are raised by depressing levers on the left and the right of the loom.

A peg plan used on a dobby loom. This example is for 16 shafts.

A treadle loom with six shafts and six pedals. The shafts in this example are raised by depressing the pedals. Each pedal can be tied from one to five shafts depending on the pattern or structure of the fabric.

A 16-shaft dobby loom. This is operated by a single pedal that, when depressed, engages with the mechanism programmed by the peg plan.

A 24-shaft electronic dobby loom. The lifting plan is entered using a key pad. Two pedals are used to raise the shafts and to change to the next pattern row.

WARP INFORMATION

The choice of warp yarn is dependent on the type of finish you are hoping to achieve. Typically the yarn must be of a suitable strength to undergo a consistent tight tension, and to avoid broken threads as you weave. You will have established from your initial visual research the surface quality you require – whether it is smooth, textured or a combination; single-colour or striped; dense, evenly sett or open. The warp threads are usually called ends. Once you have made your choice then the following information should be recorded on the specification sheet:

- The type of yarn, e.g. silk, wool, cotton, viscose.
- The count of the yarn. In twisted yarns, this is indicated by a number such as 2/30's or 4/4's or 3/12's; the first figure gives the number of strands in the thread, and the second number, the thickness of each strand. Filament yarns usually have one number indicating how many strands make up the thread. The individual strands are called trams, so a 12-tram filament silk has 12 strands forming the one thread.
- The correct density of cloth. To obtain this you will need to calculate the number of ends per cm/inch. There is a basic technique using a ruler. The yarn is wrapped around the ruler evenly, leaving a space that is the same thickness as the yarn. This will be filled by the weft yarn when weaving. Normally 2.5cm (1in) is a sufficient distance to wrap.
- The width of the warp, which is needed to ensure that the warp is placed centrally on the beam, and will also indicate the width of the cloth when woven.
- The length of the warp, which is needed to indicate how much you intend to weave. There will be wastage from the start of the weaving (due to tying the warp threads onto the front beam), at the end of the warp (where yarn is unable to be woven as it is attached to the back beam) and through the shafts.
- The total number of ends. This is needed to indicate how many threads to wind to achieve the correct width of fabric.
- A warping plan.

When calculating the length of the warp, once you have decided how much you want to weave, add on an extra metre/yard. This will cover tying on, end-of-weave wastage, experimentation and take-up by the weft. As you weave, the warp threads go over and under the weft, and so will need to cover more distance.

To ensure that the yarn you plan to use in the warp is strong enough to undergo tensioning, you will need to test it. Unwind a length of yarn measuring about 50cm (20in). With one end in your left hand and the other in your right, pull it to a tight tension. Try this a few times. If the yarn breaks, avoid using it in your warp because you will have problems with broken ends as you weave.

Warp yarn wrapped evenly around a ruler over 2.5cm (1in) to calculate how many ends per cm (inch) to use the yarn in the warp.

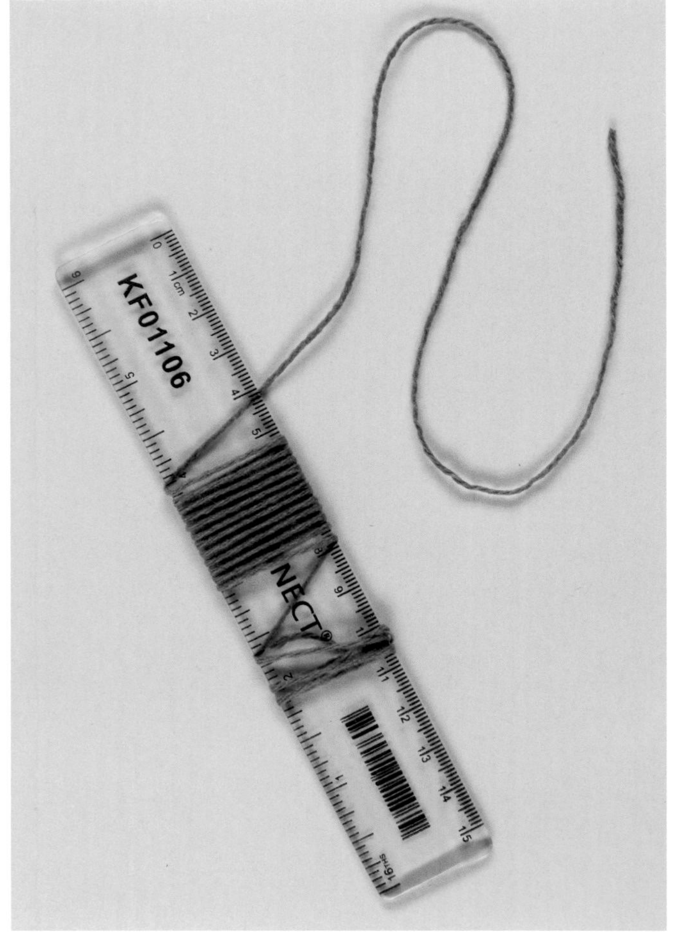

IF YOU ARE USING TEXTURED, HAIRY OR WOOLLEN YARNS IN YOUR WARP THEN MAKE SURE THAT THEY ARE NOT TOO CLOSELY SETT. WHEN CALCULATING YOUR ENDS PER CM/INCH, GIVE ENOUGH SPACE TO EACH END TO AVOID RUBBING AND WEAKENING AS YOU WEAVE.

THE WARPING PLAN

The warping plan is needed to show how many ends you need to wind for your warp to achieve the required width and design. It is an easy-to-read chart that will tell you how many ends to wind for each colour/yarn and in what order. The example shown here uses a single type of yarn in three different colours and features one **repeat**. You repeat the plan to achieve the desired width.

Warping plan

Yarn type and colour						
2/60 silk pink				8		
2/60 silk olive		8				8
2/60 silk silver	48		12		12	

There are 96 ends in this repeat. If the 2/60 silk is 19 ends per cm (48 ends per inch) then the repeat is 5cm (2in) wide. Repeat five times and the weave is 25cm (10in) wide.

Read the columns in turn, and begin with winding 48 silver ends. Once you have wound the 48th end, break this yarn off and tie in the next colour (olive), wind eight ends and so on.

If you are producing a design that has a non-repeating composition, then a table showing the complete warp design for the width of the cloth should be created.

Above: Upright warping mill. The warp yarn is wrapped around the mill in a spiral to the pre-determined length.

Below: Detail of the warping posts at the top of the warping mill. The warp yarn is wound to form a cross between the second and third post.

SPREADING THE WARP ONTO THE BEAM

There are different methods of transferring your warp onto the beam, but the principles are the same. Your warp must be placed centrally on the back beam, and be spread evenly across the prescribed width of the cloth design to maintain an even tension across the warp. The spreader or raddle will help control the warp. It resembles a large-scale comb that has gaps or dents of equal size, divided by metal bars or wooden rods through which the ends are passed. A 2's spreader (or 2-inch spreader) will have 2 dents to an inch.

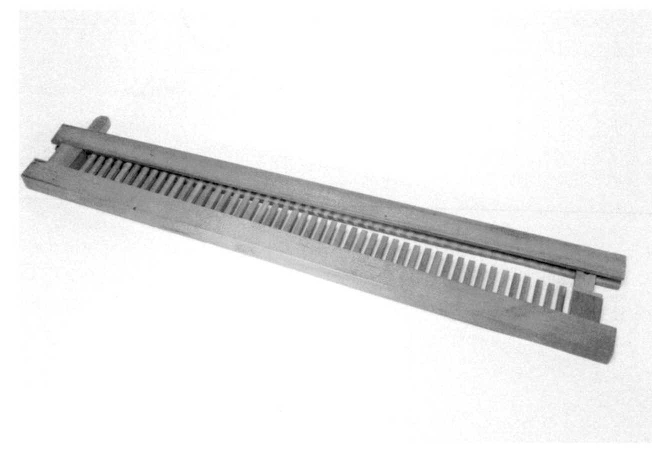

Above: Wooden raddle (spreader).

Divide the number of warp ends per cm/inch by the number of dents (gaps) in the spreader. The resulting number will be how many ends of warp need to be placed into each dent (gap).

For example:

Warp yarn is 48 ends per inch.
Using a 2's spreader divide 48 by 2 = 24 ends per dent

It is essential to keep an even tension across the warp as it is wound onto the beam.

Below: The warp yarn is divided equally into the dents of the raddle before winding the warp onto the beam.

THE THREADING PLAN

The threading plan, or 'draft', indicates which thread is going onto which shaft and in what order. Shaft 1 is closest to you as you thread up. Each shaft is a frame that holds the **heddles**, which can be made from wire or strong yarn. Each heddle has an eye in its centre through which individual threads are passed using a tool called a 'threading hook'.

A colour or symbol can be used to identify each different end on the plan if you are using a combination of yarns or colours.

The threading plan is read from left to right, and each X represents a warp end. In the example here, the first end is thread onto shaft 1, the second onto shaft 2 and so on. This example is commonly known as a **straight draft** (see p.50) and is a repeat of six ends using six shafts.

Threading plan

Shaft						
6						X
5					X	
4				X		
3			X			
2		X				
1	X					

Shafts with wire heddles.

Wire heddles.

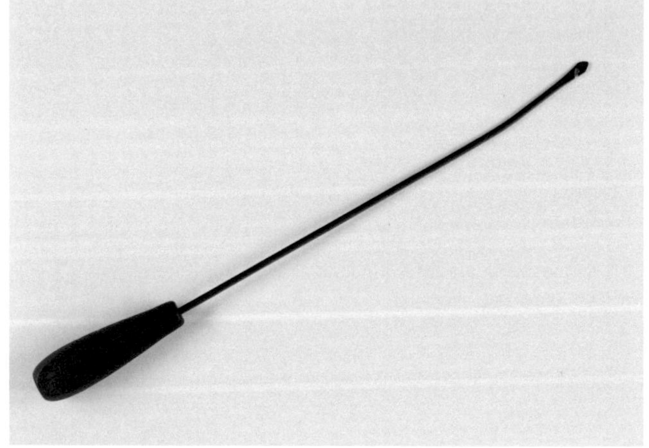

Threading hook.

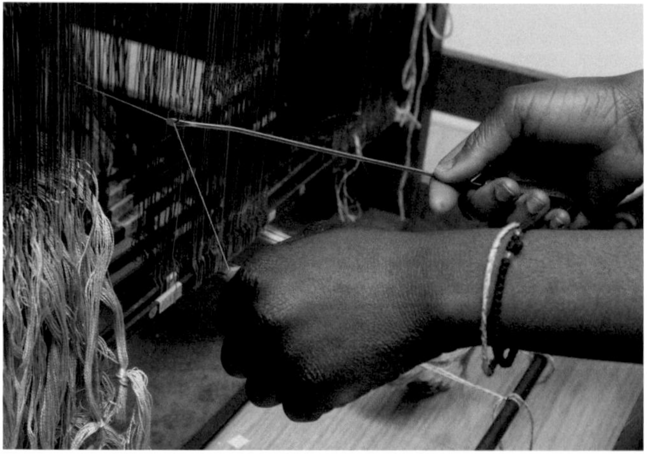

Pulling the warp yarn through the eye in the heddle with a threading hook.

THE REED PLAN

After completing the threading of the warp ends onto the shafts, they are then passed through a **reed** using a reed hook. The reed is a much finer version of the spreader/raddle with metal intersections, and is used to divide the warp yarn evenly across the front of the loom. The gaps in between each metal intersection are also called 'dents'. Ideally two ends are threaded through each dent to create a smooth even cloth, so calculating which reed to use is easy. Just divide your ends per cm/inch by two, and the resulting number is the reed to use.

For example: 48 ends per inch ÷ 2 = 24's reed (24-dent reed; 24 dents to the inch)

You can use more open reeds such as a 16's with 3epd (ends per dent), a 12's with 4epd or an 8's at 6epd. The fewer dents to the cm/inch there are, the greater the likelihood of a natural line or gap appearing in the finished cloth.

When the denting is complete, the reed is placed inside a frame known as the **sley** (or batten/beater). This moves backward and forward, and is used to **beat** the weft yarn into place when weaving.

If a design feature such as spacing and cramming is required, then you must produce a **denting plan**.

A reed hook.

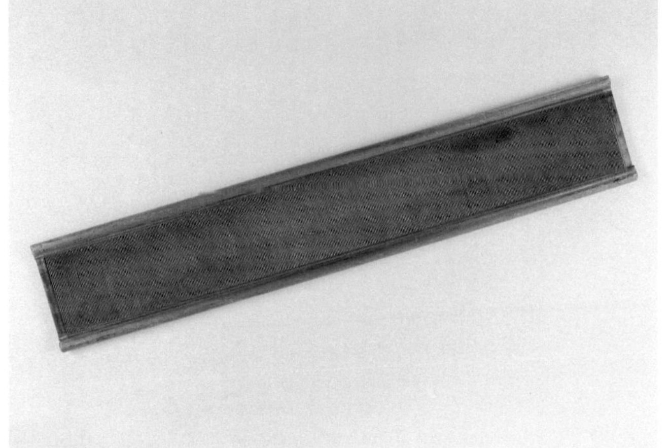

A reed.

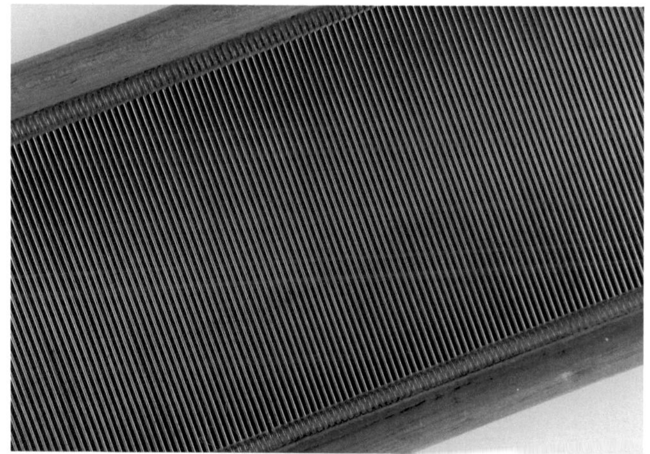

A close-up of the wires separating the dents in the reed.

A spaced and crammed denting plan

The number in each box indicates how many threads are in each dent. The more threads, the denser the cloth; the fewer threads, the more open the cloth.

4	4	4	4	3	3	3	3	2	2	2	1	1	1	1	1	1	2	2	2	3	3	3	3

THE REED PLAN WITH THE THREADING PLAN

On your point paper, you can colour in the squares below the threading plan to indicate how many threads are in each dent in the reed that you are using. Use this simple but effective method of recording the information, which is particularly helpful whenever you are spacing or cramming, or are using yarns with different setts. (The yarn sett is the density of yarn in 1 cm/inch.)

A reed plan with the threading plan: regular denting

Shaft																		
6						X						X						X
5					X						X						X	
4				X						X						X		
3			X						X						X			
2		X						X						X				
1	X						X						X					
Reed plan	■	■			■	■			■	■			■	■			■	■
			■	■			■	■			■	■			■	■		

A reed plan with the threading plan: spacing and cramming

Shaft																		
6						X						X						X
5					X						X						X	
4				X						X						X		
3			X						X						X			
2		X						X						X				
1	X						X						X					
Reed plan	■		■		■		■	■			■	■				■	■	■
		■		■		■			■	■			■	■	■			

ENSURE THAT AN OPEN REED IS USED WHEN USING TEXTURED, THICK OR HAIRY YARNS, AS THE WIRE INTERSECTIONS CAN RUB AND WEAKEN THEM IF SETT TOO CLOSELY, RESULTING IN BROKEN ENDS.

TENSIONING THE WARP YARN

Once the denting is complete, and before you can start weaving, the next step is to secure the warp ends to create a tight, even tension through the warp. This is achieved by tying the warp ends to the stick attached to the front beam on the loom.

- It is very important to create an even tension across the warp.
- Odd loose ends may catch on the shuttle when weaving, causing them to break.
- If there are large sections of loosely tensioned warp, the weft yarn will not beat down evenly across the weaving.
- Loose threads may not be raised high enough by the shuttle, causing visible mistakes in the weaving.

Tying on the warp yarn in a single knot.

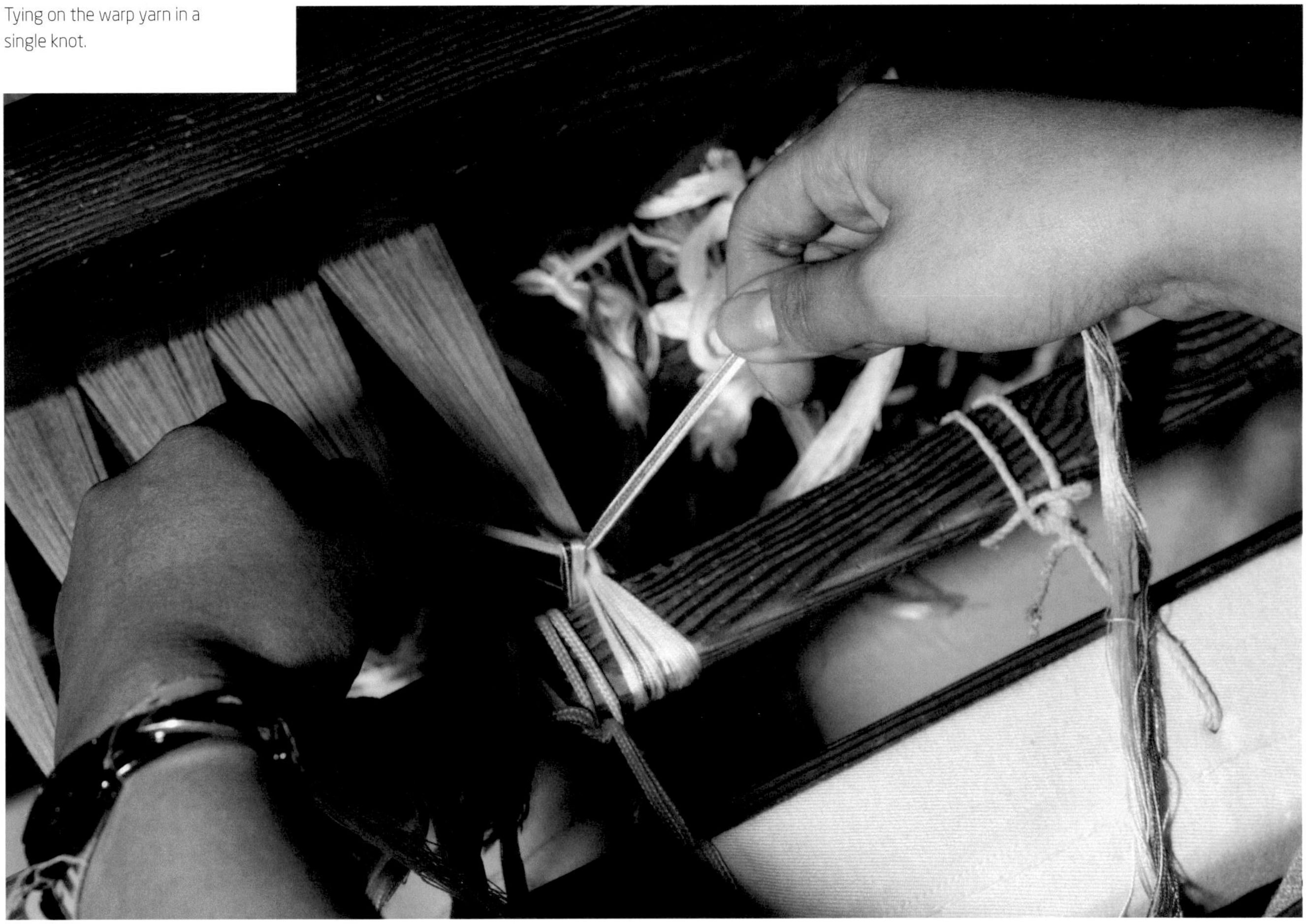

Securing the warp yarn, keeping the tension even.

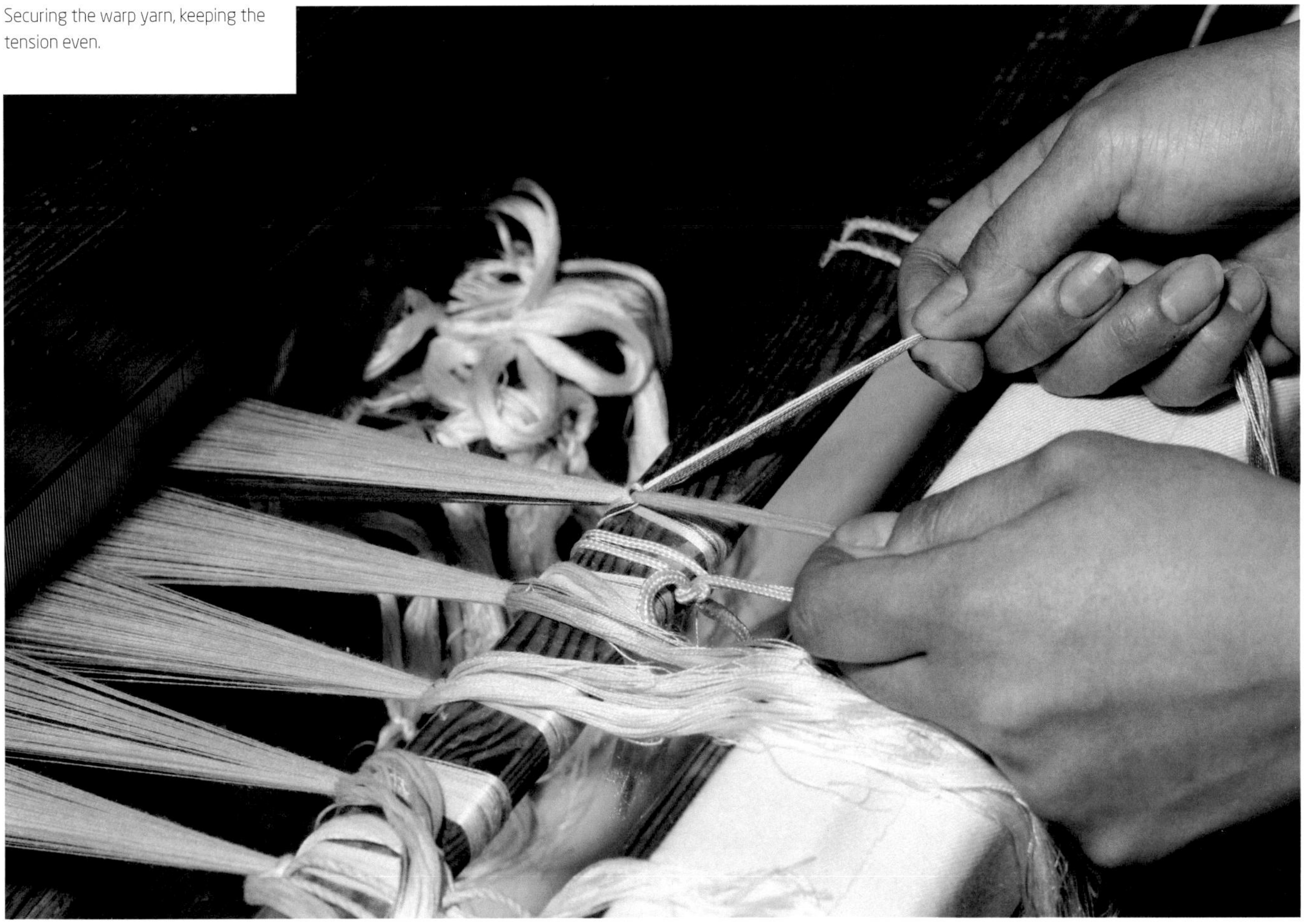

TYING ON A TRADITIONAL YARN

STEP 1

Starting either on the left or the right of the dented warp yarn, take a bundle of consecutive ends – about 2.5cm (1in) across. Smooth the yarn by pulling through any loose ends.

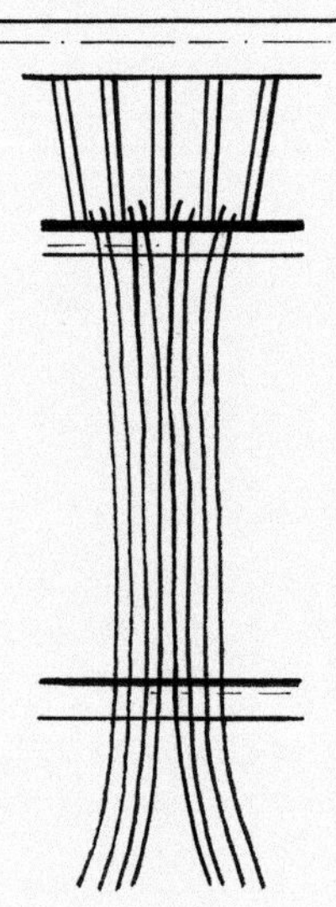

STEP 2

Split the bundle in half – two 1.25cm (½in) bundles. Take the bundles over the stick and bring them up on either side of the original bundle.

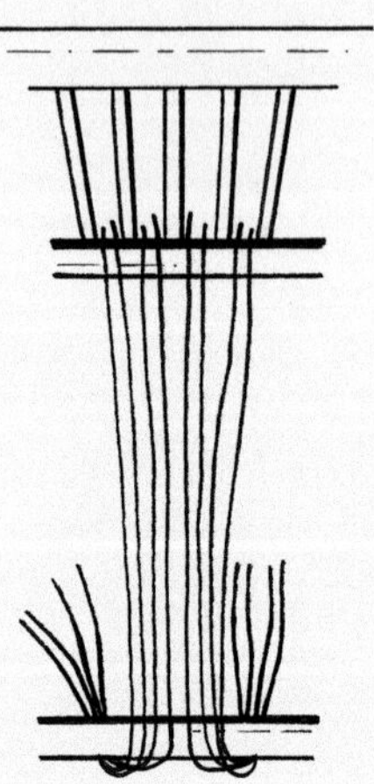

STEP 3

Tie them in a single knot on top of the original bundle.

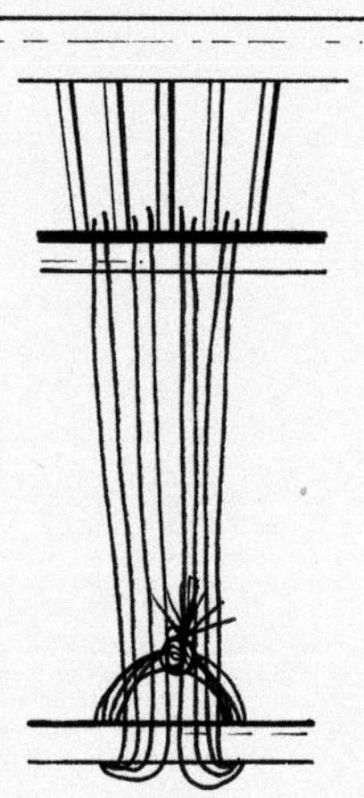

STEP 4

Repeat the process across the width of the warp. Starting in the centre, tighten the single knot, and tie another knot on top.

Go to the group on the left and tie in the same way. Now go to the right of the centre and tie in the same way. Repeat by alternating each side of the centre until the warp is secure.

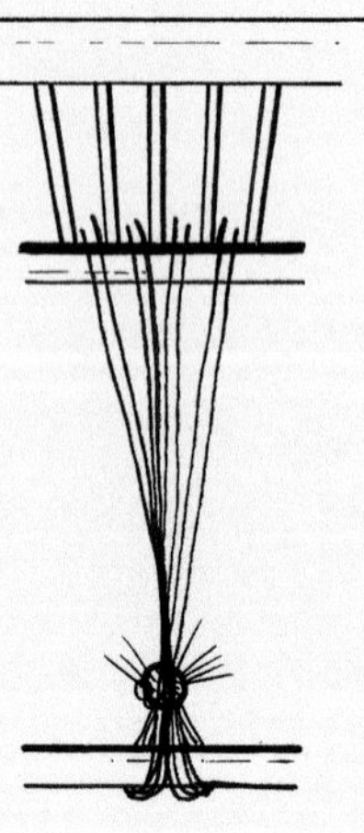

SLIGHTLY WET FINGERS WILL GIVE BETTER FRICTION.

TYING ON A SLIPPERY YARN

Nylon monofilament, silk filament and shiny viscose yarns are not held well with a knot – they tend to slip and release the tension achieved before the process is complete. The following method will give an even tension.

STEP 1

Starting either on the left or the right of the dented warp yarn, take a bundle of consecutive ends – about 2.5cm (1in) across. Smooth the yarn by pulling through any loose ends.

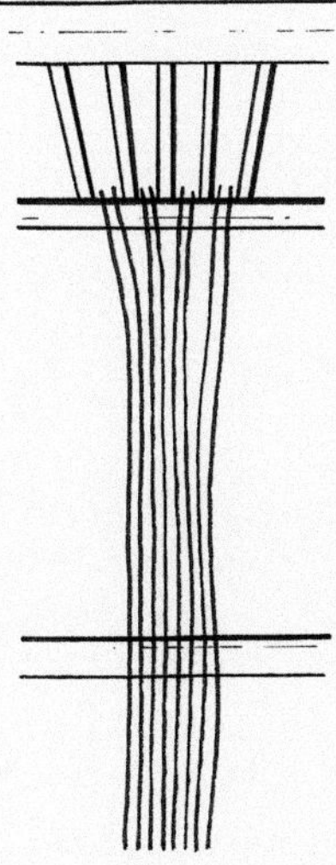

STEP 2

Keeping a good tension, tie a knot in the end of the bundle. Repeat across the width of the warp.

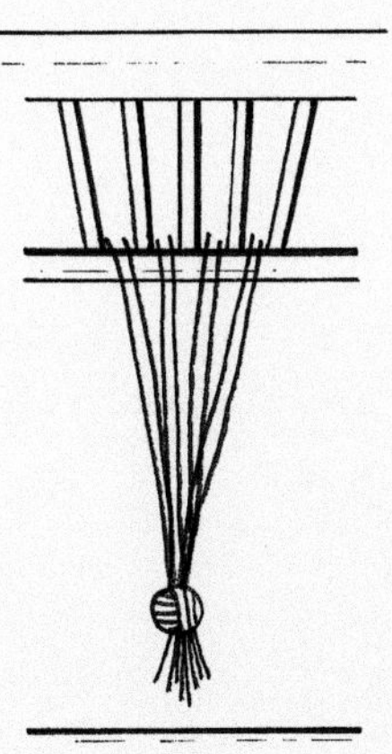

THE KNOT ON EACH BUNDLE SHOULD BE APPROXIMATELY 5CM (2IN) AWAY FROM THE STICK TO ALLOW FOR ANY ADJUSTMENTS.

STEP 3

Tie a length of strong cord to the stick to the left of where the warp yarn has been dented – you will need enough cord to go through each bundle and around the stick in turn until you reach the last bundle.

Pass the longest end through the first bundle of yarn above the knot.

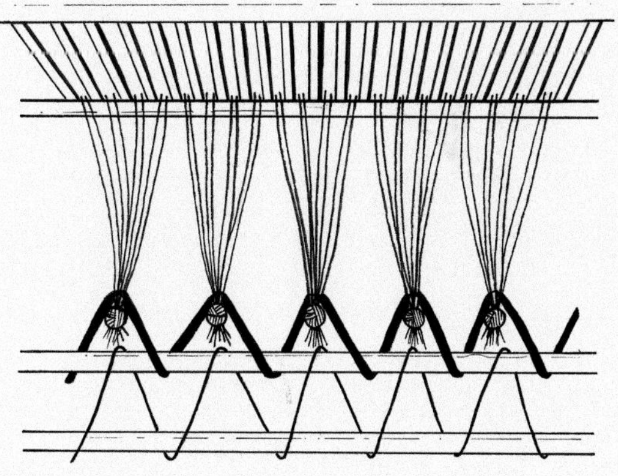

Take the cord over and under the stick and through the next bundle of yarn. Pull the cord to achieve an even tension in each bundle as you go.

Repeat to the end and tie off the cord around the stick.

THE LIFTING PLAN

This shows which shafts are to be lifted and in which order. There should be a lifting plan for each design that you weave. When experimenting or combining different plans, write down the order in which you lift the shafts to give a new lifting plan.

In the example here, the numbers on the left are the sequence of the pattern. The numbers along the bottom relate to the number of shafts. The X indicates that a shaft is to be lifted. Each individual weft thread is known as a **pick**. This is a **plain-weave** structure with repeats over two weft picks.

When weaving, shafts 1, 3 and 5 are lifted and a weft pick is inserted and placed in position by the reed. The shafts are lowered, shafts 2, 4 and 6 are lifted, then a weft pick is inserted and placed in position by the reed. Repeat this process and you have a plain-weave cloth, the simplest structure in woven cloth.

THE WEFT PLAN

If more than one type or colour of yarn is being used in the weft then a weft plan will record what yarns you have used, and in what order. It is a good idea to record the sequence as you weave each design.

USING THE WEFT YARN

The selected weft yarn is wound onto a bobbin using a bobbin winder. This is then placed into a shuttle. Following the lifting plan sequence, lift the shafts and pass the shuttle through the raised warp threads, allowing the yarn to unwind from the bobbin across the width of the cloth. Lower the shafts and beat the weft into place using the reed and repeat the action through the lifting sequence. Try to get into a regular rhythm while weaving. Irregular pressure when beating the weft into place will be visible.

There are several types of shuttle, the most common being a boat or roller shuttle. These will easily accommodate most yarns, but if a particularly thick yarn is being used then a stick shuttle is more convenient.

You may need to record how many picks per cm/inch there are in your weave design on the specification sheet. A picking glass (magnifier) can be used to count the number of threads once the cloth is removed from the loom.

A lifting plan

Lifting sequence							
2		X		X		X	
1	X		X		X		
	1	2	3	4	5	6	Shaft

A weft plan

Type of yarn																	
2/30 silk blue	8						4						2				
2/60 silk olive			8						4						2		
2/60 silk white					8						4						2
Silk noil		1		1		1		1		1		1		1		1	

Front view, from top to bottom: stick shuttle, roller shuttle, boat shuttle.

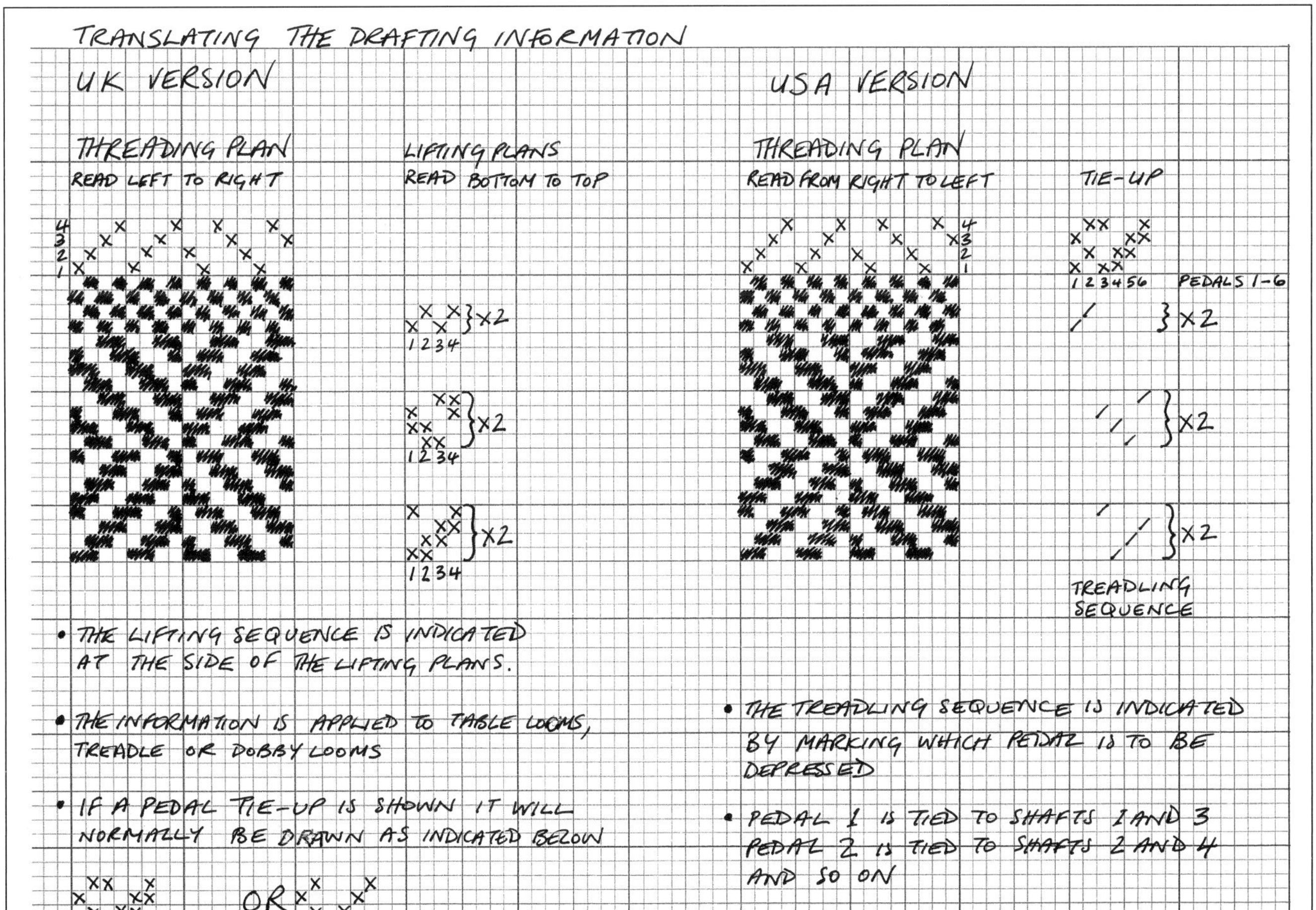

TRANSLATING THE DRAFTING INFORMATION

UK VERSION

THREADING PLAN
READ LEFT TO RIGHT

LIFTING PLANS
READ BOTTOM TO TOP

×2
1234
×2
1234
×2
1234

USA VERSION

THREADING PLAN
READ FROM RIGHT TO LEFT

TIE-UP
123456 PEDALS 1–6

×2
×2
×2

TREADLING SEQUENCE

- THE LIFTING SEQUENCE IS INDICATED AT THE SIDE OF THE LIFTING PLANS.
- THE INFORMATION IS APPLIED TO TABLE LOOMS, TREADLE OR DOBBY LOOMS
- IF A PEDAL TIE-UP IS SHOWN IT WILL NORMALLY BE DRAWN AS INDICATED BELOW

OR

123456 → PEDALS ← 123456

- THE TREADLING SEQUENCE IS INDICATED BY MARKING WHICH PEDAL IS TO BE DEPRESSED
- PEDAL 1 IS TIED TO SHAFTS 1 AND 3
PEDAL 2 IS TIED TO SHAFTS 2 AND 4
AND SO ON

WINDING THE BOBBIN FOR USE IN A ROLLER OR BOAT SHUTTLE

STEP 1

Place the bobbin securely on the long metal pin on the bobbin winder.

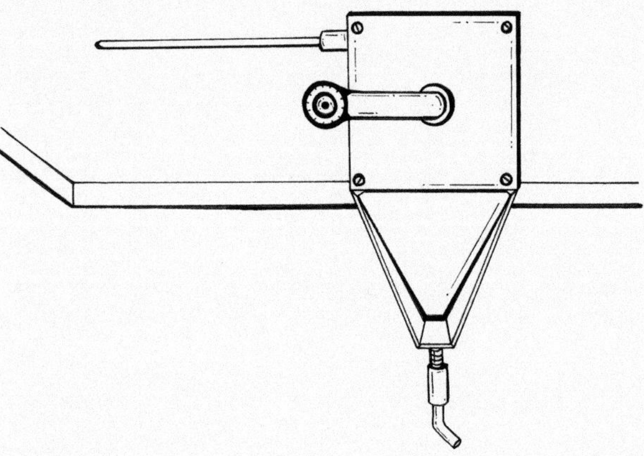

STEP 2

Wrap the yarn around the bobbin by hand for a few turns until it is secure.

Hold the thread and begin to wind the yarn slowly around the bobbin using the handle, which turns in a clockwise direction. Begin by winding a section of yarn at one end of the bobbin – try not to get too near the edge as the yarn may fall away from the end of the bobbin when weaving. Start either on the left or right.

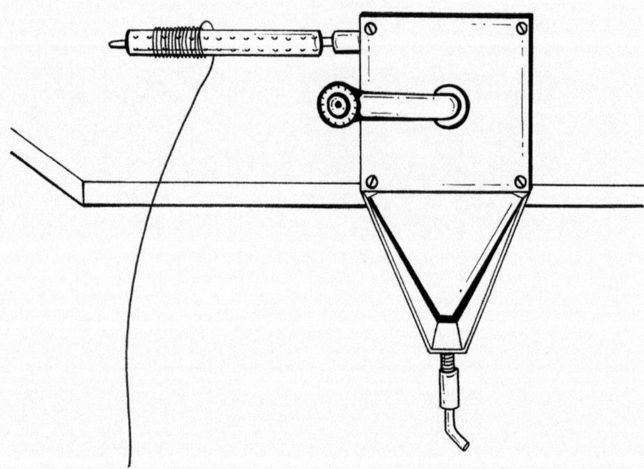

STEP 3

After this, wind another section of yarn onto the opposite end of the bobbin.

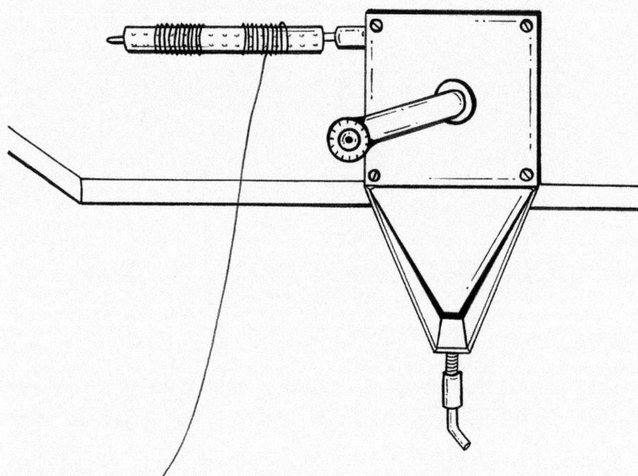

STEP 4

Once the two ends have been wound, fill in the centre evenly until a torpedo shape is made. As you become more confident and proficient you will find that you can go at a faster speed when winding your bobbins.

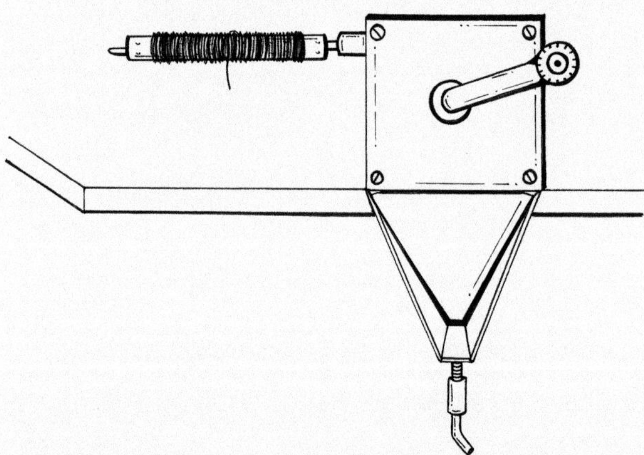

Tension: Try to keep a firm tension when you are winding the bobbin.

- If you wind the yarn too loosely it may fall away from the ends of the bobbin when weaving.
- If you wind the yarn too tightly it may cut into the earlier layers and not be able to be released smoothly when weaving.

Thick yarns: If you are using a particularly thick yarn in the weft, then you will not be able to wind a great deal of the yarn onto a bobbin before the torpedo shape becomes too fat to sit in the roller or boat shuttle.
Try using a stick shuttle, as this will accommodate more yarn.

FINISHING DETAILS

When you have completed the weaving, you may wish to finish the fabric either by:

- Steam pressing.
- Gentle hand washing.
- Milling/scouring by hand.
- Machine washing.
- Heat pressing.

If you do so, then you need to record certain details before you commence the process. When the samples are off the loom, measure the width and length of each piece, and weigh them individually. Repeat the process after finishing. This will allow you to make note of any shrinkage that takes place and to what percentage. If you machine wash the fabric, then it is very important to record the temperature and programme used, particularly when using different types of wool as well as elastic and shrink yarns.

CLOTH WEIGHT

Occasionally you may be asked to provide the weight of your cloth, either as a requirement for a competition entry, or by someone in the textile industry. This will give an indication of whether the cloth is lightweight or heavy.

1. Measure the length and width of the sample and calculate the area.

Length × width = area

2. Weigh the sample in grams/ounces.

3. Calculate the cloth weight per square metre/yard by following either of the equations below.

METRIC CALCULATION EXAMPLE

10,000 square cm = 1 square m

The area of the sample is 26 30cm = 780 square cm

The sample weighs 3g

The weight per square metre: $^3/_{780}$ × 10,000 = 38.46

The weight of the cloth per square metre is 38.5g

IMPERIAL CALCULATION EXAMPLE

1,296 square in = 1 square yd

The area of the sample is 10 × 12in = 120 square in

The sample weighs 2oz

The weight per square yard: $^2/_{120}$ × 1,296 = 21.6

The weight of the cloth per square yard is 21½oz

DYEING

You will have more control over your design decisions if you are in a position to dye your own yarns. You will need to calculate the amount of yarn that you should dye for each colour in your warp, which will ensure that you have enough for the proposed plan. If you do not dye enough the first time round, you will never achieve exactly the same shade or tone, no matter how closely you follow your original recipe.

The calculation:

Multiply the number of warp ends for each colour by the warp length and add on 10 per cent to cover shrinkage or breakage.

Example:

Red $^{2}/_{30}$ cotton: 40 ends × 4m/yd = 160m/yd + 10% = 176m/yd

If the colour is also needed for use in the weft then additional metres/yardage can be added. This is calculated by multiplying the picks per cm/inch by the width of the cloth and the length of the design. The picks per cm/inch depend on the structure you are using, but normally a plain-weave structure will be the same number of picks per cm/inch as ends per cm/inch using the same yarn.

Example if the design uses one weft colour:

Red $^{2}/_{30}$ cotton: 16 picks × 25cm wide × 30cm long = 12,000 ÷ 100 = 120m

(40 picks x 10in wide × 12in long = 4,800in ÷ 36 =

133$^{1}/_{3}$yd)

When using more than one colour in the design, then from the original calculation, estimate the percentage of each colour you intend to use.

If you are experimenting, then use your inspirational work to judge how much or little you may use.

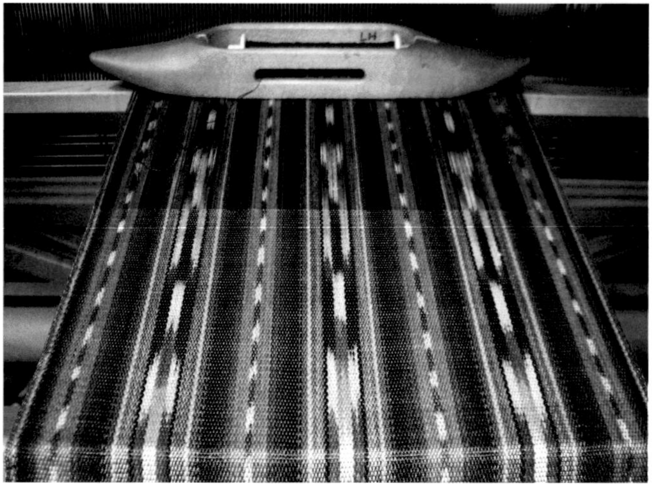

Example of tie-dyed warp woven in plain weave. Smaill sections of the warp are wound separately and tie-dyed.

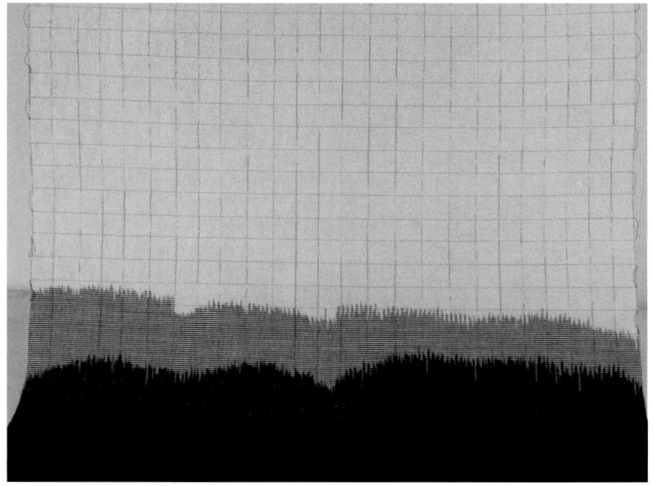

Example of dip-dyed warp. The varied grey check is created by dip-dyeing the hank and using it in the warp and the weft.

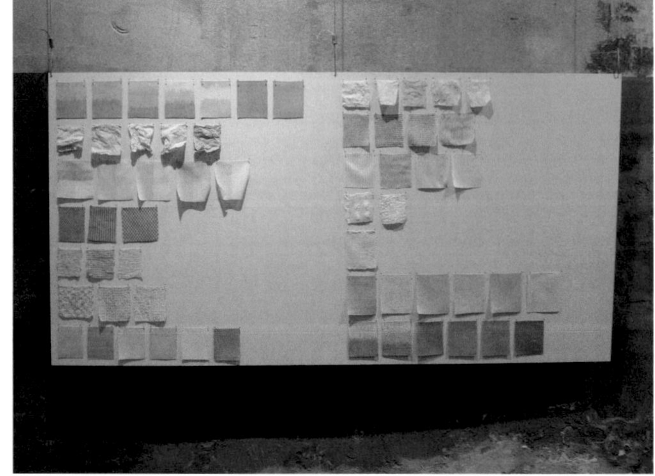

A collection of experiments using plain weave with a variety of warp and weft yarns and dyeing techniques.

INSPIRATION AND VISUAL RESEARCH

There are several decisions to make before you start weaving, such as what yarn to use with what weave structure, what colours and in what proportion – will it be a plain warp or striped; will the required effect be created through texture, colour or both?

Giving consideration to these elements will help you to produce woven fabrics that are considered and designed for their function, be it for practical use or for decoration. Getting the colour, yarn and structure right is essential to creating the most beautiful and exciting fabric designs, and it also makes the process much more satisfying for the weaver.

Inspiration comes in many forms, and helps you to make the initial decisions when designing your fabric.

RECORDING INFORMATION

Drawing gives the most individual and original response to your subject matter – it is your choice as to what you record for development into woven fabric designs. The information that you record can be diagrammatical, realistic or impressionistic. Drawing is your personal interpretation of what is before you, and it is the quality of that information that is important when recording things that excite you. Have confidence!

You can use whatever medium or technique best suits you. Your interpretation may well be inspired by the subject. You can use line, colour, texture or collage, make individual studies or compositions, work on a small or large scale, and be delicate or dynamic.

Photography is another way of recording your inspiration and will support your drawing in enabling you to develop ideas from pictures as the project progresses. Proportion, colour and composition are all important considerations when using your camera.

Above: Inspirational drawings of vegetables with woven designs.

Below: Inspirational drawings using books and dolls. Also shows yarn wrap, fashion visualization and the woven fabric design.

Top: Inspirational imagery of natural forms with the woven fabric design.

Middle left: The circus as inspiration with the woven fabric design.

Middle right: Floral inspiration and design development with the woven fabric design.

Bottom: The circus as inspiration with the woven fabric design.

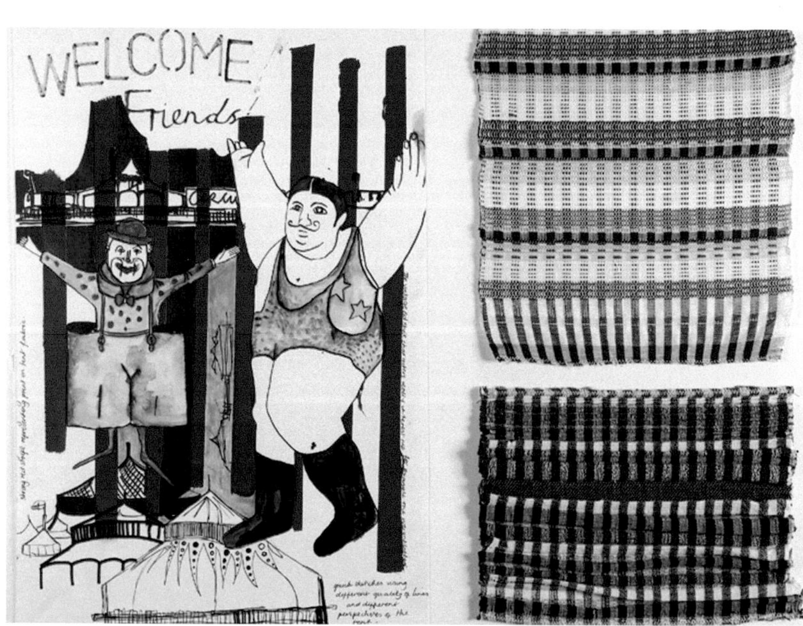

THEMES AND INSPIRATION

You may be given a theme or topic, or you may be in a position to decide your own. Whatever the situation, your topic should excite and inspire you, sustaining experimentation and diverse translations, which will provide a wealth of information for development into woven fabric.

Here are just a few suggestions:

- Select items to draw – perhaps individual objects that interest you.
- Make a 'themed set' using a collection of objects/flowers/fabric, etc., that are suggested by the topic.
- Be inspired by current and topical events.
- Get out and about. Draw cityscapes or landscapes.
- Look at natural forms and the patterns found there.
- Investigate mechanics, science and invention.

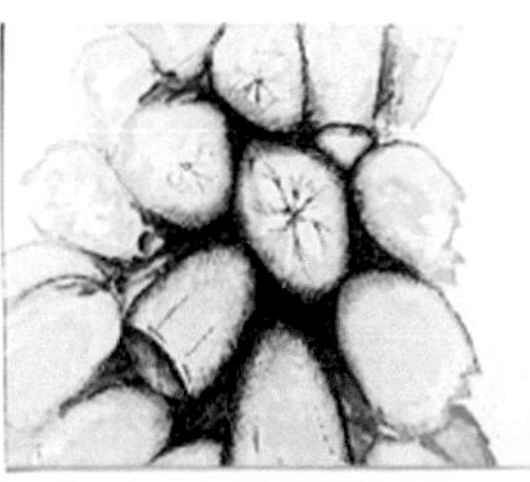

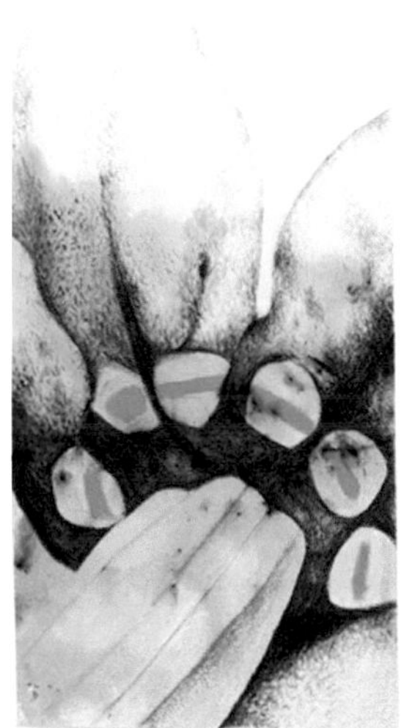

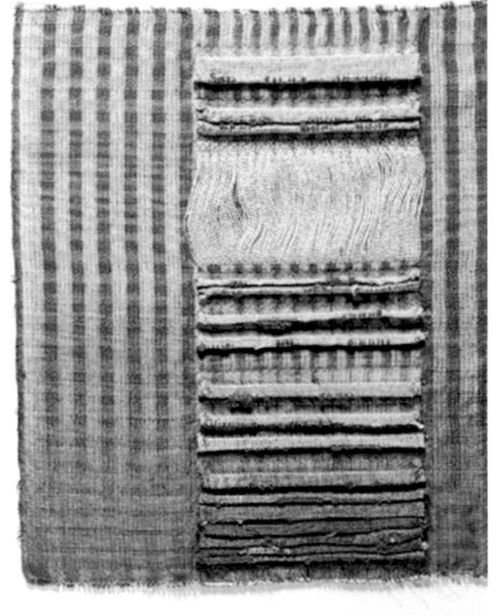

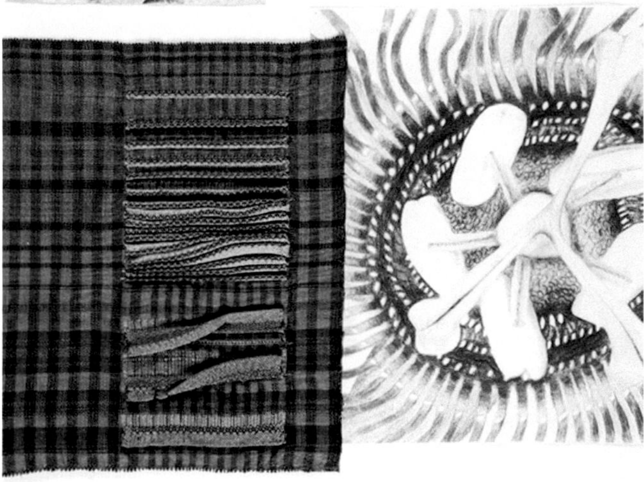

Top: Inspirational drawings of flowers with the woven fabric design.

Bottom: Inspirational drawings of flowers with the woven fabric design.

TRANSLATING DRAWINGS INTO WOVEN DESIGNS

When you have explored your theme sufficiently to sustain experimentation on the loom, then it is time to look at yarns, structure, colour and composition. Your interpretations will give clues as to surface quality, colours, proportions and scale.

Normally one warp will give you several different design variations, the number being determined by how long and how wide your warp is. Typically if you plan a 4m (4yd)-long warp, and the width of the warp is 23cm (9in), then you should be able to produce ten individual designs 30.5cm (12in) in length.

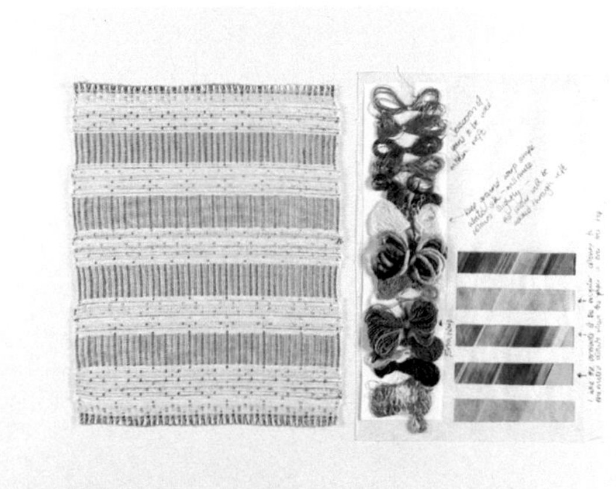

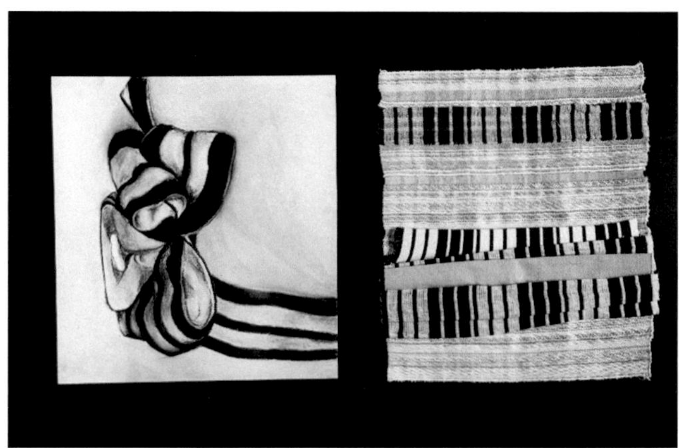

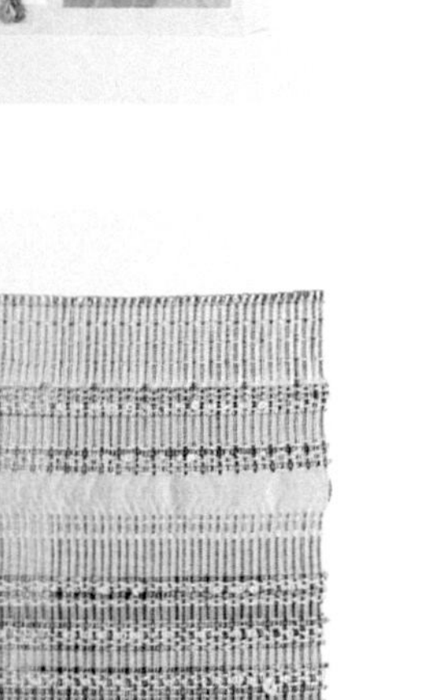

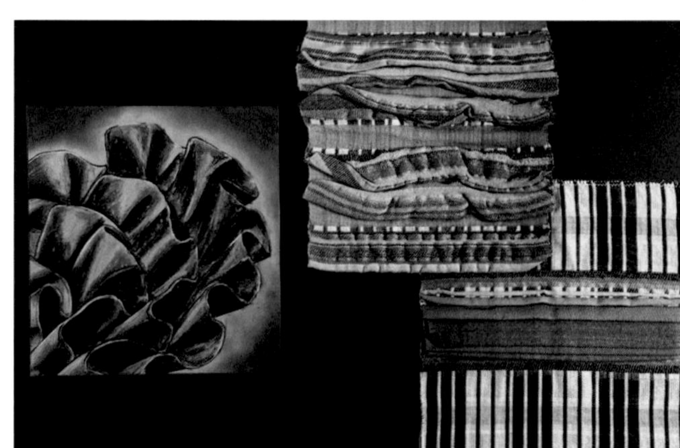

Top left: Yarn and colour inspiration with the woven fabric design.

Top right: Drawing of ribbon with the woven fabric design.

Bottom left: Paper and yarn manipulation with an image of a crowd scene with the woven fabric design.

Bottom right: Drawing of frilled ribbon as inspiration and the woven fabric designs.

GRAPHIC COMPOSITIONS

To help you decide the overall composition and proportion of your warp plan and weave design before committing to the loom, it is a good idea to produce design plans on plain paper, in a sketchbook or on graph paper, using coloured pencils or paints.

These are visual experiments that will give an impression of what the composition of your warp will be. You can indicate what structures are to be used by simulating the effect with line or with texture. Several compositions can be produced in this way to help with decision-making.

YARN WRAPS

These are a great way to test out yarns, colours and compositions before you make the warp. You can produce several designs using this system, with different colour proportions and yarn combinations for each. Looking at the proportion of colours next to each other, and the different effects achieved by introducing texture and line, will help you select the composition that you feel is most successful.

- Use a strip of stiff card about 5 × 15cm (2 × 6in). Use longer strips for more complex compositions.
- Select yarns that best reflect the combinations in your visual research. These yarns could be fine or thick, textured or smooth.
- Use ribbons as a substitute for colours or yarns that are not available.
- Attach the first thread in the repeat with tape to the reverse of the card, and begin to wrap the yarn around the card, sitting each thread next to its neighbour.
- When the required width is wound, secure the thread on the reverse and attach the next yarn in the sequence in the same way until your design is complete.

Remember that the number of threads wound around the card to produce the wrap does not represent the number of 'ends' to be used in the warp. This is decided when the number of ends per cm/inch of the selected yarn is calculated.

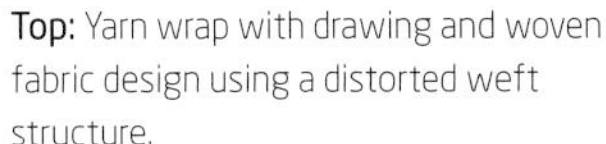

Top: Yarn wrap with drawing and woven fabric design using a distorted weft structure.

Middle and bottom: The yarn has been wound in sections alternating between horizontal and vertical wraps. The overall effect is a complex series of layered stripes.

2
PLAIN WEAVE

PLAIN WEAVE

Plain-weave fabrics are typically very strong. The structure they employ has the most intersections of warp and weft and so binds the cloth closely together.

The plain-weave construction is uniform and is based on a repeat unit of two warp ends (threads) and two weft picks (threads) crossing over and under each other in alternate order.

Diagram of plain-weave structure

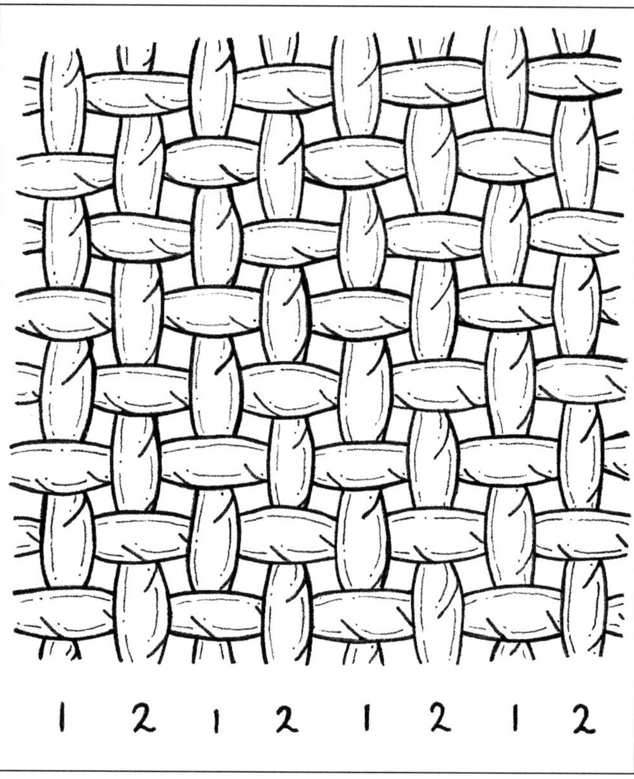

Plain-weave structure using a cotton warp and a slub yarn in the weft to create a textured surface.

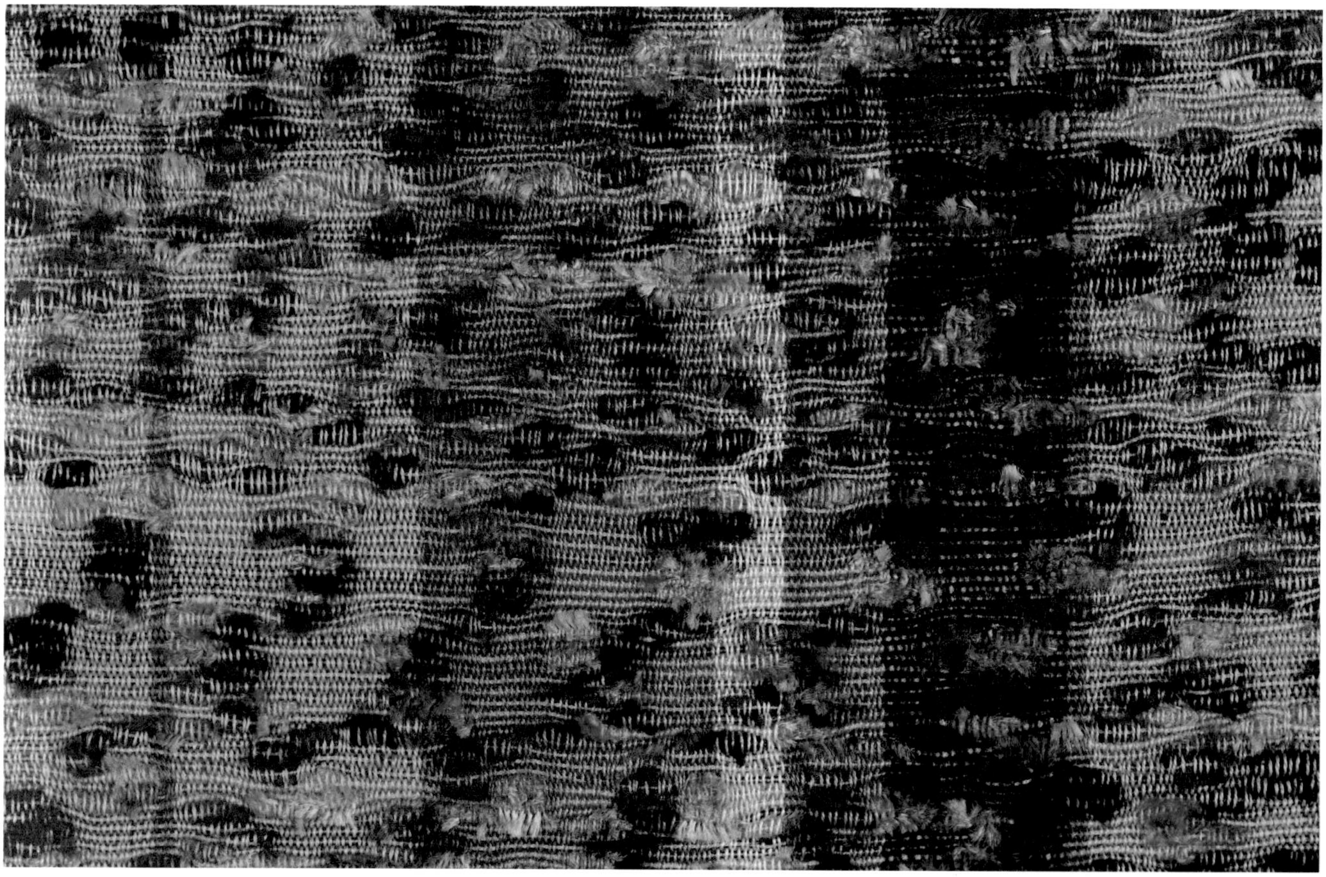

PLAIN WEAVE ON TWO, THREE AND FOUR SHAFTS

In theory, all you need to produce a plain-weave cloth are two shafts with the warp ends threaded on shafts 1 and 2 alternately. When weaving, shaft 1 is lifted and a weft pick inserted and placed in position by the reed. The shaft is lowered and shaft 2 is lifted, a weft pick inserted and placed in position by the reed. Repeat this process and you have a plain-weave cloth.

It may be necessary to use four shafts to produce a good plain weave. For instance, if your warp yarn is very fine there will be a large number of ends per cm/inch, which could mean that on two shafts the heddles would be too crowded, taking up a greater space and restricting the lift of the shaft. This could also cause the yarn to rub and weaken, resulting in frayed or broken ends.

Normally, if using wire heddles, the maximum number that will fill an inch-wide (2.5cm) space is 24, so on two shafts there will be 48 in total. So 48epi (ends per inch or 2.5 cm) is the maximum yarn sett that can be used and repeated on two shafts. The yarn sett is the density of yarn in 1 inch or cm.

Plain weave on 2 shafts

Threading									Lifting plan		X		
										X			
											X		
2		X		X		X		X	2	X			
1	X		X		X		X		Shaft	1	2		

Plain weave on 3 shafts

Threading									Lifting plan		X	
										X		X
3			X				X				X	
2		X		X		X		X		X		X
1	X				X				Shaft	1	2	3

Plain weave on 4 shafts

Threading									Lifting plan		X		X
4				X				X		X		X	
3			X				X				X		X
2		X				X				X		X	
1	X				X				Shaft	1	2	3	4

Wire heddles crammed on the shaft.

POTENTIAL FAULTS IN PLAIN WEAVE

Although it is the simplest weave structure, plain weave can be the most difficult cloth to produce without showing any faults. This is because there is no weave pattern as such to disguise any irregularities, so they are immediately noticeable. Assuming that there are no mistakes in the threading, reed or lifting plans, any of the following can result in a faulty appearance:

- Irregular warp tension, where there are slack ends or groups of ends across the width of the cloth.
- Irregular beating of the weft picks where there has been a varying degree of reed impact on the fell (edge) of the cloth. Try to get into a regular rhythm when weaving.
- Knots and spinning faults in the yarn, which are particularly visible when weaving fine cloth.
- Poor, patchy dyeing of warp and weft yarn.

Plain-weave fabric using a space-dyed ribbon yarn and a two-tone twist yarn.

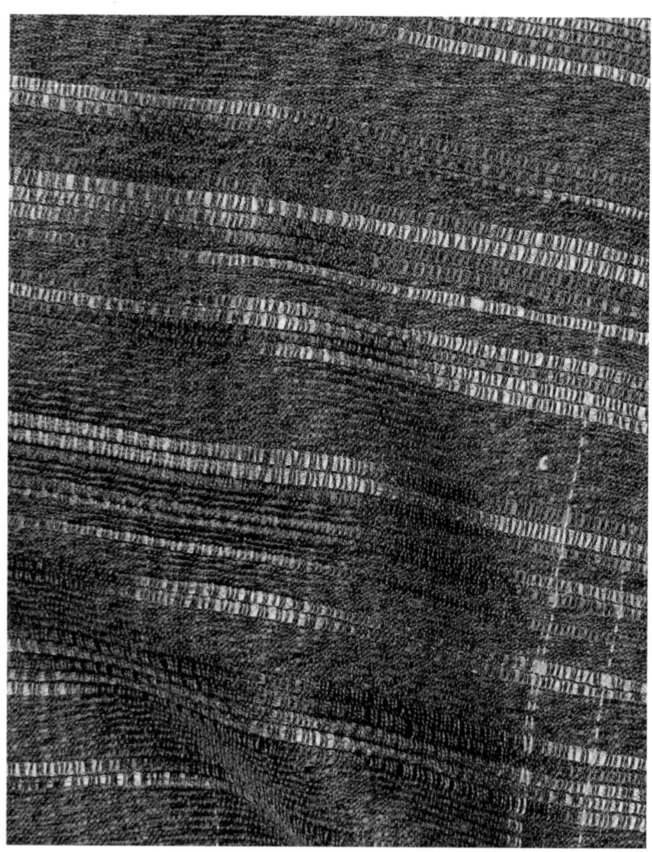

Plain-weave structure with hand-looped feature in spun silk.

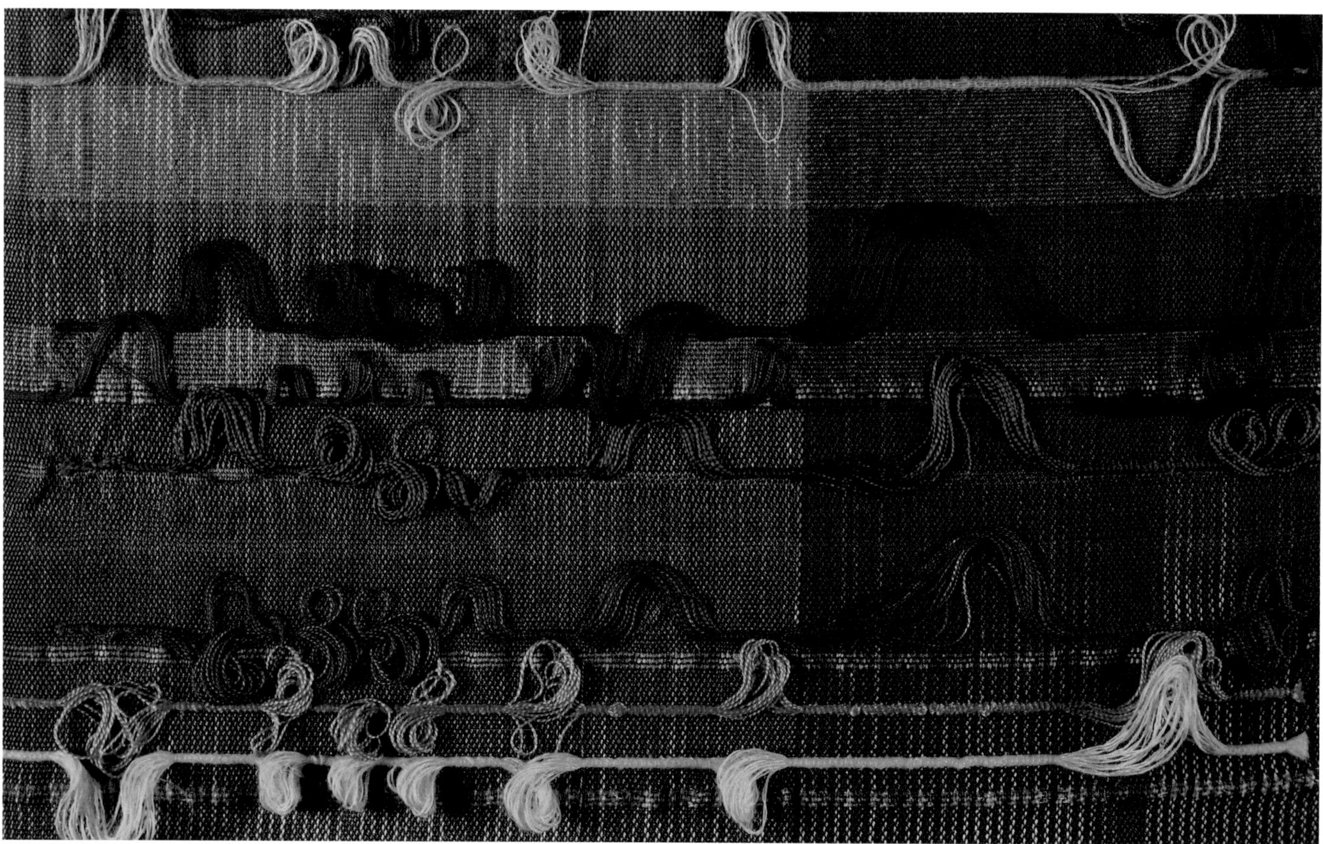

PLAIN-WEAVE VARIATIONS

Plain weave is the simplest structure and is typically woven on a two-end unit, over one and under one, but there are a considerable number of variations that will result in an exciting range of design options.

It can be woven in many weights and qualities using just one type of yarn in warp and weft. Feature yarns can be introduced to create a fancy stripe or check, either as single ends or blocks of contrasting texture and thickness. Using contrasting colours will give you an endless and unique collection of stripes and checks, while dip-dyeing and tie-dyeing your warp yarn will create more complex designs and patterns.

BASIC RIBBED CLOTHS

There are two basic types of ribbed cloth: warp-faced and weft-faced. In warp-faced cloth there are more warp ends showing, whereas in weft-faced cloth you see more weft yarn.

A warp-faced rib weave is formed by using a high density of fine warp ends – at least double the number of ends per cm/inch than for a regular plain-weave cloth. The weft yarn is much thicker than the warp ends and, when weaving, is completely covered by the warp. The result is a stiff, durable cloth. If you wind several fine threads together on the bobbin to make one thick filament thread, the resulting fabric has a softer, more pliable finish. The resulting rib is horizontal.

Plain-weave warp-faced ribs. Alternating colours on a multiple-striped warp in filament silk using eight shafts.

A weft-faced rib can be formed by using a coarse or thick yarn in the warp that is highly tensioned, with a fine weft yarn used to cover the warp when weaving. To create a softer finish to the cloth, you can make your own filament yarn by threading several fine warp ends through each heddle. The result is a vertical rib.

Weft-faced rib weave in cotton and fancy chenille yarn.

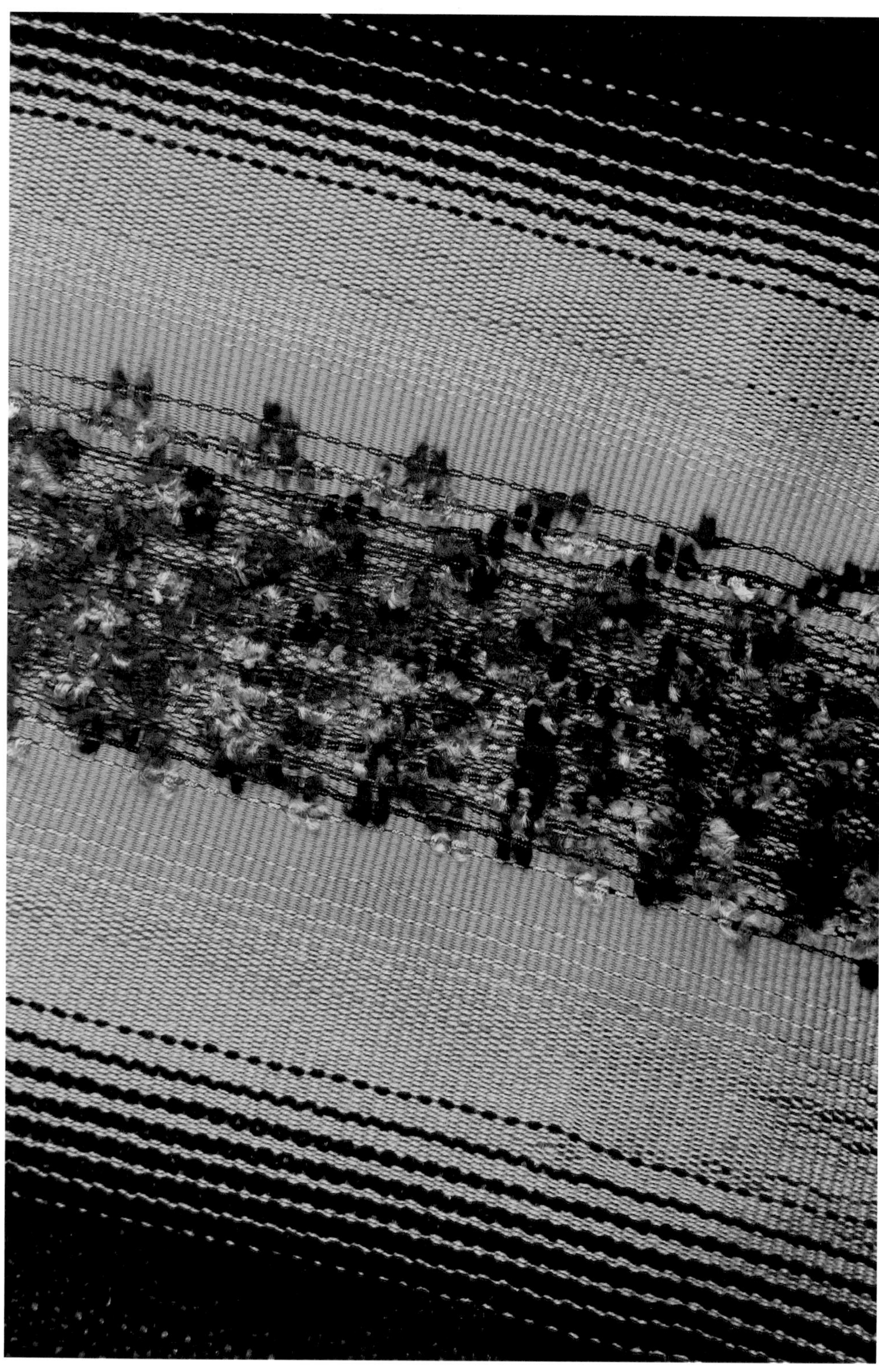

CRAMMING AND SPACING

Vertical stripes can be formed by varying the density of the yarn in the reed. Basically, once you have calculated the number of ends per cm/inch that you will use for your yarn, if you use more ends to the cm/inch then you have a denser, tighter fabric; if you use fewer ends per cm/inch, then your fabric will be more open. Always have multiples of a common denominator for ease of working out which reed to use.

Metric example: your yarn is 48 ends per 2.5cm for a normal sett.

Use a reed with 12 dents per 2.5cm (48 dents per 10cm) with either: 6 ends per dent (72 ends per 2.5cm), 5epd (60 ends per 2.5cm), 4epd (48 ends per 2.5cm), 3epd (36 ends per 2.5cm), 2epd (24 ends per 2.5cm) or 1epd (12 ends per 2.5cm).

Or use a reed with 16 dents per 2.5cm (64 dents per 10cm) with either: 5epd (80 ends per 2.5cm), 4epd (64 ends per 2.5cm), 3epd (48 ends per 2.5cm), 2epd (32 ends per 2.5cm) or 1epd (16 ends per 2.5cm).

Imperial example: your yarn is 48 ends per inch for a normal sett.

A 12's reed can be used to produce setts of 72epi (with 6 ends per dent), 60epi (5epd), 48epi (4epd), 36epi (3epd), 24epi (2epd) and 12epi (1epd).

Alternatively, a 16's reed can be used to produce setts of 80epi (with 5 ends per dent), 64epi (4epd), 48epi (3epd), 32epi (2epd) and 16epi (1epd).

The change can be gradual or abrupt, can be a large or a small repeat, and since colour and yarn texture can also play a part, the possibilities for the designer are great. The resulting fabric will have a strong visual impact, although the function may be limited, since the open sections of the cloth are unstable.

Using coarse, textured or hairy yarns will reduce the movement of the yarn from the tightly packed areas into the spaces and add stability to the spaced areas. Using smooth or shiny yarns may lead to a slippery fabric, resulting in movement and instability.

You can also experiment with cramming more ends per dent than usual, and leaving several dents empty. It is probably best to do this as a repeat pattern, as random spaces can look like a series of mistakes in your design.

Diagram of spacing and cramming using plain weave and 2 x 2 twill

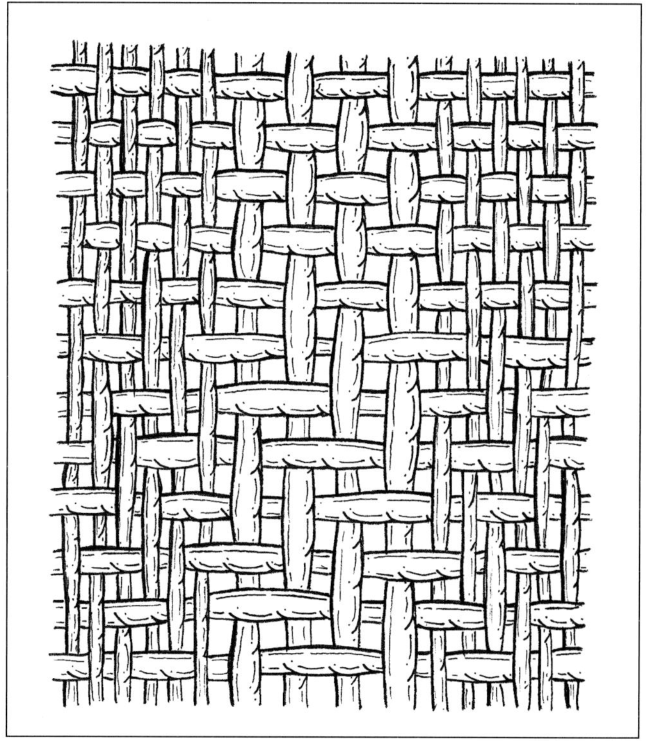

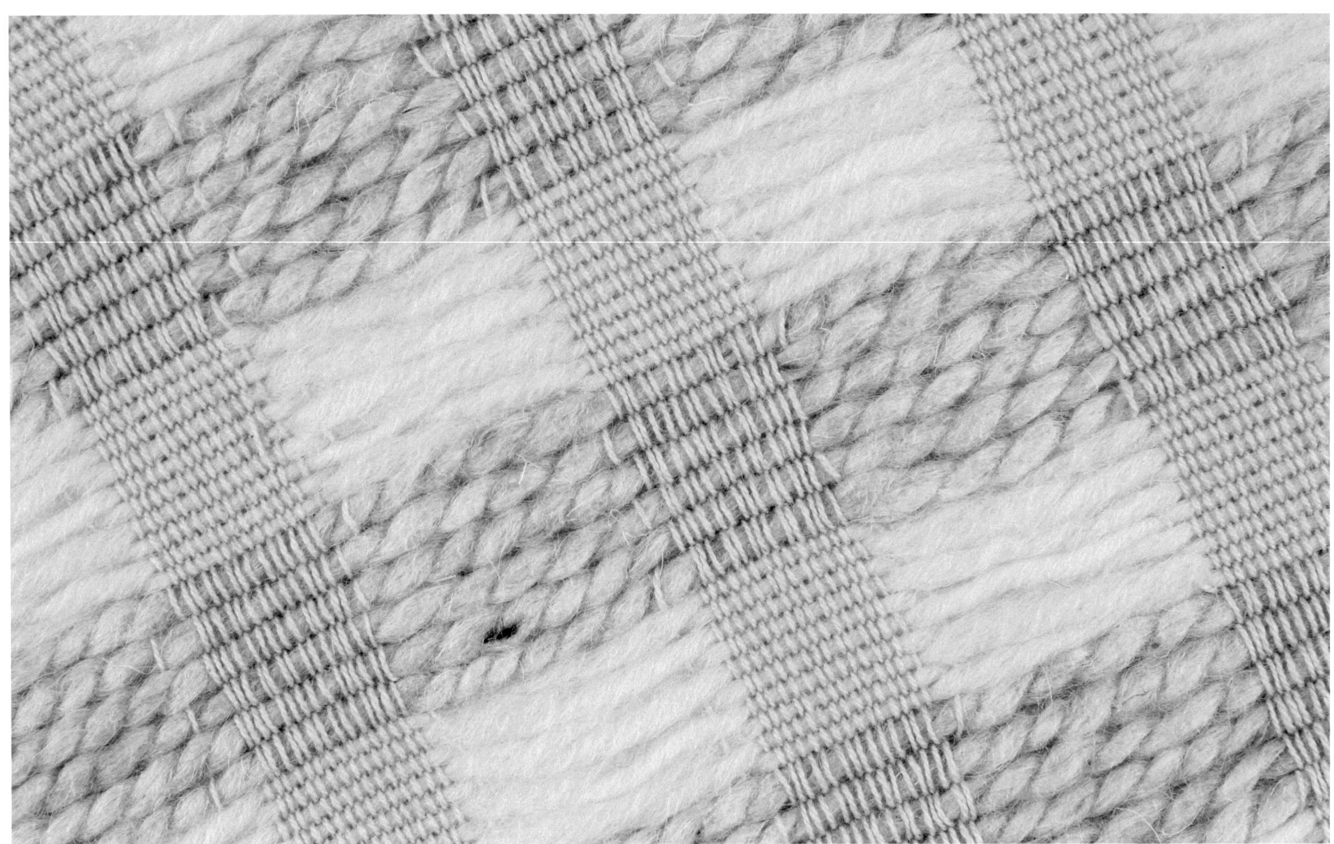

Example of regular spaced cramming and spacing using a cotton warp and wool weft.

Gradual denting

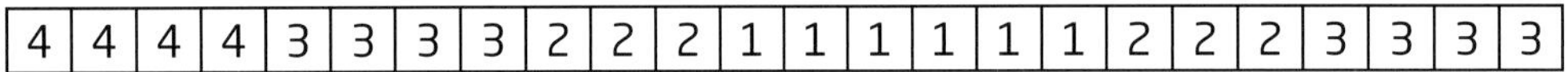

4	4	4	4	3	3	3	3	2	2	2	1	1	1	1	1	1	2	2	2	3	3	3	3

Regular-spaced denting

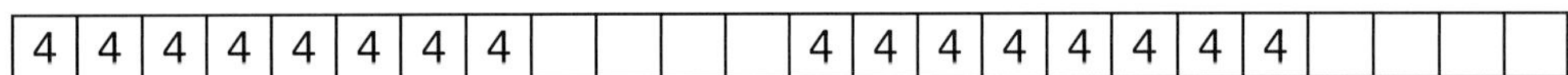

4	4	4	4	4	4	4	4					4	4	4	4	4	4	4	4				

The number in each box represents the number of ends in each dent. If the box is empty, then there are no ends in that dent.

Weft spacing can be achieved by varying the pick density and is controlled by the impact of the beater on the fell of the cloth as you are weaving. Controlling the regularity is not easy, but you can create the effect providing no regular pick density is required.

To give a regular space, you can try inserting a small rod, straw or stick between your usual weft yarn during weaving. When the finished fabric is removed from the loom, these weft additions can be removed to leave a gap between the regular weave. Try washing the finished fabric first to relax the yarn, and it may move less when the gap is revealed.

Use regular warp and weft spacing to create a fabric that has an open chequerboard effect.

HOPSACK WEAVE OR BASKET WEAVE

This is based on an extension of the plain weave, where, rather than one thread, two or more threads are used as one unit. If your threading plan is a regular threading on shafts 1, 2, 3 and 4 in sequence, then you can lift shafts 1 and 2 together, and insert two weft picks. This is followed by lifting shafts 3 and 4, and inserting a further two weft picks.

Diagram of hopsack weave

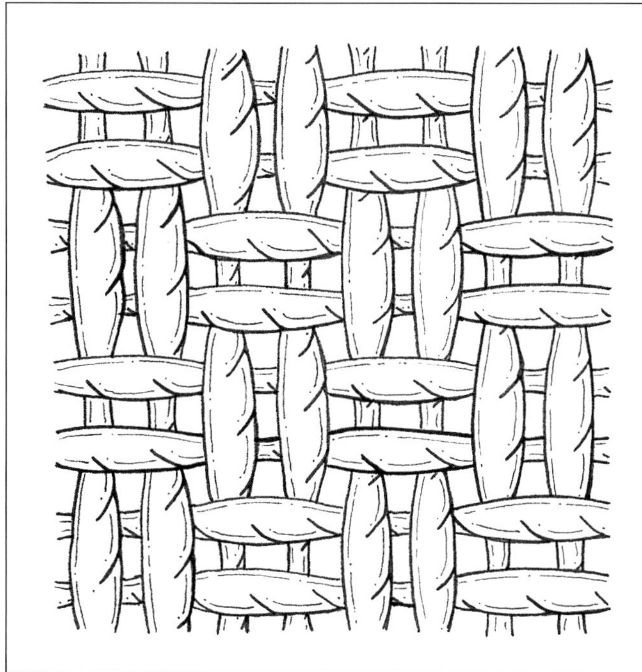

Regular hopsack on 4 shafts

Threading									Lifting plan			X	X
4				X				X				X	X
3			X				X			X	X		
2		X				X				X	X		
1	X				X				Shaft	1	2	3	4

Alternatively, you could plan to create the effect at the threading stage, and thread two or more ends in sequence on one shaft i.e. 1.1, 2.2, 3.3, 4.4.

Regular hopsack on 4 shafts

Threading									Lifting plan		X		X
4							X	X			X		X
3					X	X				X		X	
2			X	X						X		X	
1	X	X							Shaft	1	2	3	4

To give an interesting texture over two shafts, try alternating one end on shaft 1 and then two ends on shaft 2.

Irregular hopsack on 2 shafts

Threading							Lifting plan		X
4								X	
3									X
2		X	X		X	X		X	
1	X			X			Shaft	1	2

3
TWILL WEAVES

TWILL WEAVES

There are many variations of twill weave and, while all have a distinctive diagonal, they can change appearance depending on the thickness of your warp and weft yarn, the number of shafts you use, and the threading pattern and lifting plan. With just a few shafts you can use contrasts and movement in your weave designs to create fantastic patterns – and the more shafts at your disposal, the more dramatic the outcome.

All twill-weave constructions can be recognized by a diagonal line running across the fabric. The line is created by floats in the warp or the weft, or in more complex patterns, a combination of both. The length of the float varies from one twill to another, and the diagonal line can run either from the left or from the right.

A twill cloth is softer to handle than a plain-weave cloth because the yarn intersections are less frequent, making it more flexible and giving better draping qualities.

FLOATS

Floats are warp or weft threads that pass over more than one of the opposite set. In structures such as twills and satin or sateen weaves, the float can pass over as many as 15 threads or more. When using very fine yarn at 32 ends per cm (96 ends per inch), for example, this is quite acceptable and produces a cloth that is practical for use. When using heavier yarns, the number of threads the float passes over will need to decrease to give a suitable finish. If the fabric is woven too loosely – the floats are too long – then the fabric structure will slip, and you will either have to change the weave to a tighter structure, or increase the ends per cm/inch.

TWILLS OVER THREE SHAFTS

When constructing a twill weave, you need a minimum of three shafts. In the simplest, most basic twills, the intersections in the weave move one end sideways for each weft pick.

Straight draft over 3 shafts

Threading							Lifting plan	A						B		
3			X			X		X		X						X
2		X			X				X	X					X	
1	X			X				X	X					X		
							Shaft	1	2	3				1	2	3

Point draft over 3 shafts

Threading					Lifting plan	A				B				C		
3			X			X		X				X		X		X
2		X		X			X	X			X				X	
1	X					X	X			X				X		X
					Shaft	1	2	3		1	2	3		1	2	3

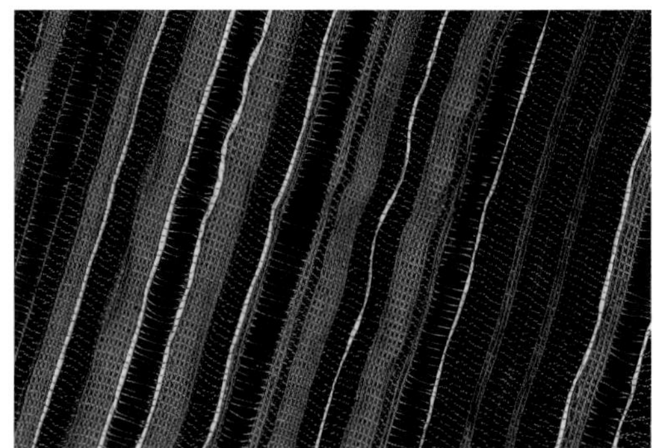

Combination of six-shaft twill weaves.

Combination of six shaft twill weaves with plain weave.

In both examples, Lifting plan A will result in a warp-faced twill, as there are more warp floats on the surface of the cloth; in Plan B there is only one warp thread lifting out of the three in the sequence, so resulting in a weft-faced twill.

It is impossible to create a plain weave from a straight draft threading plan over three shafts, as you begin and finish the repeat on an odd number. To overcome this you could use a point draft, which alternates between odd and even shafts in the threading plan. Lifting plan C gives plain weave. Your twill will be automatically reversed with a point draft, creating a zigzag pattern across the fabric.

A 2 x 2 reverse twill weave on four shafts. The warp has been dip-dyed in two sections before winding onto the loom.

THREADING PLANS

The threading plan, or draft, describes the sequence in which warp ends are threaded. There are different terms to describe these set-ups.

A **straight draft** indicates that the warp ends are threaded onto each shaft in sequence, i.e. on four shafts the order is shaft 1, 2, 3 then 4 and repeated until all warp ends are threaded. So on eight shafts the repeat is from 1 to 8, and on 16 shafts it will be 1 to 16 repeated.

A **point draft** is the term used for a threading plan that reverses at the point it reaches the last shaft being used in the sequence, i.e. on four shafts the order is shaft 1, 2, 3, 4, 3, 2. You will notice that the repeat ends on shaft 2. If you were to end on shaft 1, and were to continue to shaft 1 for the next repeat, then there would be two threads side by side on the same shaft, which would appear as an obvious mistake. This principle should be followed on all point drafts, whether on four or 24 shafts.

A **block draft** is the term used when a number of shafts are nominated for a group of ends, and a second, third or fourth set of shafts nominated for further groups of ends. For instance, when using a four-shaft loom, shafts 1 and 2 will be used for block one, and shafts 3 and 4 for block two. The number of threads in each block will be determined by the design. If there are more shafts available, then more blocks can be created. (See also p.70.)

RECORDING TWILL WEAVES

The pattern of twills can be written down numerically. The first number indicates how many warp ends are lifting, and the second number how many warp ends remain down and are covered by the weft.

For example, in the three-shaft twill shown:

- Lifting plan A will be a 2 × 1 twill.
- Lifting plan B will be a 1 × 2 twill.

Complex patterns can also be recorded in this way.

EXAMPLES OF TWO BLOCKS USING EIGHT SHAFTS EACH

The warp is wire and nylon monofilament with a wire and monofilament weft using various eight-shaft twills over two blocks of four shafts each.

1 x 7 twill, plain weave and crêpe weave forming blocks of contrasting structures. Cotton warp and filament silk weft. Two blocks each on eight shafts.

Various eight-shaft twills and plain weave on two blocks, each block threaded on eight shafts. Spun silk warp and weft.

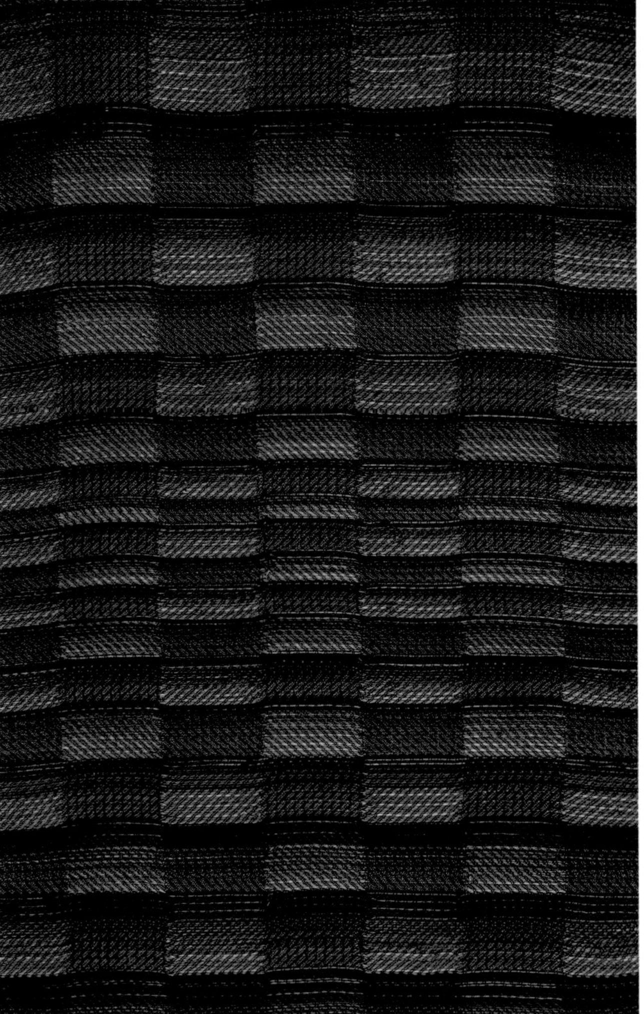

1 x 7 against 4 x 2 x 1 x 1 twill. Spun silk warp and weft. Two blocks each on eight shafts.

Reverse twills and straight twills with plain weave. Cotton warp and weft. Two blocks each on eight shafts.

EXAMPLES OF TWILLS USING BLOCK THREADING OVER THREE BLOCKS ON 24 SHAFTS USING EIGHT-SHAFT WEAVES

Various eight-shaft twills and plain weave on three blocks, each block threaded on eight shafts. Spun silk warp and weft.

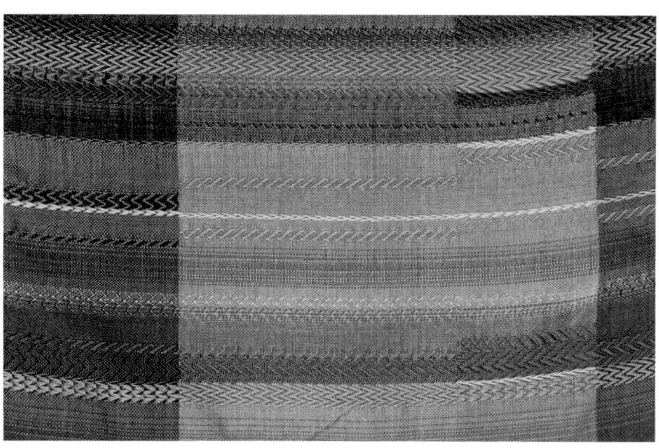

Various eight-shaft twills and plain weave on three blocks, each block threaded on eight shafts. Spun silk warp and weft.

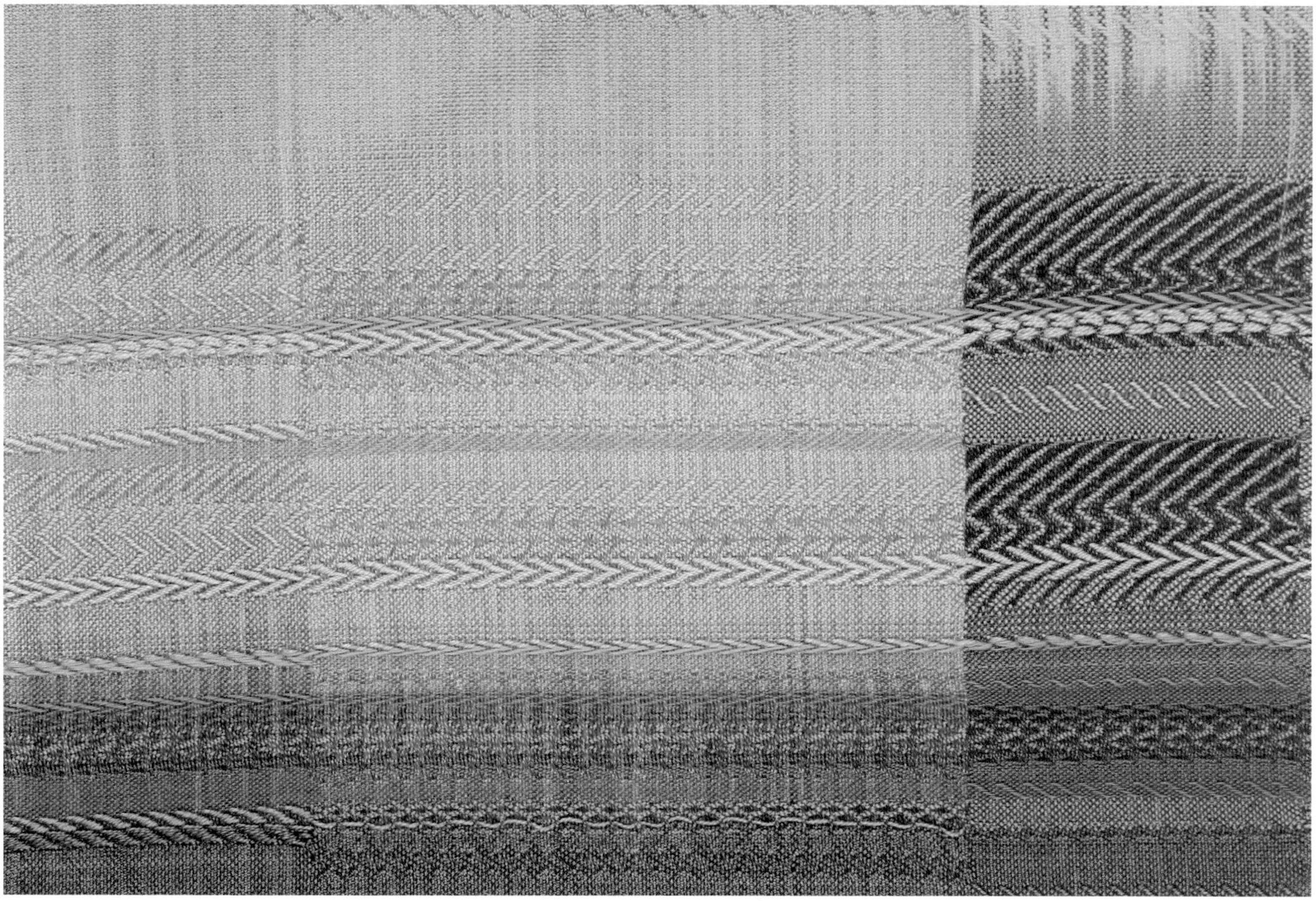

Various eight-shaft twills and plain weave on three blocks, each block threaded on eight shafts. Spun silk warp and weft.

TWILLS USING A STRAIGHT DRAFT OVER FOUR SHAFTS

There are several types of twill that can be created over four shafts, which will result in different visual effects through the length of warp or weft float.

1. BALANCED TWILL

The warp and weft floats are the same length and the cloth is identical on the back and front. The threading plan is a straight draft over four shafts and the lifting plan has two ends raised and two down, which move in sequence for each pick through the pattern. So, the sequence is to raise shafts 1 and 2, then 2 and 3, then 3 and 4 and finally 4 and 1. This is one repeat, and is known as a 2 × 2 twill.

If the lifting plan is reversed, a zigzag pattern is created vertically through the fabric, and the floats in warp and weft will be longer at the point of reversal.

2 x 2 twill

Threading									Lifting plan	X			X
4				X				X				X	X
3			X				X				X	X	
2		X				X				X	X		
1	X				X				Shaft	1	2	3	4

2 x 2 twill reversed

									Lifting plan	X			X
										X	X		
											X	X	
												X	X
Threading										X			X
4				X				X				X	X
3			X				X				X	X	
2		X				X				X	X		
1	X				X				Shaft	1	2	3	4

Diagram of 2 x 2 twill

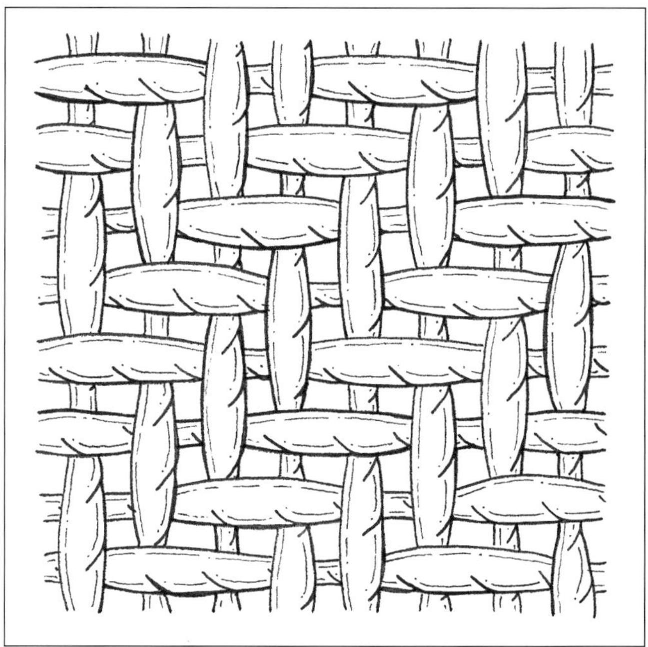

Reverse 3 x 1 twill in spun silk.

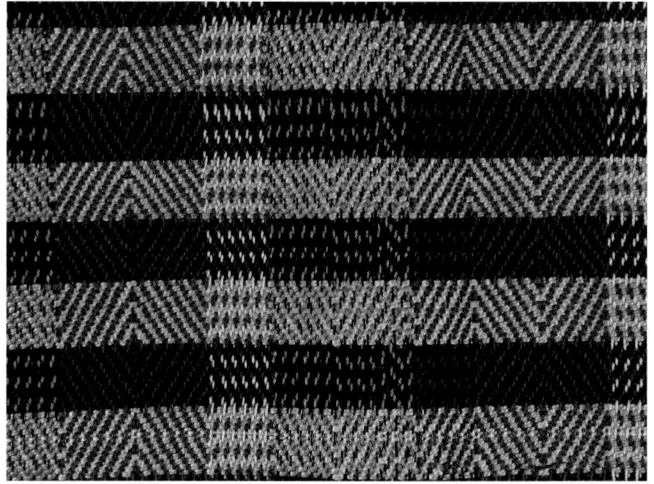

Reverse 2 x 2 twill in spun silk.

2. WARP-FACED TWILL

This twill has the majority of warp threads visible on the cloth surface. The number of ends lifting in each row of the pattern is three out of the four, and is known as a 3 × 1 twill. The sequence is to raise three threads and leave one down for each of the lifts. The warp colour is more visible.

3 x 1 twill

Threading									Lifting plan	X	X		X
4				X				X		X		X	X
3			X				X				X	X	X
2		X				X				X	X	X	
1	X				X				Shaft	1	2	3	4

3 x 1 twill reversed

									Lifting plan	X	X		X
										X	X	X	
											X	X	X
										X		X	X
Threading										X	X		X
4				X				X		X		X	X
3			X				X				X	X	X
2		X				X				X	X	X	
1	X				X				Shaft	1	2	3	4

Diagram of 3 x 1 twill

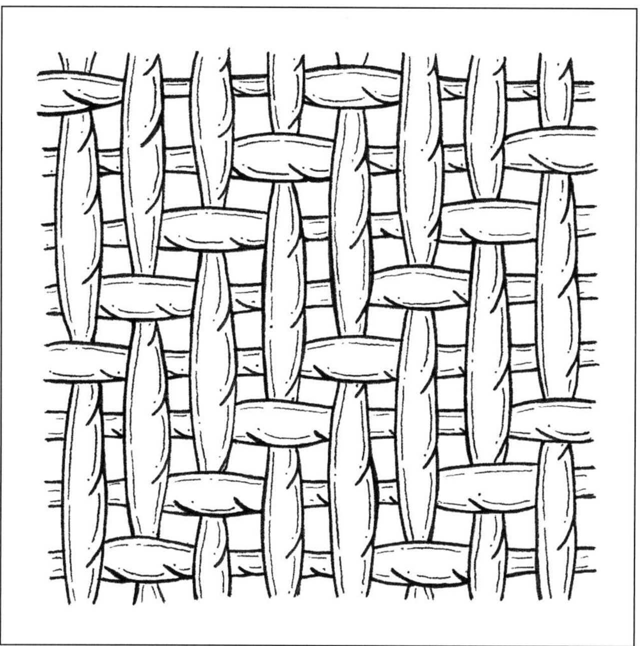

THE TWILL ANGLE

The angle of the twill line is determined by the ratio of ends and picks in the weave construction. An equal number of picks to ends, using the same thickness of yarn, will produce a twill line of 45 degrees. If there are twice as many ends to picks, the angle gets shallower, while twice as many picks to ends makes the angle steeper.

Twill angle A (twice as many picks), B (equal number of picks to ends), C (twice as many ends)

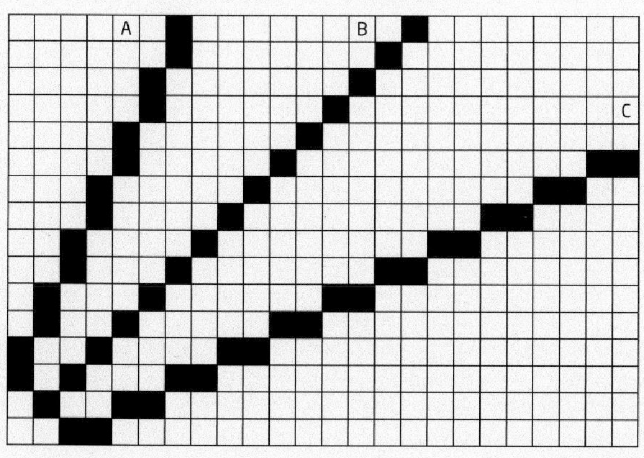

3. WEFT-FACED TWILL

This twill has the majority of weft threads visible on the surface. The number of ends lifting in each row of the pattern is one out of four and is known as a 1 × 3 twill.

Diagram of 1 x 3 twill

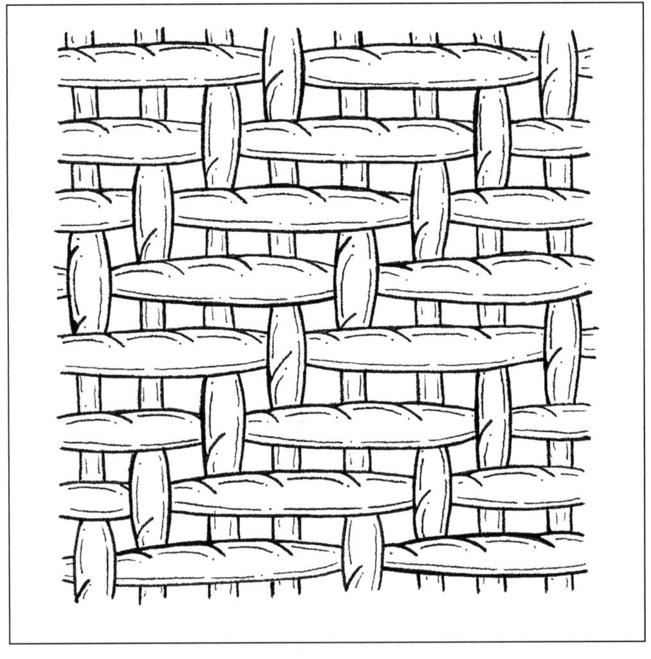

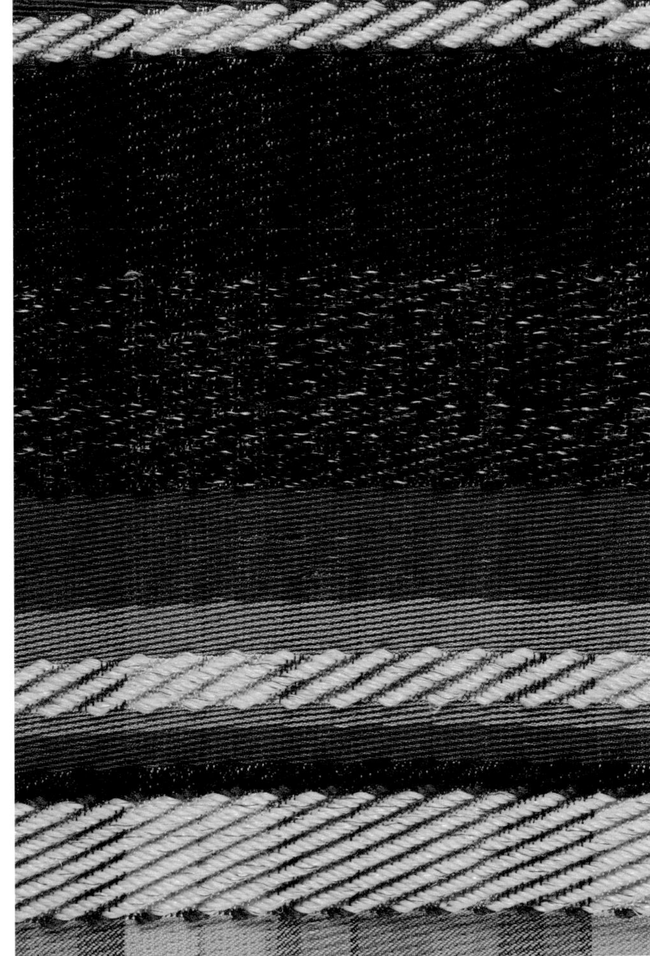

1 x 3 twill

Threading									Lifting plan	X	X		X
4				X				X		X		X	X
3			X				X				X	X	X
2		X				X				X	X	X	
1	X				X				Shaft	1	2	3	4

1 x 3 twill reversed

									Lifting plan				X
										X			
											X		
												X	
Threading													X
4				X				X				X	
3			X				X				X		
2		X				X				X			
1	X				X				Shaft	1	2	3	4

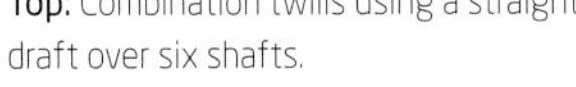

Top: Combination twills using a straight draft over six shafts.

Bottom: Combination of six-shaft twills and plain weave.

4. HERRINGBONE TWILL

This is a variation on the 2 × 2 balanced twill, with a reverse in the lifting plan.

2 x 2 herringbone twill

Threading									Lifting plan		X		X
4				X				X		X	X		
3			X				X			X		X	
2		X				X						X	X
1	X				X				Shaft	1	2	3	4

2 x 2 reverse herringbone twill

									Lifting plan			X	X
										X			X
										X	X		
											X	X	
Threading										X			X
4				X				X				X	X
3			X				X				X	X	
2		X				X				X	X		
1	X				X				Shaft	1	2	3	4

5. SHADED TWILL

If you gradually move from weft-faced to warp-faced twill in your lifting plan, and back again, you can create a subtle shadowing effect. Each pattern repeats over four lifts. Repeat each section to create a more striking effect.

Shaded twill

X			X	
		X	X	
	X	X		
X	X			2 x 2 twill
X		X	X	
	X	X	X	
X	X	X		
X	X		X	3 x 1 twill
X			X	
		X	X	
	X	X		
X	X			2 x 2 twill
X				
			X	
		X		
	X			1 x 3 twill
1	2	3	4	Shaft

Combination of twills using two blocks of 8 shafts.

TWILLS USING A POINT DRAFT ON FOUR SHAFTS

If you thread up the loom using a point draft, then you will create a reverse twill pattern horizontally across the cloth. You can use the same lifting plans as in the examples using a straight draft, and the zigzag will occur naturally because of the sequence in the threading.

Note: The threading repeat in examples A and B finish on shaft 2. As stated earlier, if you were to continue to shaft 1, then there would be two threads side by side on the same shaft, which would appear as an obvious mistake. This principle should be followed on all point drafts, whether on four or 24 shafts.

A. Point draft over 4 shafts

Threading						
4				X		
3			X		X	
2		X				X
1	X					

B. Alternative point draft over 4 shafts

Threading										
4				X				X		
3			X						X	
2		X				X				X
1	X				X		X			

C. Point and straight draft combination

Threading																						
4				X				X				X				X						X
3			X				X		X				X				X				X	
2		X				X				X				X				X		X		
1	X				X						X				X				X			

THE WEAVE PATTERN ON PAPER

The weave plan, or draw-down, helps the weaver to understand and visualize the structure of a particular weave. It gives you the opportunity to try different options on paper before committing to threading the loom. You may decide to put different threading plans side by side for a more striking pattern.

Creating a weave plan

When creating a weave plan you will need your threading and lifting plans to work from. The example here shows a straight draft on four shafts with a 2 × 2 twill pattern.

- Assume that the warp threads are black and the weft threads white.
- On point paper, begin several rows down, in the squares below the threading plan. Allow at least the length of the lifting plan so that you have space for an entire repeat.
- Below the threading plan, start working from the bottom row of squares up.
- Following the first pattern row in the lifting plan, colour in all squares below the corresponding threads where the warp is lifting. So as the first and second shafts are lifting: colour in the first and fifth squares from the left, to correspond with the first shaft, and then the second and sixth squares, to correspond with the second shaft.
- Leave the remaining squares white to represent the weft threads that will be covering the black warp threads that are not raised.
- Go to the second row of the lifting plan and the second row in the weave plan. Colour in the squares corresponding to the threads on shafts 2 and 3, and leave the remainder white.
- Move up in sequence until you have completed at least one repeat, and continue if you want to see a larger area of pattern.

2 x 2 twill over a 4-shaft straight draft

Threading									Lifting plan	X			X
4				X				X				X	X
3			X				X				X	X	
2		X				X				X	X		
1	X				X				Shaft	1	2	3	4
	■			■	■			■					
			■	■			■	■					
		■	■			■	■						
	■	■			■	■							

1 x 3 twill over a 4-shaft point draft

Threading											Lifting plan				X
4				X				X						X	
3			X						X				X		
2		X				X				X		X			
1	X				X		X				Shaft	1	2	3	4
				■				■							
			■						■						
		■				■				■					
	■				■		■								
				■				■							
			■						■						
		■				■				■					
	■				■		■								

DISTORTED TWILLS

By disturbing the threading pattern, you can create a broken or curved twill pattern. The more shafts at your disposal, then the more complex the pattern potential. The examples that follow over the next few pages are over either six or eight shafts.

Broken twill – The **twill line** in the threading is interrupted and advances out of sequence in a broken line. This will give you a disturbed pattern in all of your designs. If you also want to achieve a regular twill pattern, then you can use a straight draft, and apply the same principle to the lifting plan.

Curved or undulating twill – This effect relies on varying the number of ends threaded on each shaft in a straight draft. The firmness of the fabric varies, and is tighter where the threads advance in a single progression, and tends to get looser the more threads that are repeated on each shaft. This is caused by the floats being longer than usual. You can also create movement through spacing and cramming the warp threads in the reed (see p.41).

Disturbed twill – The twill line sequence is interrupted at regular intervals, and advances in sequence in a straight line.

Disturbed reverse twill – This effect is achieved when the twill line is interrupted, reverses and then continues in a regular sequence until it reverses again.

Curved and straight twill in spun silk

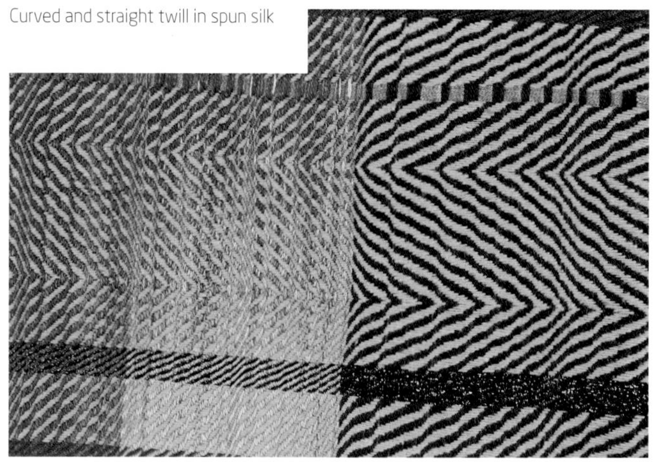

Curved twill in spun silk.

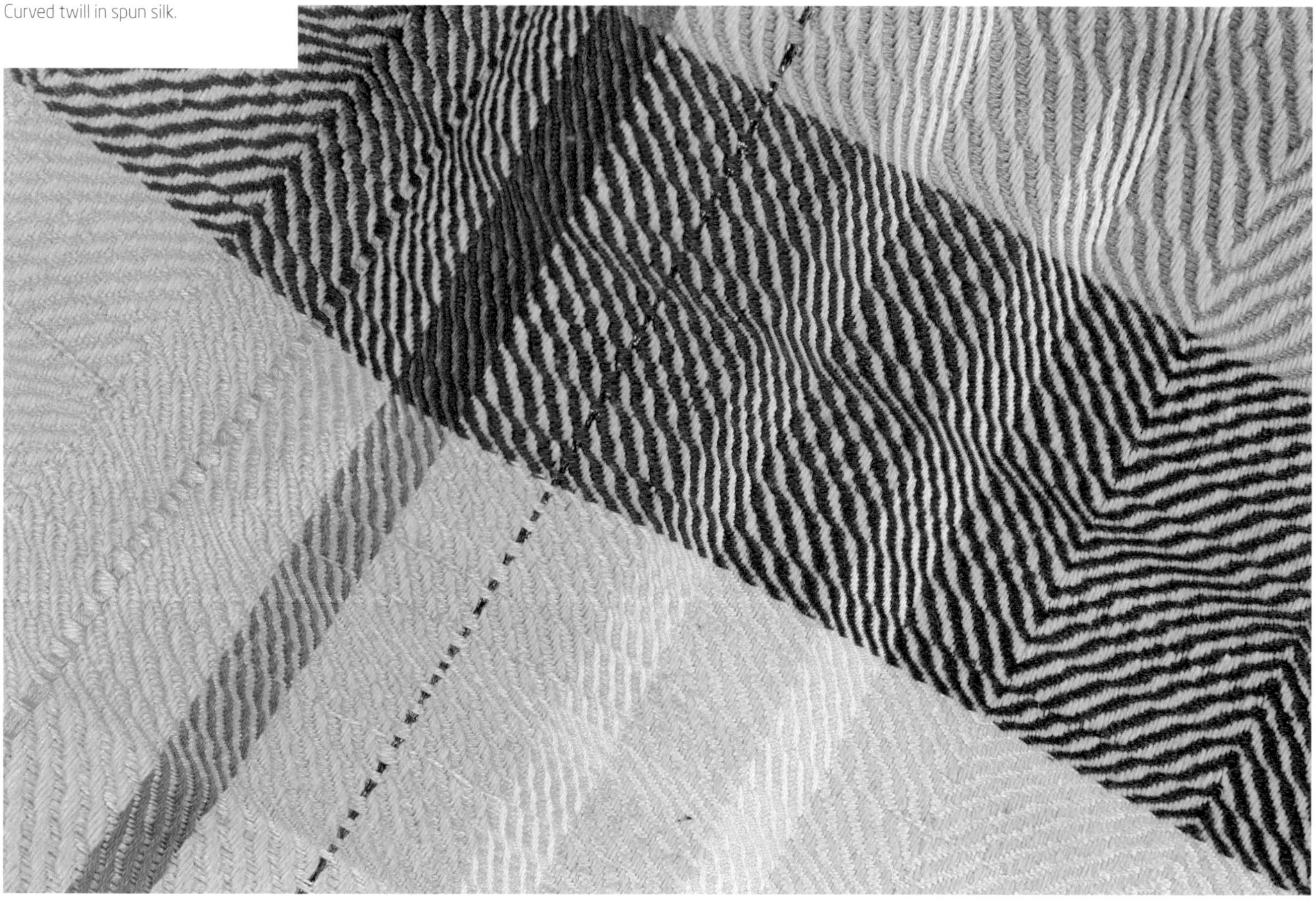

DISTORTED TWILLS OVER SIX SHAFTS

Broken twill over 6 shafts

3 x 3 twill

Threading																			
6								X				X				X			
5							X				X				X				
4				X										X				X	
3			X										X				X		
2		X				X				X									
1	X				X				X										

Lifting plan						
	X	X				X
	X				X	X
	X			X	X	X
			X	X	X	
		X	X	X		
	X	X	X			
Shaft	1	2	3	4	5	6

Curved twill over 6 shafts

3 x 3 twill

Threading																														
6										X	X									X	X								X	
5							X	X	X										X									X		
4					X	X												X								X	X			
3			X	X													X							X	X					
2		X													X	X							X							
1	X											X	X	X								X								

Lifting plan						
	X	X				X
	X				X	X
	X			X	X	X
			X	X	X	
		X	X	X		
	X	X	X			
Shaft	1	2	3	4	5	6

The weave plan shows two repeats of the 3 × 3 twill, i.e. 12 weft picks.

Disturbed twill over 6 shafts

3 x 3 twill

Threading																							
6											X										X	
5								X			X					X				X			
4				X			X			X						X				X			
3			X			X			X						X				X				
2		X			X									X				X					
1	X												X										

Lifting plan						
	X	X				X
	X				X	X
	X			X	X	X
			X	X	X	
		X	X	X		
	X	X	X			
Shaft	1	2	3	4	5	6

Disturbed reverse twill over 6 shafts

3 x 3 twill

Threading																														
6											X											X								X
5							X			X											X						X		X	
4						X			X					X				X		X						X		X		
3			X		X								X		X		X		X						X					
2		X		X								X				X								X						
1	X										X												X							

Lifting plan						
	X	X				X
	X				X	X
	X			X	X	X
			X	X	X	
		X	X	X		
	X	X	X			
Shaft	1	2	3	4	5	6

The weave plan shows two repeats of the 3 × 3 twill, i.e. 12 weft picks.

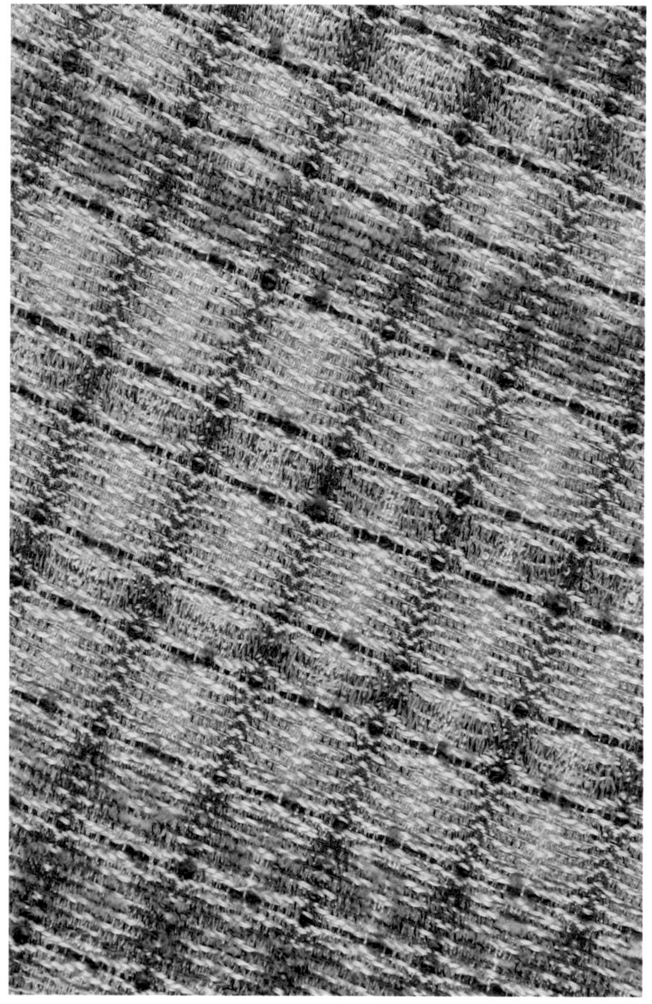

Disturbed reverse twill over six shafts in cotton and wool yarns.

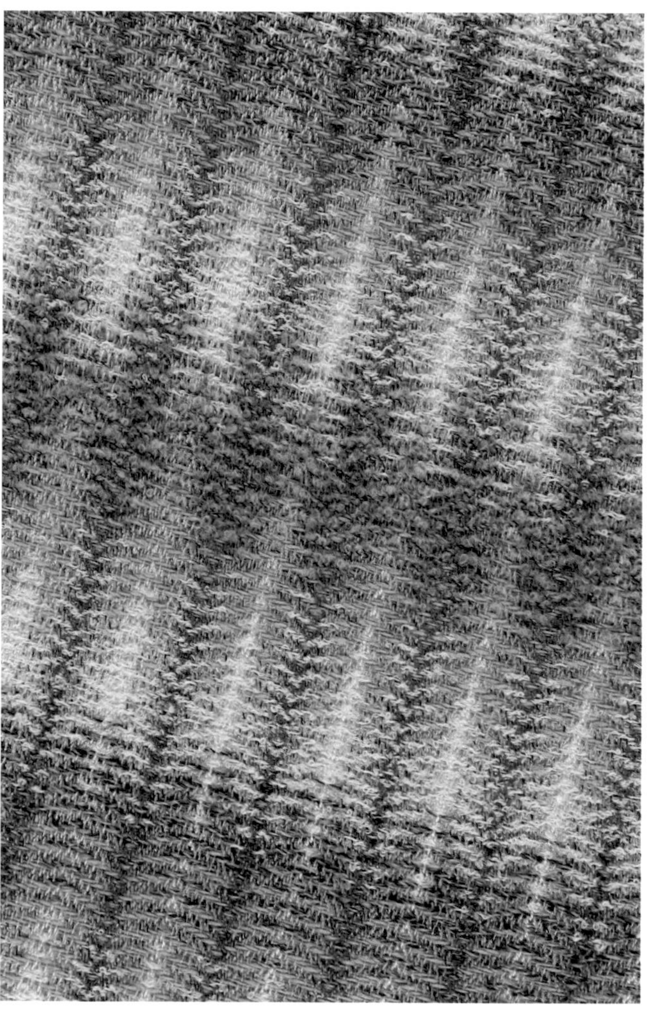

Disturbed reverse twill over six shafts in cotton and wool yarns.

1 x 5 twill

					X
				X	
			X		
		X			
	X				
X					
1	2	3	4	5	6

2 x 4 twill

X					X
				X	X
			X	X	
		X	X		
	X	X			
X	X				
1	2	3	4	5	6

3 x 3 twill

X	X				X
X				X	X
			X	X	X
		X	X	X	
	X	X	X		
X	X	X			
1	2	3	4	5	6

3 x 3 twill with alternate weft colours (A and B)

b			X	X	X	
a	X	X				X
b		X	X	X		
a	X				X	X
b	X	X	X			
a				X	X	X
b	X	X				X
a			X	X	X	
b	X				X	X
a		X	X	X		
b				X	X	X
a	X	X	X			
	1	2	3	4	5	6

4 x 2 twill

X	X	X			X
X	X			X	X
X			X	X	X
		X	X	X	X
	X	X	X	X	
X	X	X	X		
1	2	3	4	5	6

5 x 1 twill

X	X	X	X		X
X	X	X		X	X
X	X		X	X	X
X		X	X	X	X
	X	X	X	X	X
X	X	X	X	X	
1	2	3	4	5	6

2 x 2 x 1 x 1 twill

X			X		X
		X		X	X
	X		X	X	
X		X	X		
	X	X			X
X	X			X	
1	2	3	4	5	6

1 x 1 x 1 x 3 twill

	X				X
X				X	
			X		X
		X		X	
	X		X		
X		X			
1	2	3	4	5	6

3 x 1 x 1 x 1 twill

X	X		X		X
X		X		X	X
	X		X	X	X
X		X	X	X	
	X	X	X		X
X	X	X		X	
1	2	3	4	5	6

herringbone

		X		X	X
	X	X			X
X	X	X			
X	X		X		
X			X	X	
			X	X	X
1	2	3	4	5	6

Diagram of 3 x 3 twill

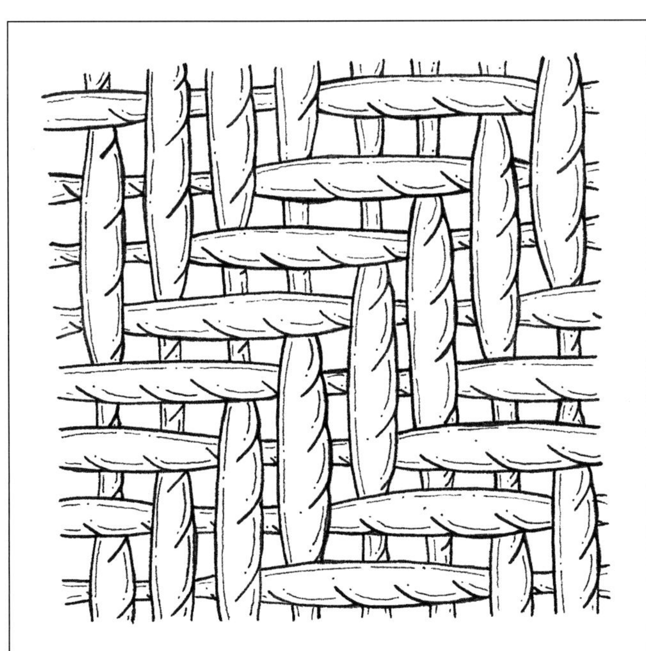

Diagram of 3 x 3 twill using alternate weft colours

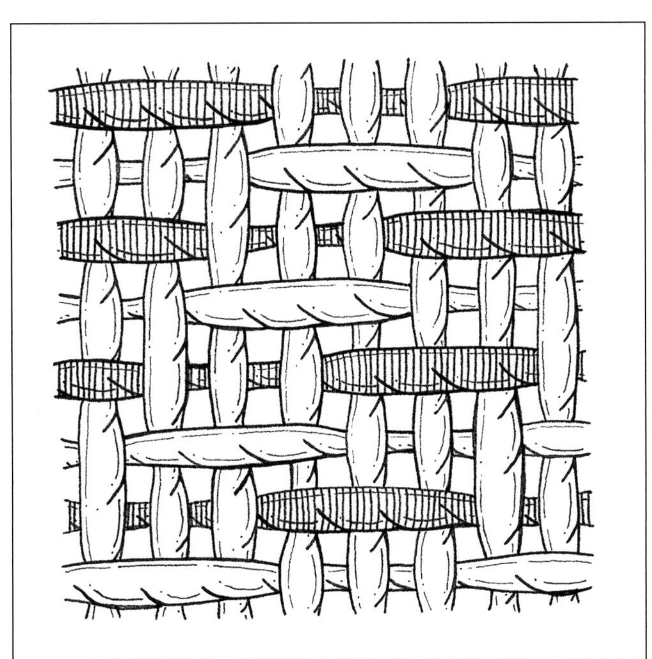

EXAMPLES USING ONE OR A COMBINATION OF THE SIX-SHAFT TWILLS

1 x 5 twill with plain weave.

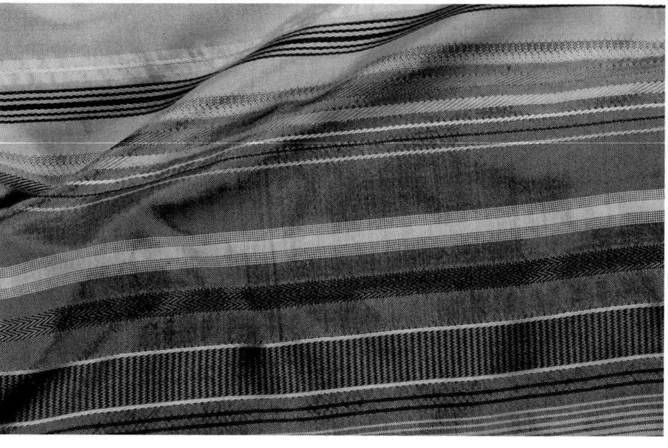

Combination of six-shaft twills.

Combination of six-shaft twills with plain weave.

3 x 3 twill. The fine filament silk weft woven across the thicker wool warp distorts the structure to give a textured effect.

Combination of 1 x 5 and herringbone twills in filament silk, spun silk and wool.

1 x 5 twill in filament silk, spun silk and wool.

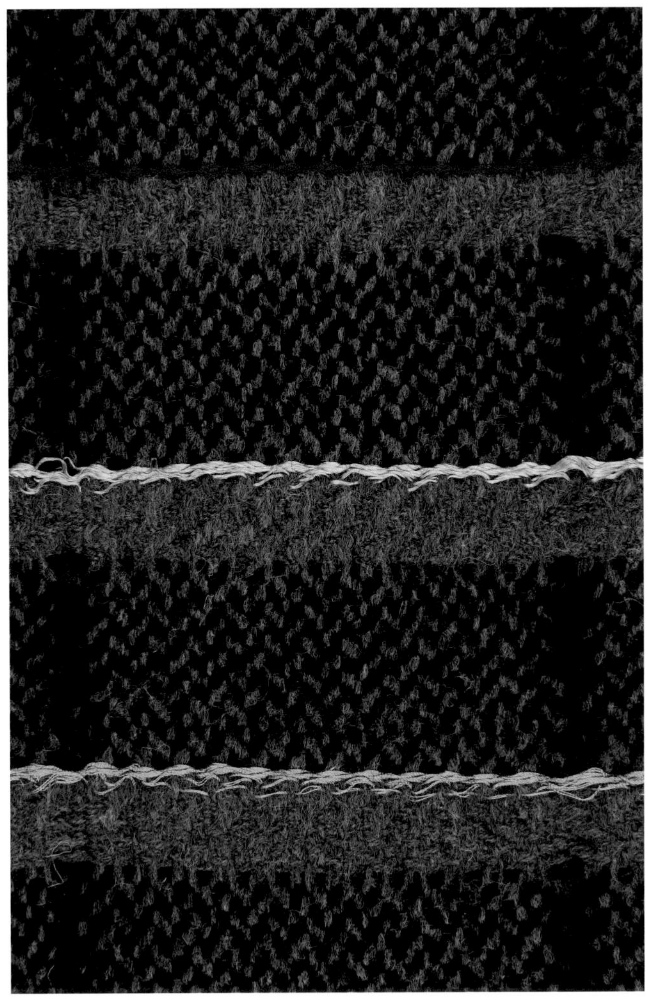

Herringbone twill with plain weave and 1 x 5 twill, in wool and filament silk.

1 x 5 twill in filament silk, spun silk and wool.

1 x 5 twill in cotton and wool.

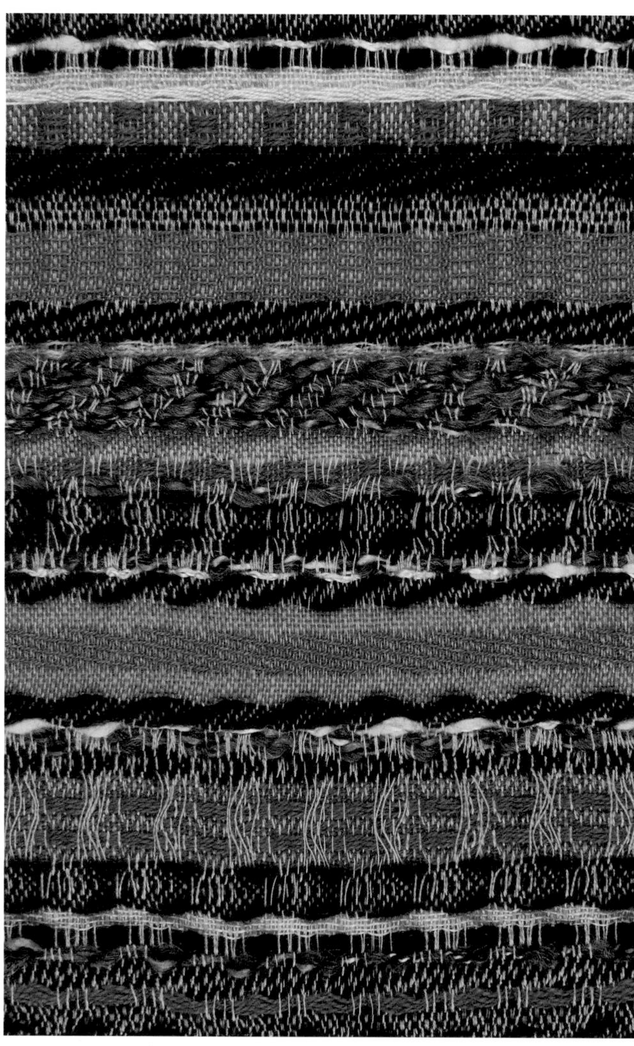

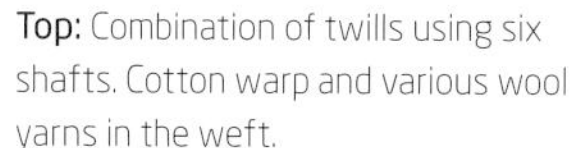

Top: Combination of twills using six shafts. Cotton warp and various wool yarns in the weft.

Bottom left: Various twills over six shafts including 1 x 5 and 3 x 3 against plain weave. The thick wool in the 1 x 5 twill section causes the fine cotton warp to contract, distorting the cloth to form a natural pleat. This is evident only when the weaving is removed from the loom.

Bottom right: Combination of twills using six shafts. Cotton warp and various wool yarns in the weft.

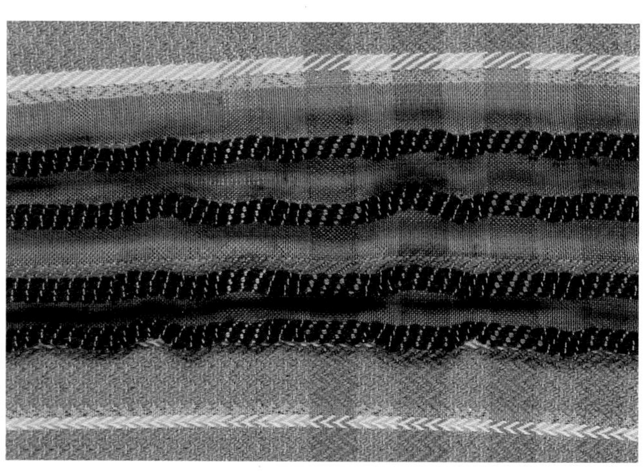

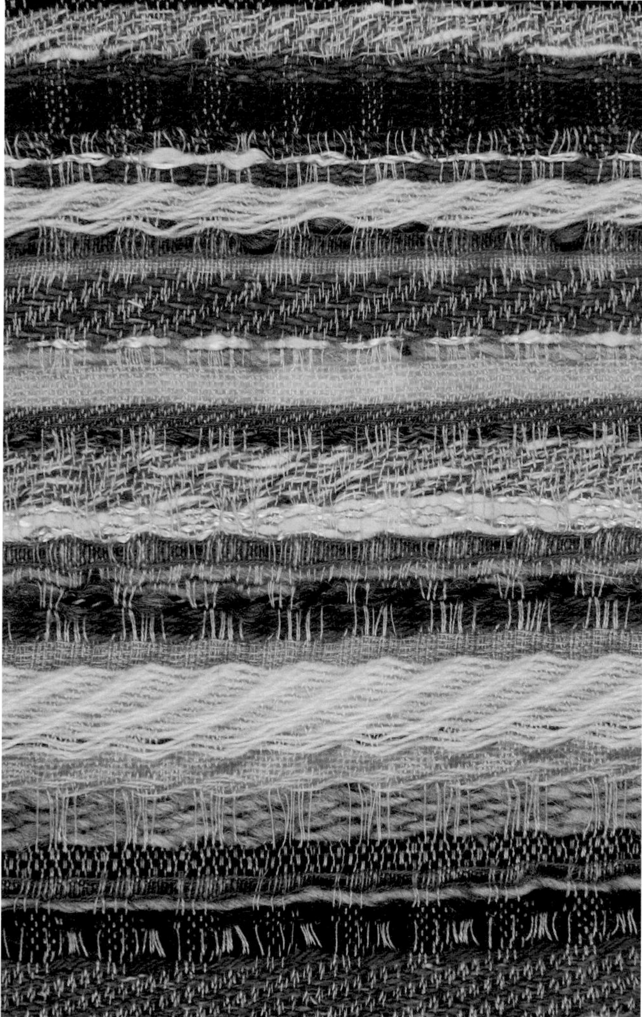

DISTORTED TWILLS OVER EIGHT SHAFTS

Curved twill over 8 shafts

Threading																														
8															X	X												X	X
7												X	X	X												X	X		
6								X	X	X	X														X				
5					X	X	X																	X					
4				X	X																			X						
3			X																		X	X								
2		X																	X	X	X									
1	X																	X												

3 x 2 x 1 x 2 twill

Lifting plan	X	X			X			X
	X			X			X	X
			X			X	X	X
		X			X	X	X	
	X			X	X	X		
			X	X	X			X
		X	X	X			X	
	X	X	X			X		
	1	2	3	4	5	6	7	8

Disturbed reverse twill over 8 shafts

Threading																														
8																	X												X
7												X				X											X		
6											X		X		X										X		X			
5								X		X				X										X		X				
4				X				X		X												X		X						
3			X		X		X														X		X							
2		X				X														X										
1	X																		X											

3 x 2 x 1 x 2 twill

Lifting plan	X	X			X			X
	X			X			X	X
			X			X	X	X
		X			X	X	X	
	X			X	X	X		
			X	X	X			X
		X	X	X			X	
	X	X	X			X		
	1	2	3	4	5	6	7	8

1 x 7 twill

	X						X
X						X	
					X		
				X			
			X				
		X					
	X						
X							
1	2	3	4	5	6	7	8

2 x 6 twill

X							X
						X	X
					X	X	
				X	X		
			X	X			
		X	X				
	X	X					
X	X						
1	2	3	4	5	6	7	8

3 x 5 twill

X	XX						X
X						X	X
					X	X	X
				X	X	X	
			X	X	X		
		X	X	X			
	X	X	X				
X	X	X					
1	2	3	4	5	6	7	8

4 x 4 twill

X	X						X
X						X	X
					X	X	X
				X	X	X	X
			X	X	X	X	
		X	X	X	X		
	X	X	X	X			
X	X	X	X				
1	2	3	4	5	6	7	8

5 x 3 twill

X	X	X	X				X
X	X	X				X	X
X	X				X	X	X
X				X	X	X	X
			X	X	X	X	
		X	X	X	X		
	X	X	X	X	X		
X	X	X	X	X			
1	2	3	4	5	6	7	8

6 x 2 twill

X	X	X	X	X			X
X	X	X	X			X	X
X	X	X			X	X	X
X	X			X	X	X	X
X			X	X	X	X	X
		X	X	X	X	X	X
	X	X	X	X	X	X	
X	X	X	X	X	X		
1	2	3	4	5	6	7	8

7 x 1 twill

X	X	X	X	X			X
X	X	X	X	X		X	X
X	X	X	X		X	X	X
X	X	X		X	X	X	X
X	X		X	X	X	X	X
X		X	X	X	X	X	X
	X	X	X	X	X	X	X
X	X	X	X	X	X	X	
1	2	3	4	5	6	7	8

1 x 1 x 1 x 5 twill

	X						X
X						X	
					X		X
				X		X	
			X		X		
		X		X			
	X		X				
X		X					
1	2	3	4	5	6	7	8

1 x 1 x 1 x 1 x 3 x 1 twill

	X		X	X	X		X
X		X	X	X		X	
	X	X	X		X		X
X	X	X		X		X	
X	X		X		X		X
X		X		X		X	X
	X		X		X	X	
X		X		X	X		
1	2	3	4	5	6	7	8

3 x 2 x 1 x 2 twill

X	X			X			X
X			X			X	X
		X			X	X	X
	X			X	X	X	
X			X	X	X		
		X	X	X			X
	X	X	X			X	
X	X	X			X		
1	2	3	4	5	6	7	8

2 x 1 x 4 x 1 twill

X		X	X	X			X
	X	X	X	X		X	X
X	X	X	X		X	X	
X	X	X		X	X		X
X	X		X	X		X	X
X		X	X		X	X	X
	X	X		X	X	X	X
X	X		X	X	X	X	
1	2	3	4	5	6	7	8

5 x 1 x 1 x 1 twill

X	X	X	X		X		X
X	X	X		X		X	X
X	X		X		X	X	X
X		X		X	X	X	X
	X		X	X	X	X	X
X		X	X	X	X	X	
	X	X	X	X	X		X
X	X	X	X	X		X	
1	2	3	4	5	6	7	8

When designing your own regular twill pattern, you need to ensure that the top, bottom and sides of the plan match up to give an uninterrupted diagonal line. This applies no matter how many shafts you are using.

Draw your plan on point paper. Continue the plan vertically and horizontally to ensure there is a continuous diagonal line; the number of threads lifting and the number staying down should add up to the total number of shafts being used.

EXAMPLES OF TWILL PATTERNS OVER EIGHT SHAFTS

Combination of eight-shaft twills including 1 x 7 and 4 x 4, using spun and filament silk.

Combination of eight-shaft twills including 1 x 7 and 4 x 4, using spun and filament silk.

A combination of twills using a point draft/threading plan over eight shafts.

1 x 7 twill using a point draft/threading plan over eight shafts. Cotton and viscose.

1 x 7 twill in wool yarns using a straight draft/threading plan.

4 x 4 twill with wool warp and weft using a point draft/threading plan.

Detail of a 4 x 4 twill with wool warp and weft using a point draft/threading plan.

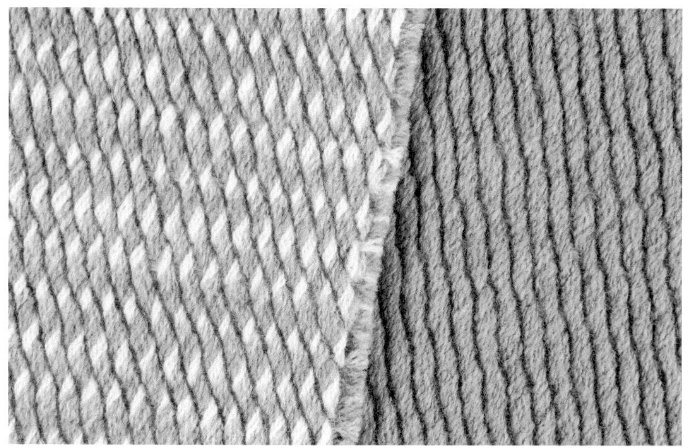

7 x 1 twill showing the face and reverse of the cloth using wool yarns in warp and weft.

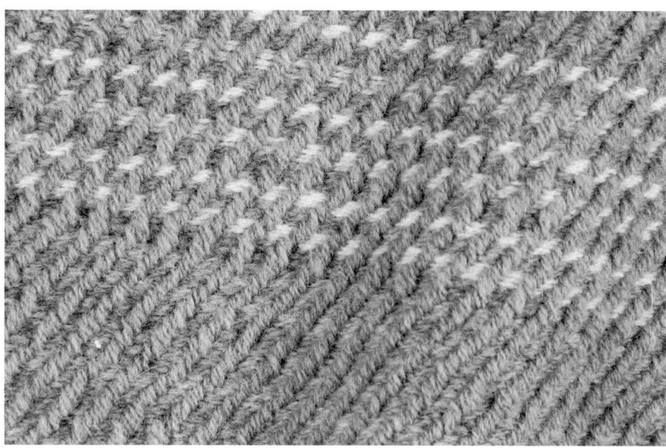

4 x 4 twill using wool yarns in warp and weft.

A 1 x 7 twill with plain weave using a nylon monofilament warp and coloured and clear lurex weft yarn.

A 4 x 4 twill with plain weave using a nylon monofilament warp and coloured and clear lurex weft yarn.

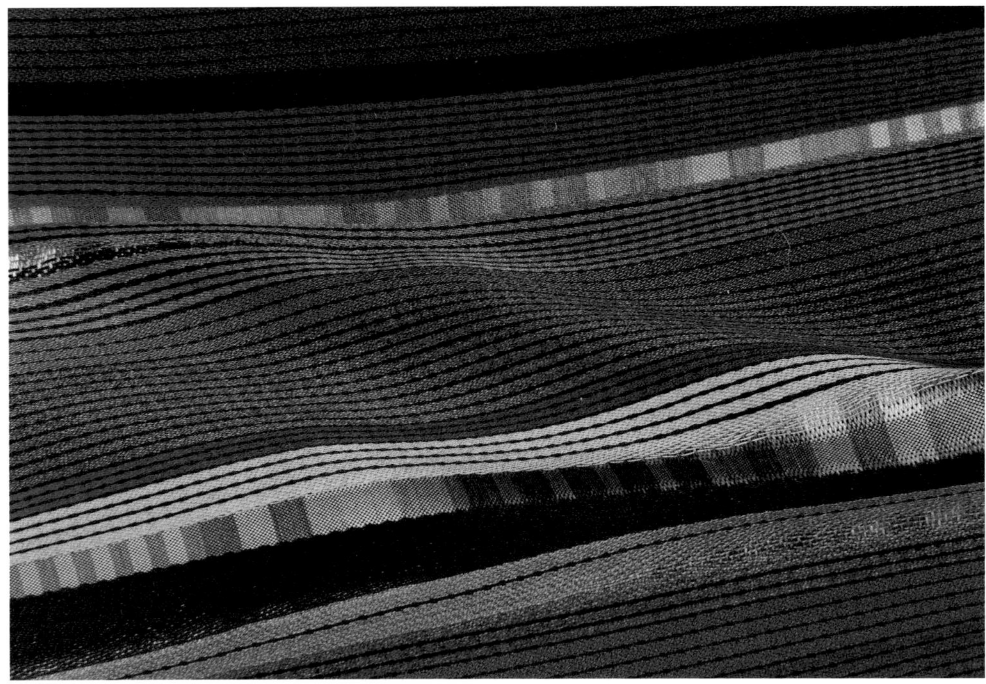

Top: 1 x 7 twill against plain weave using a cotton warp and filament silk weft to give a glossy finish.

Bottom: 1 x 7 twill using filament silk and linen in the weft.

EXAMPLES OF TWILL PATTERNS OVER 16-SHAFT POINT DRAFT

Various twill weave combinations using a point draft/threading plan over 16 shafts. Cotton warp and weft.

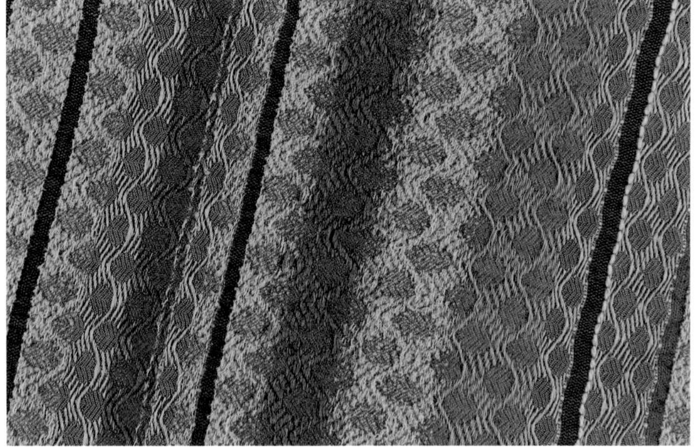

Contrasting warp- and weft-faced twill weave combination used to form patterns.

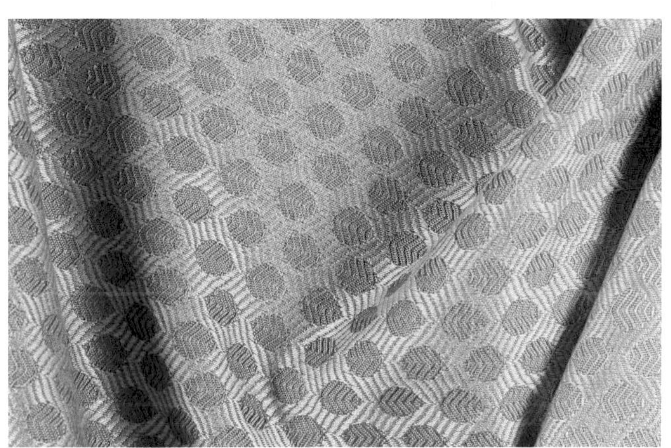

Contrasting warp- and weft-faced twill weave combination used to form patterns.

COMBINING TWILLS

When weaving the six- or eight-shaft twill examples, you can repeat one pattern throughout your fabric design, or you can use a combination of several patterns. This will give you a horizontal stripe formed by contrasting structures. However, providing that you have sufficient shafts at your disposal, it is possible to set different twill weaves side by side to create a chequerboard effect. Experimenting with different warp and weft colours and with textured and smooth yarns will create variety and contrast within the design. To create two opposing weaves side by side, you need to use a block threading plan.

BLOCK THREADING

A block threading plan, or draft, is where the total shafts at your disposal are divided by two – or three or four in some cases, depending on the number of shafts on the loom. A minimum of two shafts is needed for each block, but if a twill weave is required, then you need a minimum of three shafts per block. A prescribed number of ends are threaded onto each set of shafts, normally in a straight draft, but you could use any combination of complex threading arrangements to achieve more interesting effects.

The example here is over eight shafts, with block 1 using shafts 1 to 4, and block 2 using shafts 5 to 8. The number of times that you repeat the threading plan in each block depends on the thickness of the yarn that you use and the scale required. You can, of course, vary the widths throughout the design to give a more complex composition. Draw out the design on paper first so that you can judge which proportions work best.

Any four-shaft weaves can be used. In this example a 3 × 1 twill against a 1 × 3 twill is used, giving a warp- and weft-faced contrast. Plain weave can also be used as one of your structures, and, when set against a loose weave such as a twill, can result in curved lines being formed around the blocks. This happens because the yarn in the tight, frequent intersections of the plain-weave blocks tries to force its way into the looser twill-weave blocks.

Block threading over 8 shafts

Threading																	Lifting plan		X	X	X				X
8												X				X		X	X	X				X	
7											X				X			X	X		X		X		
6										X				X				X		X	X	X			
5									X				X								X		X	X	X
4				X				X												X		X	X	X	
3			X				X												X			X	X		X
2		X				X												X				X		X	X
1	X				X													1	2	3	4	5	6	7	8
Design																									

EXAMPLES OF TWILLS USING BLOCK THREADING ON 16 SHAFTS USING EIGHT-SHAFT WEAVES

1 x 7 twill, plain weave and crêpe weave forming blocks of contrasting structures. Cotton warp and filament silk weft. Two blocks each on eight shafts.

1 x 7 and 7 x 1 twills forming a vertical stripe through the cloth. The warp yarn is cotton, the weft yarn is filament silk. Two blocks each on eight shafts.

1 x 7 twill against plain weave using a striped cotton warp and filament silk weft in the twill to give a glossy finish. Two blocks each on eight shafts.

1 x 7 twill against plain weave using a cotton warp and filament silk weft in the twill to give a glossy finish. Two blocks each on eight shafts.

SATIN AND SATEEN WEAVES

Satin and sateen weaves are highly lustrous. The finer the yarn used, the more luxurious the finish. Both types of cloth have a soft handle, are very pliable and, because of the density of threads, the colour is more concentrated and eye-popping.

The structures are formed by breaking the twill order; unlike twill weaves that have a distinctive diagonal line, these fabrics typically have an unbroken cloth surface. The thread intersection points are called 'stitches' and are not random, but organized in such a way as to give a non-directional pattern. They are not visible because they are hidden to some extent by either warp or weft floats. The threading plan is over a straight draft and, while it is possible to weave a satin on four shafts, using 5, 6, 7, 8, 10, 12, 16 or more shafts gives a better-quality effect.

You can combine the two structures by using a block draft, where warp- and weft-faced designs contrast with each other. Experiment with horizontal and vertical colour combinations to give an exciting variety of outcomes.

TIPS FOR WEAVING SATIN OR SATEEN

- When using a satin weave, the loom preparation takes longer. The increased number of ends in the warp mean more threading.
- Setting up the loom is faster when using a sateen weave, as the warp threads are sett less densely to allow the weft to cover the warp completely. Because this is a weft-faced fabric, however, it takes longer to weave. You are able to beat down the picks more readily, resulting in more picks to the cm/inch, to create the required density.
- Once you have designed your satin, whether it is a single colour or a stripe, the colours are constant throughout and, because it is a dense sett, it will be difficult to disguise or alter the colour.
- If using sateen, you can change the colour at will as it is created through the weft.
- If you want to produce a variety of satin designs in different proportions and combinations of colours, but do not want to set up the loom for each separate design, then you can produce them in the weft. Set up the loom using yarn at a normal sett, and weave your designs as sateen. Once the warp is complete, separate each design and rotate it through 90 degrees so that the weft becomes the warp. This is also known as **railroading** your weave design.

THE SETT OF THE WARP THREADS

The number of warp threads per cm/inch is called the 'sett' and is used to describe the density of a woven cloth.

- **A normal sett is based on a plain-weave structure.**
- **A cloth has a close sett when the warp ends are crammed with more ends to the cm/inch than would normally be used to create a plain weave. This is used when weaving twills or satin structures, where there are floats creating the weave effect.**
- **A loose sett is where the warp threads are used at fewer ends to the cm/inch. It is used in weft-faced rib weaves to allow the weft thread to cover the warp.**

All three setts are used when designing a spaced and crammed weave.

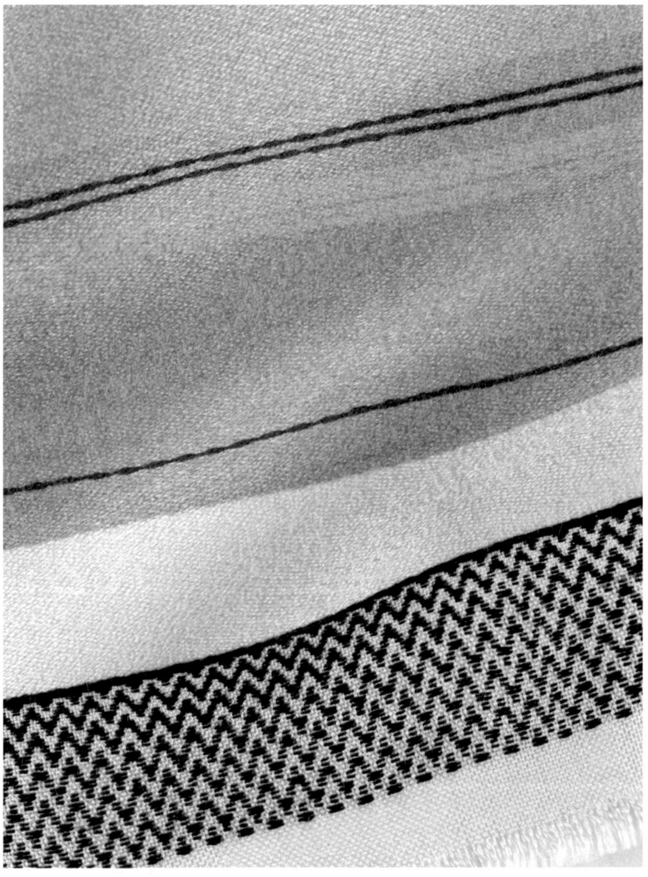

Satin weave used with reverse twill.

SATIN

This is a warp-faced cloth, created by warp floats on the surface of the cloth. A dense setting is needed to give the right quality. This is because the weave structure will be too loose if set for a plain weave. Considerably more ends per cm/inch are used than for a normal cloth. When calculating the density of the yarn to be used for a satin cloth, if the yarn selected is normally set at 20epc (48epi), then you should add at least half again to get 30epc (72epi). For an even more lustrous finish, double it to get 40epc (96epi).

If vertical stripes of satin weave are to be used as a feature in the cloth design, and are combined with weaves with more frequent intersections such as plain weave, then two separately tensioned warps are necessary. Two beams are used – one for each warp. This is because the plain-weave area will grow faster than the satin, leaving the neighbouring threads loose and lacking definition. The plain-weave section should be sett at the normal epc/epi.

The satin stripe will give a raised surface against the plain weave, created by the plain-weave structure moving in on the more loosely woven satin structure.

RAILROADING

This term is used to describe a fabric that is designed through the weft and turned through 90 degrees when taken from the loom. It is a great way to experiment with any stripe combinations, providing flexibility and variety in the number of designs you can produce. There are an unlimited number of options in yarn choice, weave structure, colour, proportion and scale.

LIFTING PLANS FOR SATIN WEAVE

4-end satin

Threading					Lifting plan	X	X		X
4				X		X	X	X	
3			X			X		X	X
2		X					X	X	X
1	X				Shaft	1	2	3	4

6-end satin

Threading													
6						X	Lifting plan	X	X	X		X	X
5					X			X	X	X	X	X	
4				X				X		X	X	X	X
3			X					X	X	X	X		X
2		X						X	X		X	X	X
1	X								X	X	X	X	X
							Shaft	1	2	3	4	3	4

8-end satin

Threading																	
8								X	Lifting plan	X	X	X	X	X		X	X
7							X			X	X		X	X	X	X	X
6						X				X	X	X	X	X	X	X	
5					X					X	X	X	X		X	X	X
4				X						X		X	X	X	X	X	X
3			X							X	X	X	X	X	X		X
2		X								X	X	X		X	X	X	X
1	X										X	X	X	X	X	X	X
									Shaft	1	2	3	4	5	6	7	8

Diagram of an 8-end satin weave

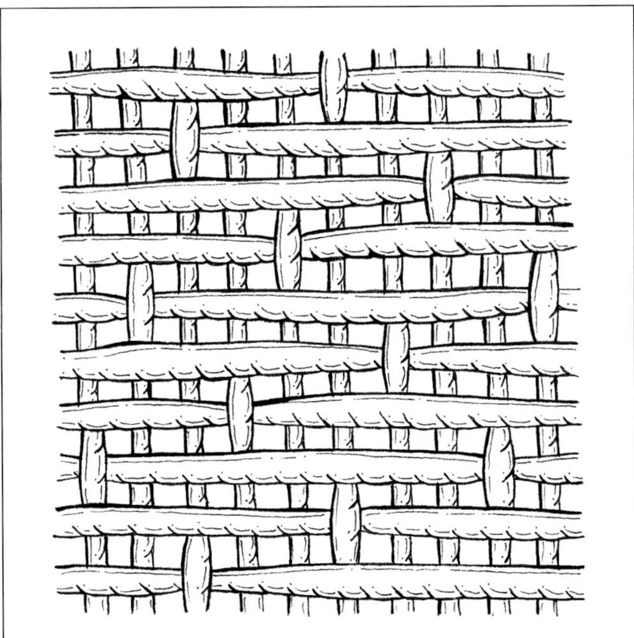

12-end satin

12												X	Lifting plan	X	X	X	X	X	X	X		X	X	X	X
11											X			X	X		X	X	X	X	X	X	X	X	X
10										X				X	X		X	X	X	X	X	X		X	X
9									X					X	X	X	X		X	X	X	X	X	X	X
8								X						X	X	X	X	X	X	X	X	X	X	X	
7							X							X	X	X	X	X	X		X	X	X	X	X
6						X								X		X	X	X	X	X	X	X	X	X	X
5					X									X	X	X	X	X	X	X	X		X	X	X
4				X										X	X	X		X	X	X	X	X	X	X	X
3			X											X	X	X	X	X	X	X	X	X	X		X
2		X												X	X	X	X	X		X	X	X	X	X	X
1	X														X	X	X	X	X	X	X	X	X	X	X
													Shaft	1	2	3	4	5	6	7	8	9	10	11	12

15-end satin

7-end satin

10-end satin

																		X	X	X		X	X	X	X	X	X
																		X	X	X	X	X	X		X	X	X
																		X	X	X	X	X	X	X	X	X	
								X	X		X	X	X	X				X	X		X	X	X	X	X	X	X
								X	X	X	X		X	X				X	X	X	X	X		X	X	X	X
X	X		X	X				X	X	X	X	X	X					X	X	X	X	X	X	X	X		X
X	X	X	X					X		X	X	X	X	X				X		X	X	X	X	X	X	X	X
X		X	X	X				X	X	X		X	X	X				X	X	X	X		X	X	X	X	X
X	X	X		X				X	X	X	X	X		X				X	X	X	X	X	X	X		X	X
	X	X	X	X					X	X	X	X	X	X					X	X	X	X	X	X	X	X	X
1	2	3	4	5				1	2	3	4	5	6	7				1	2	3	4	5	6	7	8	9	10

16-end satin

X	X	X	X	X		X	X	X	X	X	X	X	X	X	X
X	X	X	X	X	X	X	X	X	X	X	X		X	X	X
X	X	X		X	X	X	X	X	X	X	X	X	X	X	X
X	X	X	X	X	X	X	X	X	X		X	X	X	X	X
X		X	X	X	X	X	X	X	X	X	X	X	X	X	X
X	X	X	X	X	X	X	X		X	X	X	X	X	X	X
X	X	X	X	X	X	X	X	X	X	X	X	X	X	X	
X	X	X	X	X	X		X	X	X	X	X	X	X	X	X
X	X	X	X	X	X	X	X	X	X	X	X	X		X	X
X	X	X	X		X	X	X	X	X	X	X	X	X	X	X
X	X	X	X	X	X	X	X	X	X	X		X	X	X	X
X	X		X	X	X	X	X	X	X	X	X	X	X	X	X
X	X	X	X	X	X	X	X	X		X	X	X	X	X	X
	X	X	X	X	X	X	X	X	X	X	X	X	X	X	X
1	2	3	4	5	6	7	8	9	10	11	12	13	14	15	16

EXAMPLES OF SATIN WEAVE

Satin weave with reverse twill. Spun and filament silk.

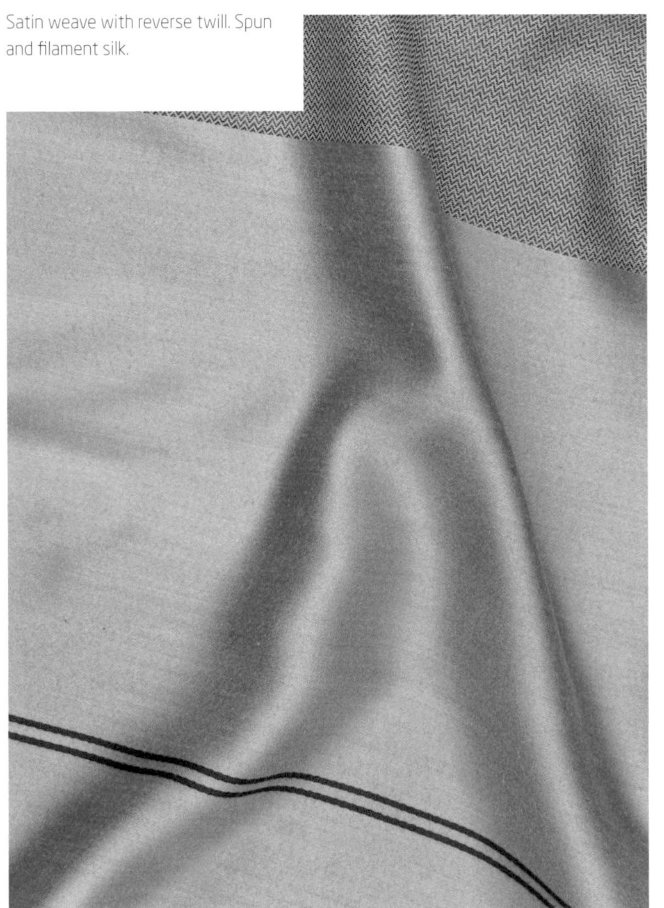

Satin weave with reverse twill. Spun and filament silk.

Satin and sateen weave in blocks. Spun and filament silk.

Satin and sateen weave in blocks. Spun and filament silk.

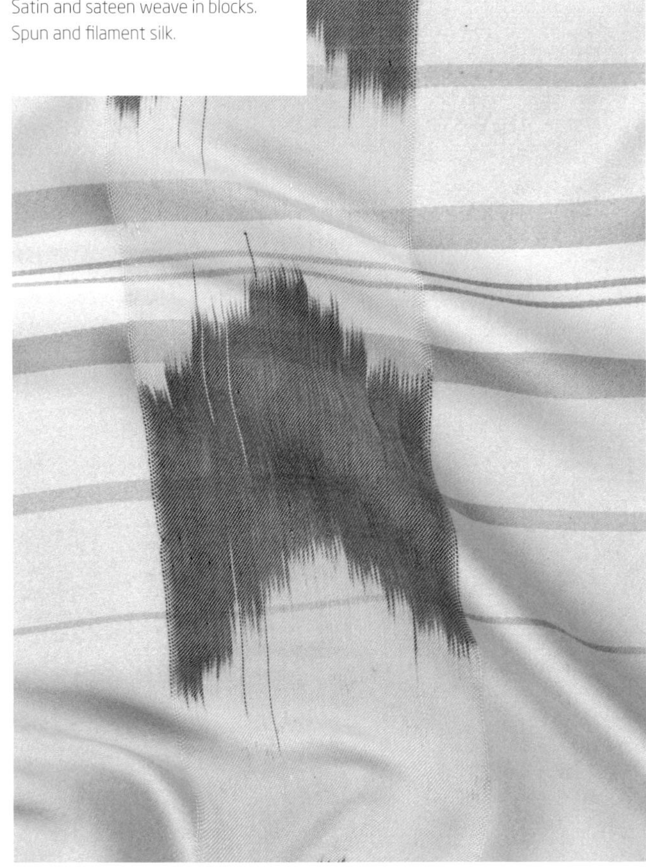

SATEEN

This is a weft-faced cloth with a preponderance of weft picks covering the warp yarn. The setting of the warp yarn is normal, allowing the weft floats to cover them.

Lifting plans for sateen weave

4-end sateen

Threading					Lifting plan				
4				X				X	
3			X						X
2		X					X		
1	X					X			
					Shaft	1	2	3	4

6-end sateen

Threading							Lifting plan						
6						X					X		
5					X								X
4				X					X				
3			X									X	
2		X								X			
1	X							X					X
							Shaft	1	2	3	4	5	6

8-end sateen

Threading									Lifting plan									
8								X								X		
7							X						X					
6						X												X
5					X										X			
4				X								X						
3			X														X	
2		X												X				
1	X										X							
									Shaft		1	2	3	4	5	6	7	8

Sateen weave with a section of the warp tie-dyed.

12-end sateen

Threading													Lifting plan												
12												X									X				
11											X					X									
10										X													X		
9									X									X							
8								X																	X
7							X													X					
6						X																			
5					X										X							X			
4				X													X								
3			X																					X	
2		X																	X						
1	X													X											
													Shaft	1	2	3	4	5	6	7	8	9	10	11	12

15-end sateen 7-end sateen 10-end sateen

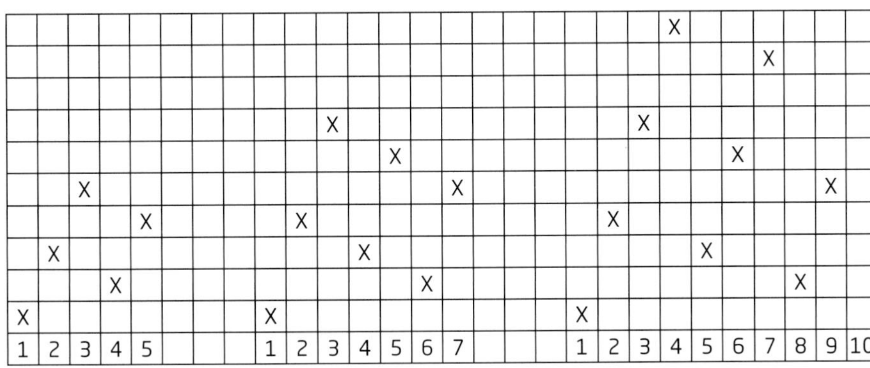

16-end sateen

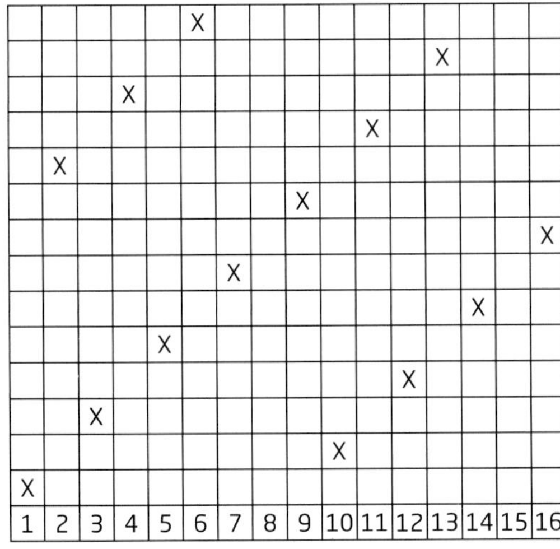

EXAMPLES OF SATIN AND SATEEN WEAVE

Satin and sateen weave in blocks. Spun and filament silk.

Satin and sateen weave showing the face and the reverse of the cloth. Spun and filament silk.

Satin and sateen weave in blocks. Spun and filament silk.

Satin and sateen weave in blocks. Spun and filament silk.

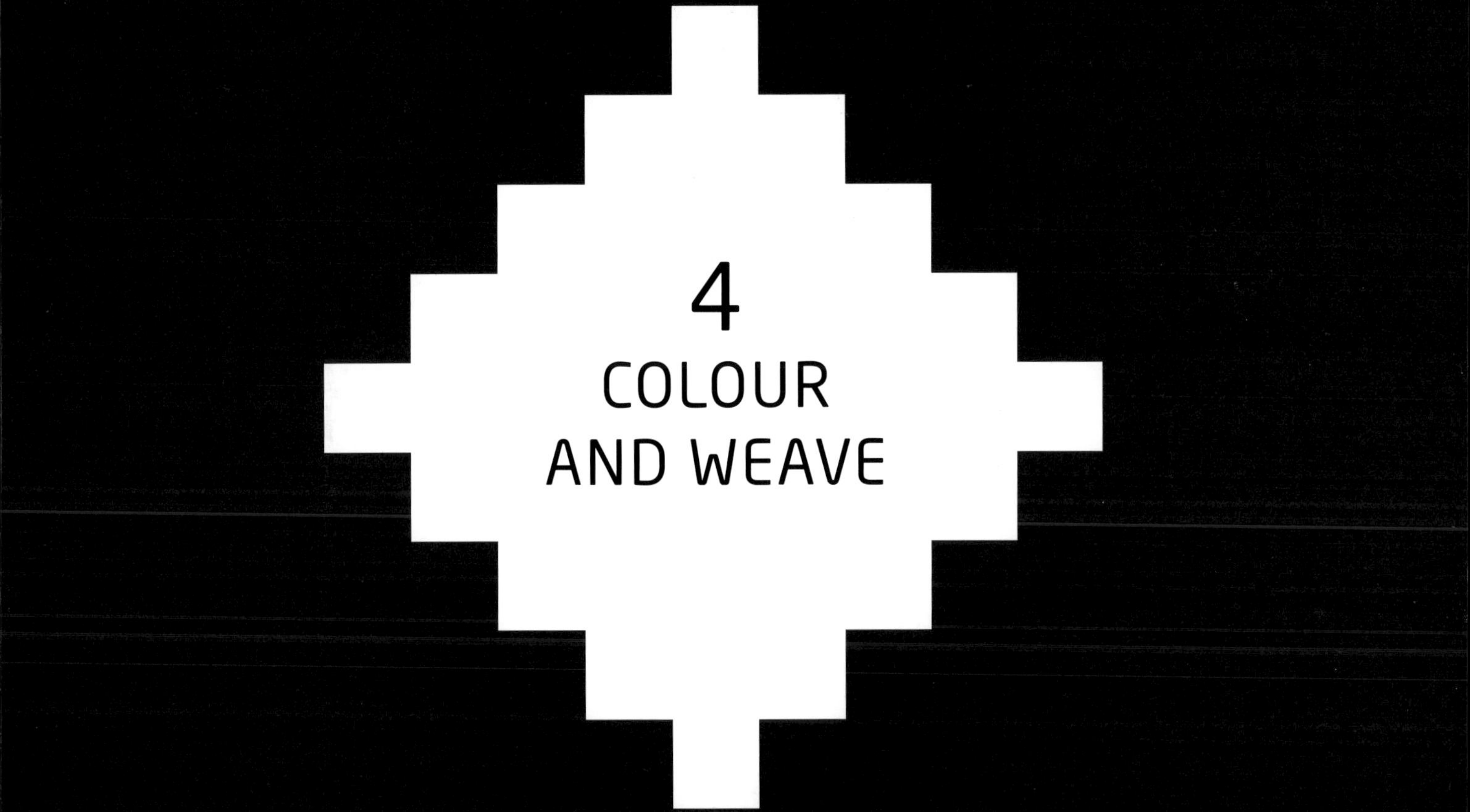

4
COLOUR AND WEAVE

COLOUR AND WEAVE

In its simplest form, a colour and weave effect is a design achieved by using two contrasting colours, combined with basic four-shaft weave structures such as plain weave or twill. The pattern is frequently quite different in appearance from either the warp and weft order or the weave structure. This is because the weave tends to break the continuity of the colours in the warp and weft.

VISUALIZING THE WEAVE STRUCTURE WITH COLOUR

There are a couple of simple exercises that can be used to enable the designer to see the effect any colour plan will produce when using a given weave structure. They allow you to work out your designs before you commit to weaving.

PAPER WEAVING

- Use thin strips of paper or ribbon of equal width and length – 1 × 15cm (3/8 × 6in) – in contrasting colours. Light against dark shows the strongest pattern.
- Plan the warp stripe. End and end – one end of each colour alternating – or two and two (two light, two dark; three light, three dark; four light, four dark, and so on). Using one proportion for each experiment to begin with will help you to understand the process more easily.
- Pin or tape your paper/ribbon to a piece of card in the warp sequence you have planned.
- Work on the basis that there is a straight draft over four shafts – if you find it easier, then number each strip of paper at the top.
- Additional paper strips in the same colours are used as the weft. Try using one of the following weave structures – plain weave, hopsack, 2 × 2 twill, 1 × 3 twill or 3 × 1 twill.
- Experiment with the weft stripe sequence – end and end, two and two etc.

1 2 3 4 1 2 3 4 1 2 3 4 1 2 3 4 1 2 3 4

2 x 2 twill and 3 x 3 weft colour sequence.

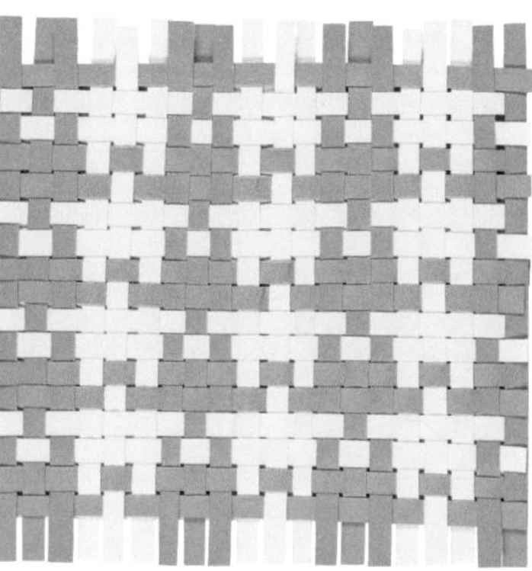

1 2 3 4 1 2 3 4 1 2 3 4 1 2 3 4 1 2 3 4

Plain weave and 2 x 2 weft colour sequence.

1 2 3 4 1 2 3 4 1 2 3 4 1 2 3 4 1 2 3 4

2 x 2 twill and 1 x 1 weft colour sequence.

1 2 3 4 1 2 3 4 1 2 3 4 1 2 3 4 1 2 3 4

1 x 3 twill and 3 x 3 weft colour sequence.

ON POINT PAPER

- On your point paper you need to record the threading plan, the sequence of warp colours, the sequence of weft colours and the lifting plan.
- Assume that the warp ends are alternating black and white, and that the weft sequence is the same.
- On the point paper, begin several rows down, in the squares below the threading plan – at least double the length of the lifting plan so that you can see a couple of repeats. Start in the bottom row of these.
- Follow the first pattern row in the lifting plan.
- Begin with a black weft. If a black end is lifting, colour in the square below the corresponding end. If a white end is lifting, leave the square white. All white ends that are not lifting, whether they are black or white, should be coloured black as they are covered by the weft colour.
- Move to the second row of the lifting plan and the weave plan.
- The second pick is white. If a black end is lifting, colour in the corresponding square black. Leave all other squares white – if it is a white end lifting it will remain white, and all yarns not lifting will be covered by the white weft.
- Move up in sequence until you have completed two repeats, and continue if you want to see a larger area of pattern.

WARP AND WEFT COLOUR SEQUENCE

Once the principles have been understood, try experimenting with the warp and weft colour sequence. The addition of a single end in a contrasting colour or texture at strategic points in the warp plan will increase the overall scale of the design and can help to separate contrasting patterns. Repeat the feature in the weft plan to create a large check.

WORKING WITH STRIPE COMBINATIONS

Experiment with stripe combinations in the warp. Either repeat the same order across the width of your design, or repeat one sequence for several ends then change to another. This will result in contrasting patterns across the width of the cloth.

Suggested combinations:

1 black, 1 white – change to 1 white, 1 black for a contrast in pattern
2 black, 2 white
3 black, 3 white
4 black, 4 white
2 black, 1 white
1 black, 2 white
3 black, 1 white
4 black, 2 white
2 black, 4 white
And so on.

PROJECT 1: END AND END WARP STRIPE

These examples use two colours in the warp – one black end (X) and one white end (O), alternating over four shafts in a straight draft. The sequence changes after two repeats.

THE THICKNESS OF YARN THAT YOU USE IS IMPORTANT. FOR A SMALL-SCALE PATTERN USE A FINE YARN. THE THICKER THE YARN YOU USE, THE LARGER THE SCALE AND THE STRONGER THE CONTRAST.

1. Plain weave: single-colour weft

Threading																	Lifting plan				
4				O				O				X				X	Black		X		X
3			X				X				O				O		Black	X		X	
2		O				O				X				X			Black		X		X
1	X				X				O				O				Black	X		X	
																	Shaft	1	2	3	4
Design																					

2. Plain weave: pick and pick weft (alternate colours)

Threading																	Lifting plan				
4				O				O				X				X	Black		X		X
3			X				X				O				O		White	X		X	
2		O				O				X				X			Black		X		X
1	X				X				O				O				White	X		X	
																	White		X		X
Design																	Black	X		X	
																	White		X		X
																	Black	X		X	
																	Shaft	1	2	3	4

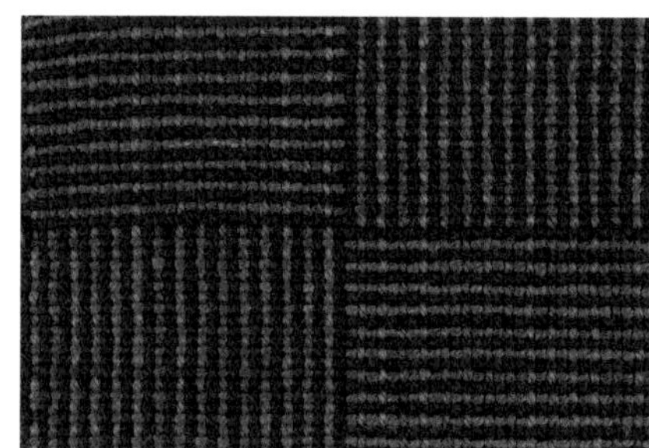

3. 2 x 2 twill: pick and pick weft

Threading																	Lifting plan				
4				O				O				X				X	Black	X			X
3			X				X				O				O		White			X	X
2		O				O				X				X			Black		X	X	
1	X				X				O				O				White	X	X		
																	White	X			X
Design																	Black			X	X
																	White		X	X	
																	Black	X	X		
																	Shaft	1	2	3	4

4. 2 x 2 twill: 2 picks black, 2 picks white in weft

Threading																	Lifting plan				
4				O				O				X				X	Black	X			X
3			X				X				O				O		White			X	X
2		O				O				X				X			Black		X	X	
1	X				X				O				O				White	X	X		
																	White	X			X
Design																	Black			X	X
																	White		X	X	
																	Black	X	X		
																	Shaft	1	2	3	4

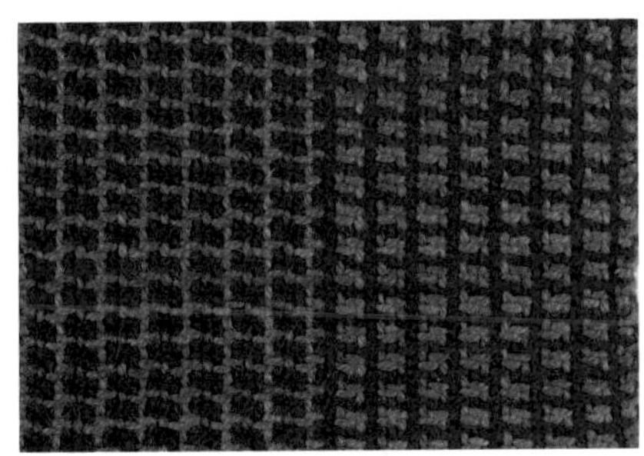

5. Hopsack weave: 2 picks black, 2 picks white in weft

Threading																	Lifting plan				
4				O				O				X				X	Black			X	X
3			X				X				O				O		White			X	X
2		O				O				X				X			Black	X	X		
1	X				X				O				O				White	X	X		
																	White			X	X
Design																	Black			X	X
																	White	X	X		
																	Black	X	X		
																	Shaft	1	2	3	4

6. Hopsack weave: pick and pick weft

Threading																	Lifting plan				
4				O				O				X				X	Black			X	X
3			X				X				O				O		White			X	X
2		O				O				X				X			Black	X	X		
1	X				X				O				O				White	X	X		
																	White			X	X
Design																	Black			X	X
																	White	X	X		
																	Black	X	X		
																	Shaft	1	2	3	4

7. 2 x 2 twill weave (odd lifts) alternating with plain weave (even lifts): pick and pick weft (black end = twill, white end = plain)

Threading																	Lifting plan				
4				O				O				X				X	White		X		X
3			X				X				O				O		Black	X			X
2		O				O				X				X			White	X		X	
1	X				X				O				O				Black			X	X
																	White		X		X
Design																	Black		X	X	
																	White	X		X	
																	Black	X	X		
																	Shaft	1	2	3	4

8. 2 x 2 twill weave (odd lifts) alternating with plain weave (even lifts): 2 picks black, 2 picks white in weft

Threading																	Lifting plan				
4				O				O				X				X	White		X		X
3			X				X				O				O		White	X			X
2		O				O				X				X			Black	X		X	
1	X				X				O				O				Black			X	X
																	White		X		X
Design																	White		X	X	
																	Black	X		X	
																	Black	X	X		
																	Shaft	1	2	3	4

PROJECT 2: 2 X 2 WARP STRIPE

These examples use two colours in the warp – two ends black (X) and two ends white (O), threaded over four shafts in a straight draft. Shafts 1 and 2 = black, shafts 3 and 4 = white.

1. Plain weave: 2 black, 2 white picks

Threading																	Lifting plan				
4				O				O				O				O	White		X		X
3			O				O				O				O		White	X		X	
2		X				X				X				X			Black		X		X
1	X				X				X				X				Black	X		X	
																	White		X		X
Design																	White	X		X	
																	Black		X		X
																	Black	X		X	
																	Shaft	1	2	3	4

2. Plain weave: pick and pick weft

Threading																	Lifting plan				
4				O				O				O				O	White		X		X
3			O				O				O				O		White	X		X	
2		X				X				X				X			Black		X		X
1	X				X				X				X				Black	X		X	
																	White		X		X
Design																	White	X		X	
																	Black		X		X
																	Black	X		X	
																	Shaft	1	2	3	4

WEFT COLOUR SEQUENCE

The order in which you use the weft yarn can change the overall design. Try altering the sequence of colours in the weft to achieve different patterns. For instance, if you are weaving a 2 × 2 twill starting with two black picks then two white picks for the sequence, try using one black, two white then one black in the sequence and see what happens.

3. 2 x 2 twill: 2 black, 2 white picks

Threading																	Lifting plan				
4				O				O				O				O	White	X			X
3			O				O				O				O		White			X	X
2		X				X				X				X			Black		X	X	
1	X				X				X				X				Black	X	X		
																	White	X			X
Design																	White			X	X
																	Black		X	X	
																	Black	X	X		
																	Shaft	1	2	3	4

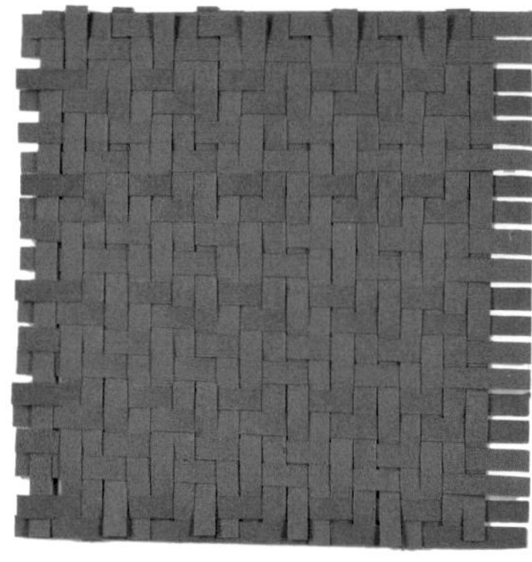

1 2 3 4 1 2 3 4 1 2 3 4 1 2 3 4 1 2 3 4

4. 2 x 2 twill: pick and pick weft

Threading																	Lifting plan				
4				O				O				O				O	White	X			X
3			O				O				O				O		Black			X	X
2		X				X				X				X			White		X	X	
1	X				X				X				X				Black	X	X		
																	White	X			X
Design																	Black			X	X
																	White		X	X	
																	Black	X	X		
																	Shaft	1	2	3	4

1 2 3 4 1 2 3 4 1 2 3 4 1 2 3 4 1 2 3 4

5. 2 x 2 twill weave (odd lifts) alternating with plain weave (even lifts): pick and pick weft (black end = twill, white end = plain)

Threading																	Lifting plan				
4				O				O				O				O	White		X		X
3			O				O				O				O		Black	X			X
2		X				X				X				X			White	X		X	
1	X				X				X				X				Black	X	X		
																	White			X	X
Design																	Black		X		X
																	White	X		X	
																	Black	X	X		
																	Shaft	1	2	3	4

6. Herringbone: 2 black, 2 white picks

Threading																	Lifting plan				
4				O				O				O				O	White			X	X
3			O				O				O				O		White	X			X
2		X				X				X				X			Black	X	X		
1	X				X				X				X				Black		X	X	
																	White	X			X
Design																	White			X	X
																	Black		X	X	
																	Black	X	X		
																	Shaft	1	2	3	4

7. Herringbone: pick and pick weft

Threading																	Lifting plan				
4				O				O				O				O	Black			X	X
3			O				O				O				O		White	X			X
2		X				X				X				X			Black	X	X		
1	X				X				X				X				White		X	X	
																	Black	X			X
Design																	White			X	X
																	Black		X	X	
																	White	X	X		
																	Shaft	1	2	3	4

Any number of combinations of stripe proportion and weave construction are possible using a limited number of shafts. Once you become more confident, you can combine different sequences of stripe in the warp and weft to achieve more complex patterns.

The effect does not have to be confined to two colours or to basic weaves using four shafts. Six- or eight-shaft twills used together with a greater variety of warp and weft colours can produce bolder and more intricate designs.

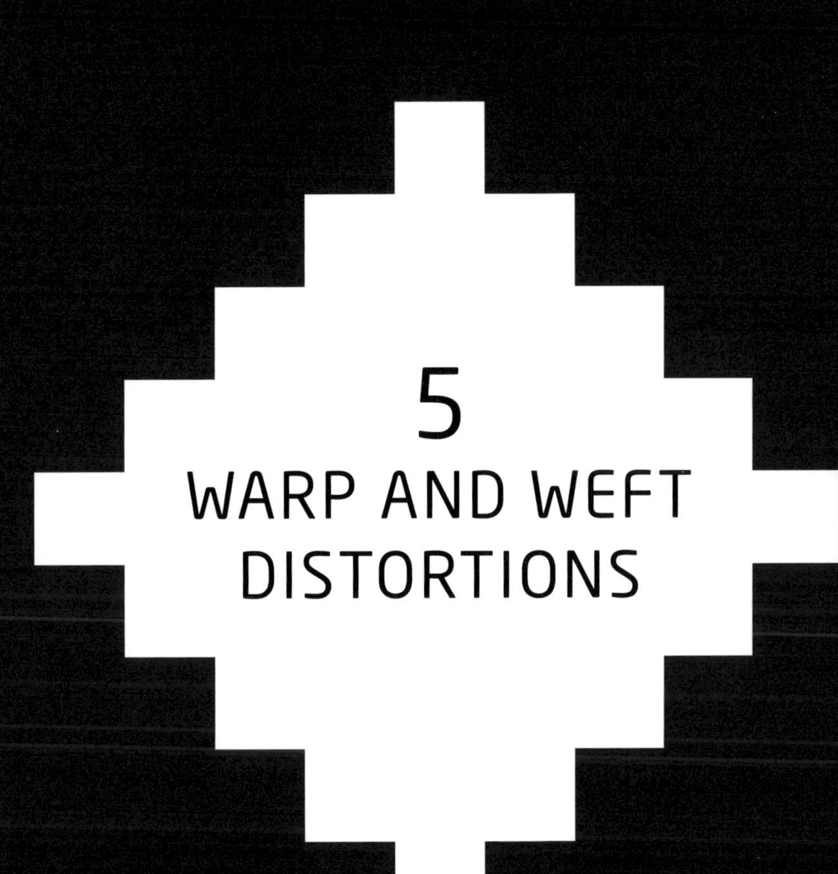

5
WARP AND WEFT DISTORTIONS

WARP AND WEFT DISTORTIONS

Distortions can be created in your fabric designs that will give exciting surface and visual effects. There are several structures and techniques that you can use to achieve different results.

- Grouped warp or weft distortions are created by using opposing weave structures, which result in curved shapes being formed within the cloth.
- Single-end distortions use additional warp or weft threads, which are woven in such a manner as to create a wavy or zigzag line floating on the surface of the cloth.
- Angling the reed creates a diagonal line across the width of the cloth.

GROUPED WEFT DISTORTIONS

The weave construction is based on alternating blocks of plain weave woven alongside blocks of floating warp ends in a chequerboard pattern. The undulating lines are formed by the opposing densely woven structure sitting alongside a loosely woven structure, with the tightly woven ends and picks naturally moving into the loosely woven areas.

The shapes that are formed are known as medallions, and can be outlined and emphasized by using a thick or contrasting coloured weft thread at the beginning of each repeat in the lifting plan.

You need only four shafts to obtain this curved structural effect; experimenting with weft yarns, colours and proportions will give endless design potential and variety.

The overall pattern could be regular, with each block using the same number of ends, or you could alternate between large and small blocks, or even produce a totally random combination of proportions. A gradual increase in the number of ends in each block will give additional movement and undulation.

Once your proportions have been planned, the thickness of the yarn used for the warp will determine the number of ends threaded in each block.

Grouped weft distortions

When following any of the lifting plans suggested, which will create a distorted weft, feature yarns to emphasize the curve should be introduced at the first pick only of each pattern. These yarns can be substantially thicker than the other weft picks to give a pronounced wave, and can be a contrasting colour or the same as the finer weft yarns, depending on the design effect required.

Distorted weft on two blocks. The yarn used is spun silk.

1. Threading plan over 4 shafts

Shaft								
4						X		X
3					X		X	
2		X		X				
1	X		X					
	----repeat----				----repeat----			

Lifting plan A: threading plan 1

Lifting Sequence					
4	X			X	One repeat
3	X		X		
2		X	X		One repeat
1	X		X		
	1	2	3	4	Shaft

For Plan A, lifts 1 to 2 should be repeated until the desired proportion is woven. Then lifts 3 to 4 should be repeated until the desired proportion is woven.

Lifting plan B: threading plan 1

Lifting Sequence					
16		X		X	One repeat
15		X	X		
14		X		X	
13		X	X		
12	X			X	
11	X		X		
10	X			X	
9	X		X		
8		X		X	One repeat
7	X			X	
6		X		X	
5	X			X	
4		X	X		
3	X		X		
2		X	X		
1	X		X		

In both lifting plans, the weft yarn forms a plain-weave structure in alternating blocks, and is trapped between warp floats in the opposing blocks. Plan B shows a slight variation, where the warp floats interchange to give grouped bundles of trapped weft floats.

EXAMPLES OF GROUPED WEFT DISTORTIONS – TWO BLOCKS PLAIN WEAVE

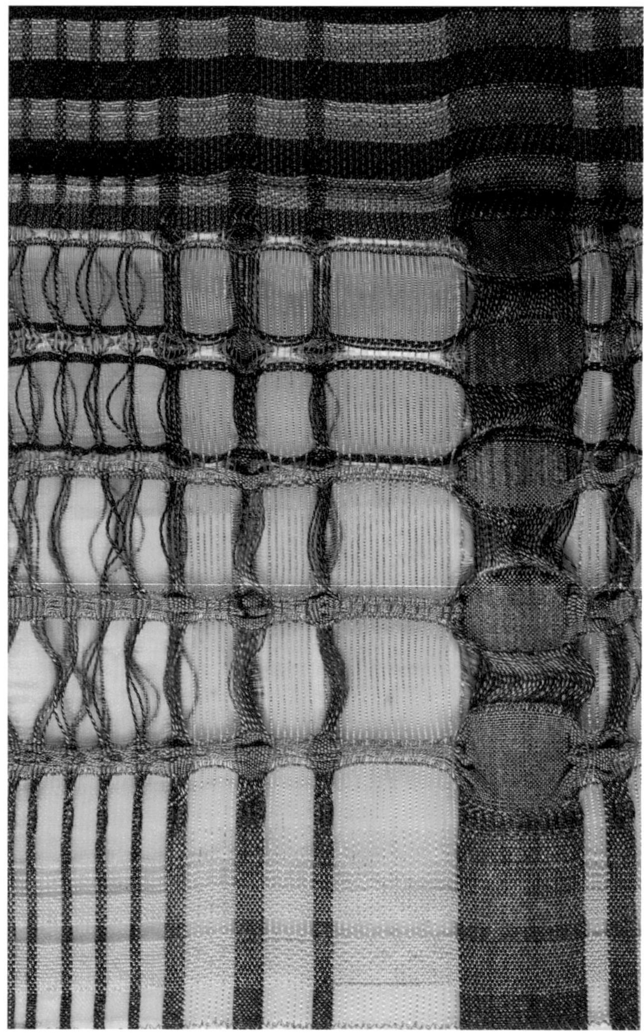

Plain-weave weft distortion on four shafts with a silk and nylon monofilament warp and weft.

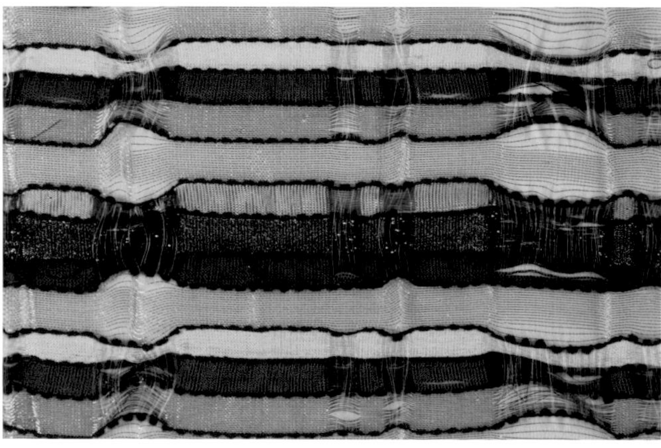

Plain-weave weft distortion with a nylon monofilament warp. Each block is threaded over two shafts. The weft yarn is lurex, filament silk and looped wool.

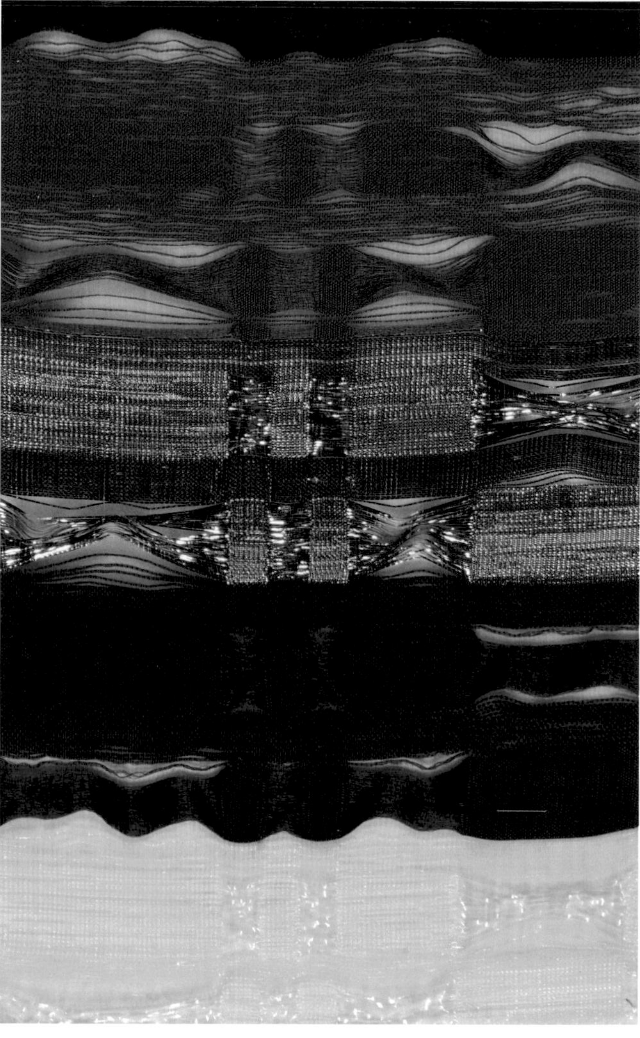

Plain-weave weft distortion with a nylon monofilament warp. Each block is threaded over two shafts. The weft yarn is lurex and filament silk.

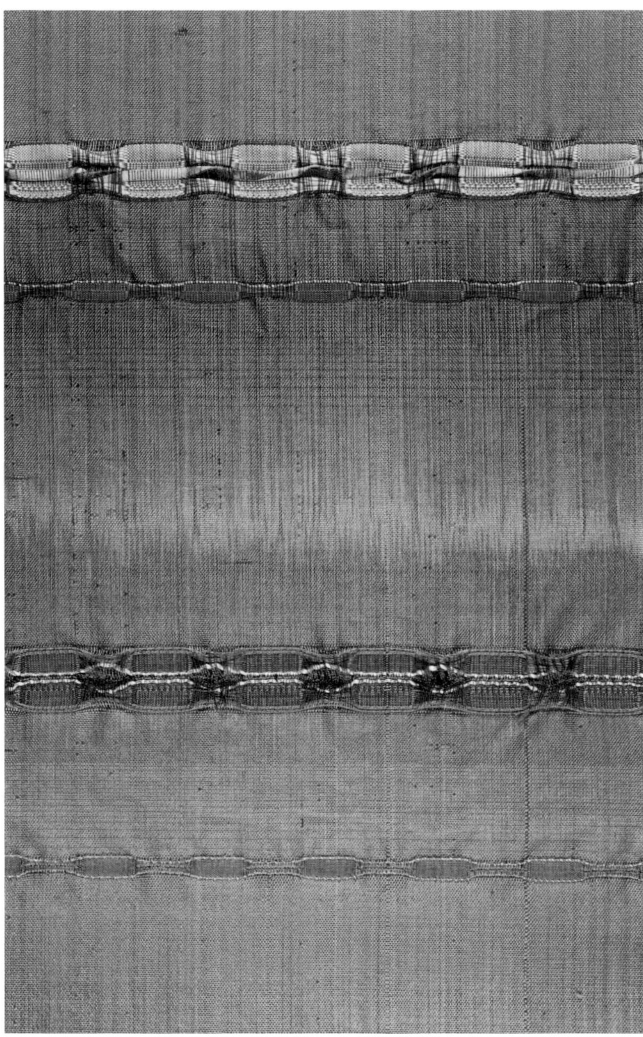

Distorted weft on two blocks against plain weave. The warp and weft are spun silk and a cotton feature yarn has been used to accentuate the curve.

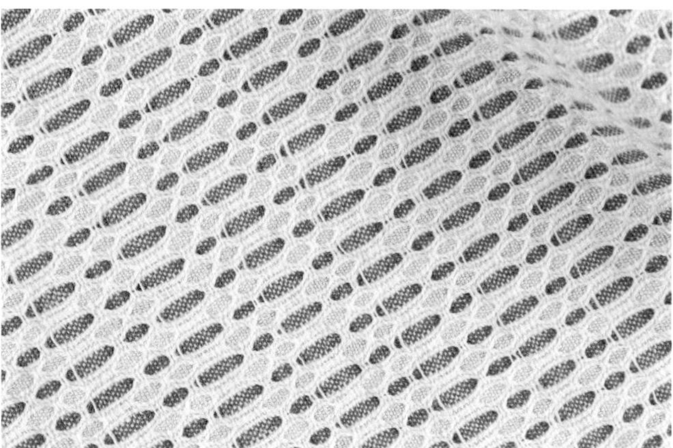

Distorted weft on two blocks.

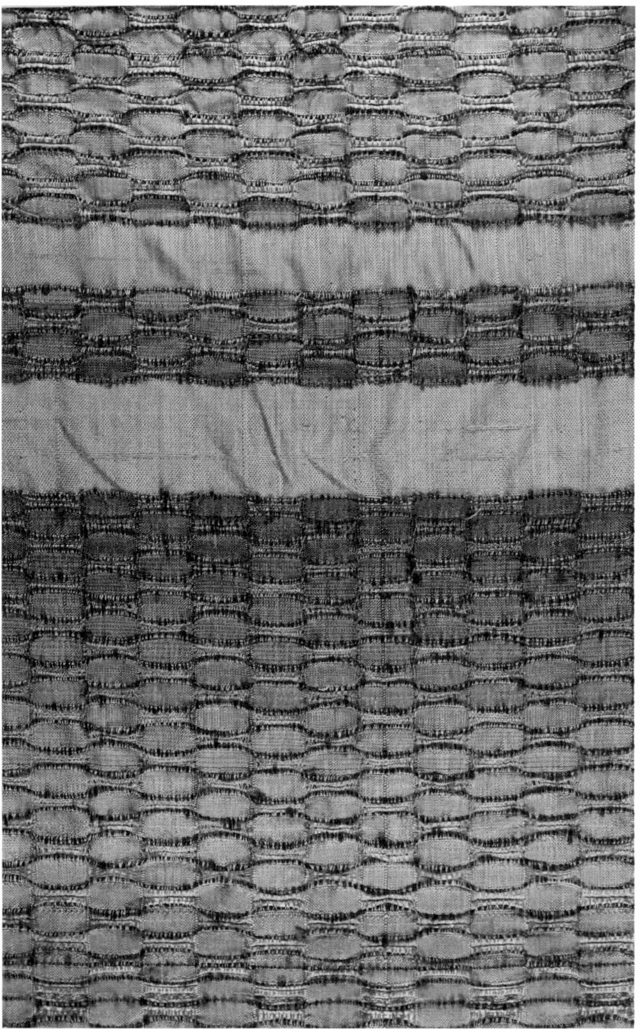

Distorted weft on two blocks against plain weave. The warp and weft are spun silk and a cotton feature yarn has been used to accentuate the curve.

Plain-weave distorted weft using spun silk yarn in the warp and weft.

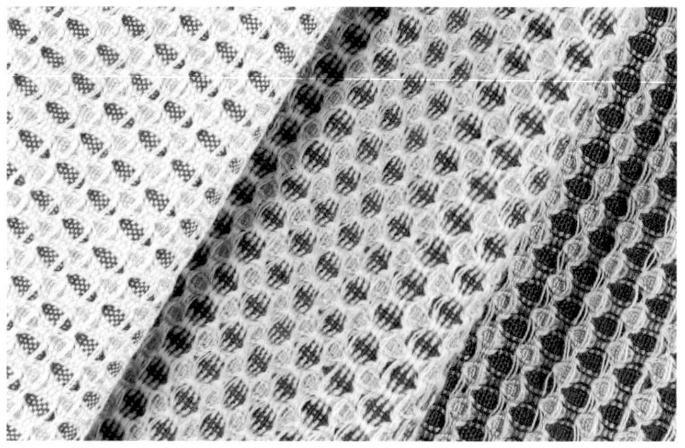

Collection of samples using distorted weft on two blocks.

Plain-weave distorted weft using unsupported clear lurex in the warp and weft. Nylon raffia has been used in the weft to accentuate the curves. The warp has been dip-dyed.

Plain-weave distorted weft. Nylon monofilament in the warp and dyed and clear lurex in the weft.

Plain-weave distorted weft. Nylon monofilament in the warp and lurex and filament silk in the weft.

Plain-weave distorted weft. Nylon monofilament in the warp and dyed and clear lurex in the weft.

Plain-weave distorted weft. Nylon monofilament in the warp and lurex and filament silk in the weft.

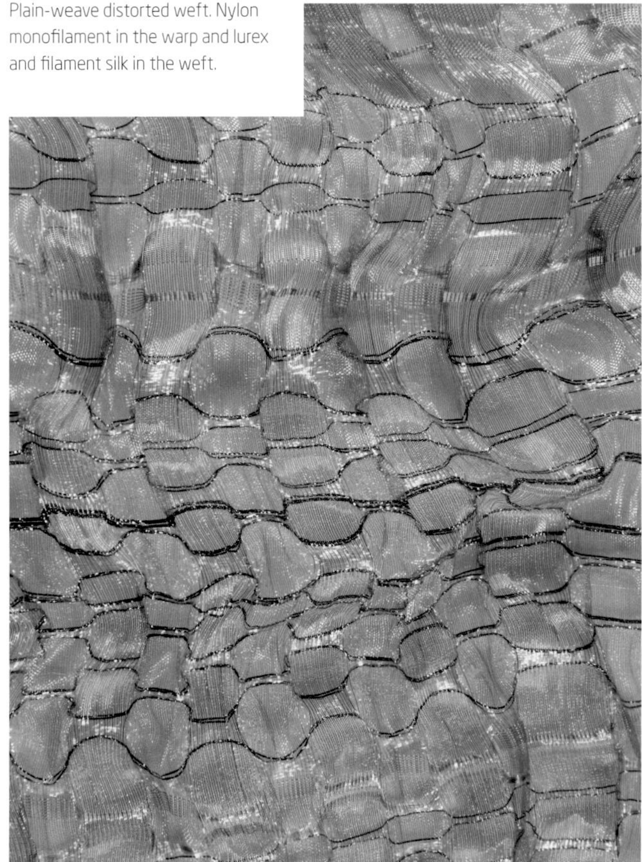

GROUPED WEFT DISTORTION USING ADDITIONAL SHAFTS

The more shafts you have available, the greater the potential to create movement within the structural pattern. You can continue to use two shafts for each block, contrasting plain weave with the warp floats. Or, if a twill weave is required, three or more shafts could be used in each block.

2. Threading plan over 6 shafts: 2 blocks

Shaft												
6									X			X
5								X			X	
4							X			X		
3			X			X						
2		X			X							
1	X			X								

---------repeat------- ---------repeat--------

Lifting plan examples: threading plan 2

Lifting sequence							
12	X	X				X	One repeat
11	X	X			X		
10	X	X		X			
9	X	X				X	
8	X	X			X		
7	X	X		X			
6			X	X	X		One repeat
5		X		X	X		
4	X			X	X		
3			X	X	X		
2		X		X	X		
1	X			X	X		
	1	2	3	4	5	6	Shaft

Lifting sequence							
12	X			X		X	One repeat
11	X				X	X	
10	X			X	X		
9	X			X		X	
8	X				X	X	
7	X			X	X		
6	X		X	X			One repeat
5		X	X	X			
4	X	X		X			
3	X		X	X			
2		X	X	X			
1	X	X		X			
	1	2	3	4	5	6	Shaft

3. Threading plan over 6 shafts: 3 blocks

Shaft																		
6														X		X		X
5													X		X		X	
4								X		X		X						
3							X		X		X							
2		X		X		X												
1	X		X		X													

---------repeat--------- ---------repeat--------- ---------repeat---------

Lifting plan examples: threading plan 3

Lifting sequence							
12	X		X			X	One repeat
11	X		X		X		
10	X		X			X	
9	X		X		X		
8	X			X	X		One repeat
7	X		X		X		
6	X			X	X		
5	X		X		X		
4		X	X		X		One repeat
3	X		X		X		
2		X	X		X		
1	X		X		X		
	1	2	3	4	5	6	Shaft

Lifting sequence							
12		X	X			X	One repeat
11	X		X		X		
10		X	X			X	
9	X		X		X		
8	X			X		X	One repeat
7	X		X		X		
6	X			X		X	
5	X		X		X		
4		X		X	X		One repeat
3	X		X		X		
2		X		X	X		
1	X		X		X		
	1	2	3	4	5	6	Shaft

EXAMPLES OVER THREE BLOCKS - PLAIN

Left and right: Plain-weave distorted weft on three blocks. Each block uses two shafts.

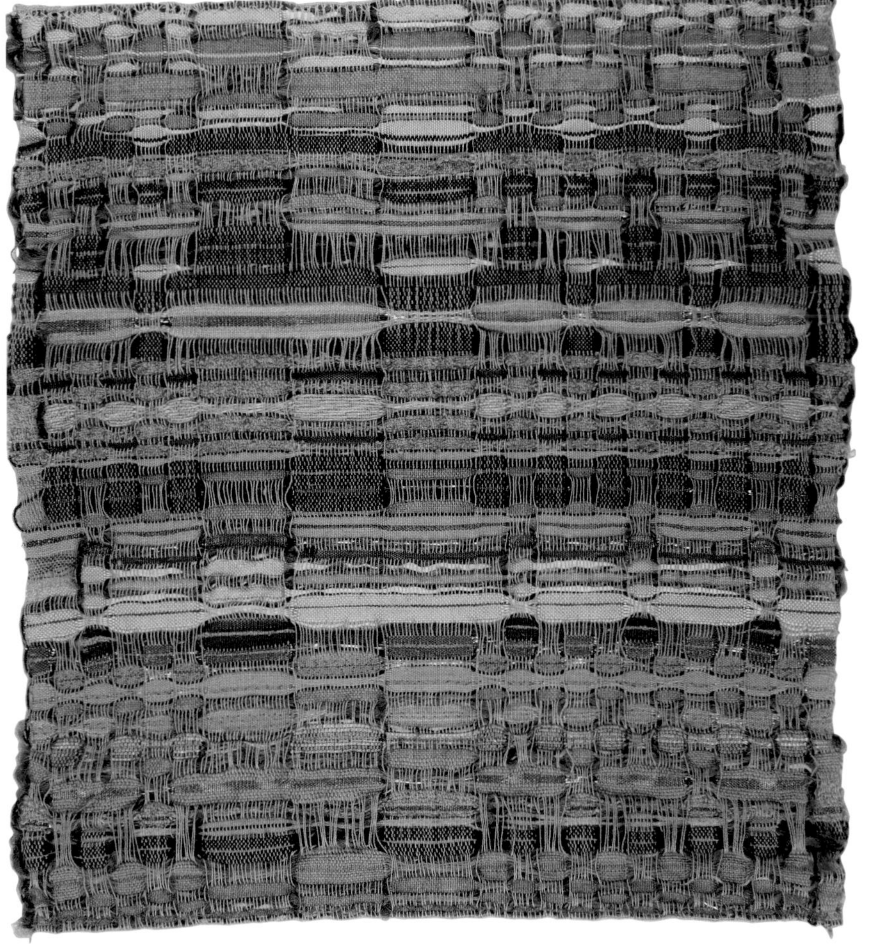

4. Threading plan over 8 shafts: 4 blocks

Shaft																
8														X		X
7													X		X	
6										X		X				
5									X		X					
4						X		X								
3					X		X									
2		X		X												
1	X		X													

----repeat---- ----repeat---- ----repeat---- ----repeat----

5. Threading plan over 8 shafts: 4 blocks reversed

Shaft																								
8														X		X								
7													X		X									
6										X		X						X		X				
5									X		X						X		X					
4						X		X														X		X
3					X		X														X		X	
2		X		X																				
1	X		X																					

----repeat---- ----repeat---- ----repeat---- ----repeat---- ----repeat---- ----repeat----

Lifting plan examples: threading plans 4 and 5

Lifting sequence									
16		X		X		X		X	One repeat
15		X		X		X	X		
14		X		X		X		X	
13		X		X		X	X		
12	X		X			X	X		One repeat
11	X		X		X		X		
10	X		X			X	X		
9	X		X		X		X		
8		X		X		X		X	One repeat
7		X	X			X		X	
6		X		X		X		X	
5		X	X			X		X	
4		X	X		X		X		One repeat
3	X		X		X		X		
2		X	X		X		X		
1	X		X		X		X		
	1	2	3	4	5	6	7	8	Shaft

Lifting sequence									
16		X		X	X			X	One repeat
15	X		X		X		X		
14		X		X	X			X	
13	X		X		X		X		
12		X	X			X		X	One repeat
11	X		X		X		X		
10		X	X			X		X	
9	X		X		X		X		
8	X			X		X		X	One repeat
7	X		X		X		X		
6	X			X		X		X	
5	X		X		X		X		
4		X		X		X	X		One repeat
3	X		X		X		X		
2		X		X		X	X		
1	X		X		X		X		
	1	2	3	4	5	6	7	8	Shaft

Lifting sequence									
16		X	X		X			X	One repeat
15	X		X		X		X		
14		X	X		X			X	
13	X		X		X		X		
12	X			X		X	X		One repeat
11	X		X		X		X		
10	X			X		X	X		
9	X		X		X		X		
8	X		X		X		X		One repeat
7	X		X			X		X	
6	X		X		X		X		
5	X		X			X		X	
4		X		X	X		X		One repeat
3	X		X		X		X		
2		X		X	X		X		
1	X		X		X		X		
	1	2	3	4	5	6	7	8	Shaft

Lifting sequence									
8	X			X	X			X	One repeat
7	X		X		X		X		
6	X			X	X			X	
5	X		X		X		X		
4		X	X			X	X		One repeat
3	X		X		X		X		
2		X	X			X	X		
1	X		X		X		X		
	1	2	3	4	5	6	7	8	Shaft

EXAMPLES OVER MULTIPLE BLOCKS

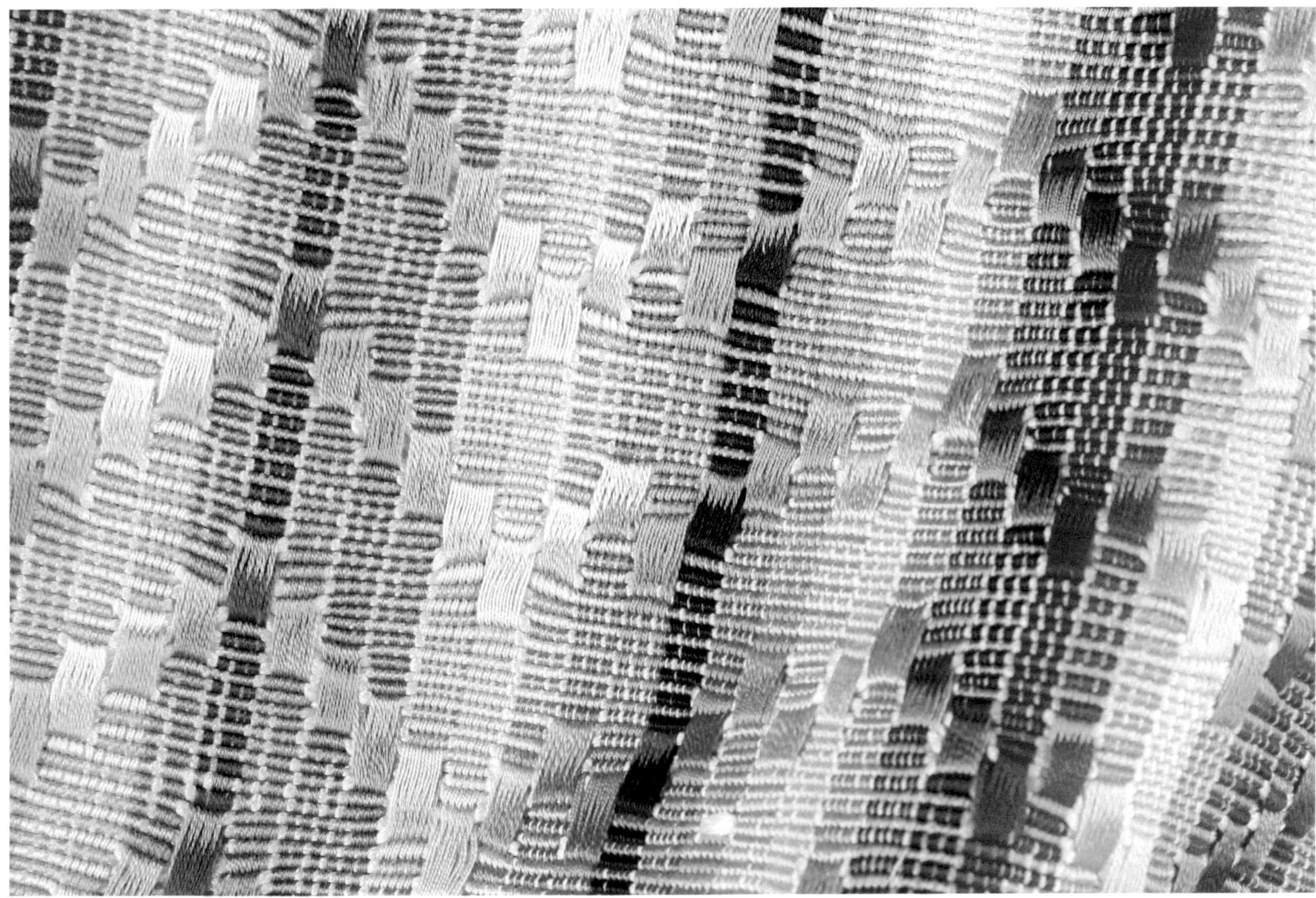

Distorted weft using six blocks arranged in a point draft/threading plan. The warp and weft are spun silk.

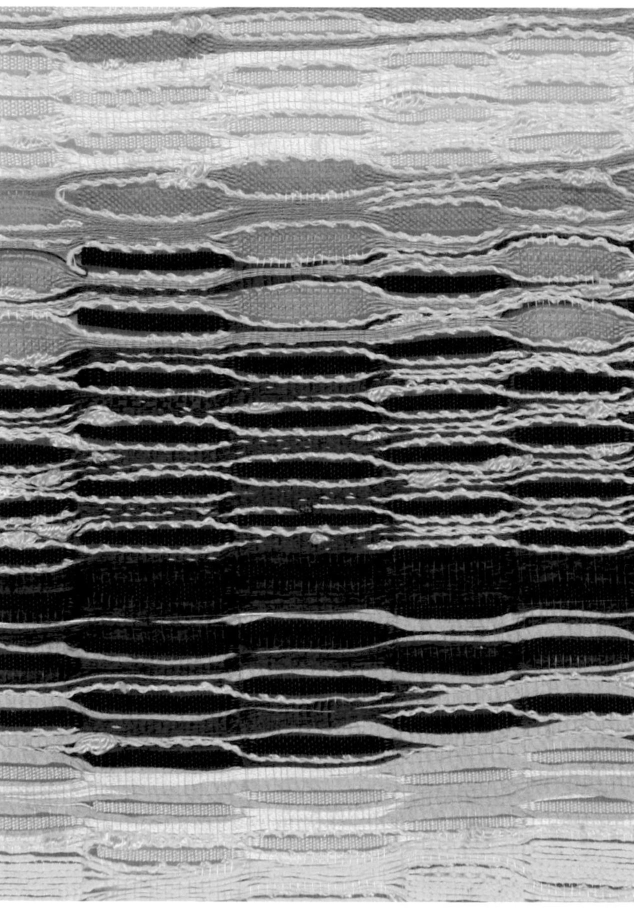

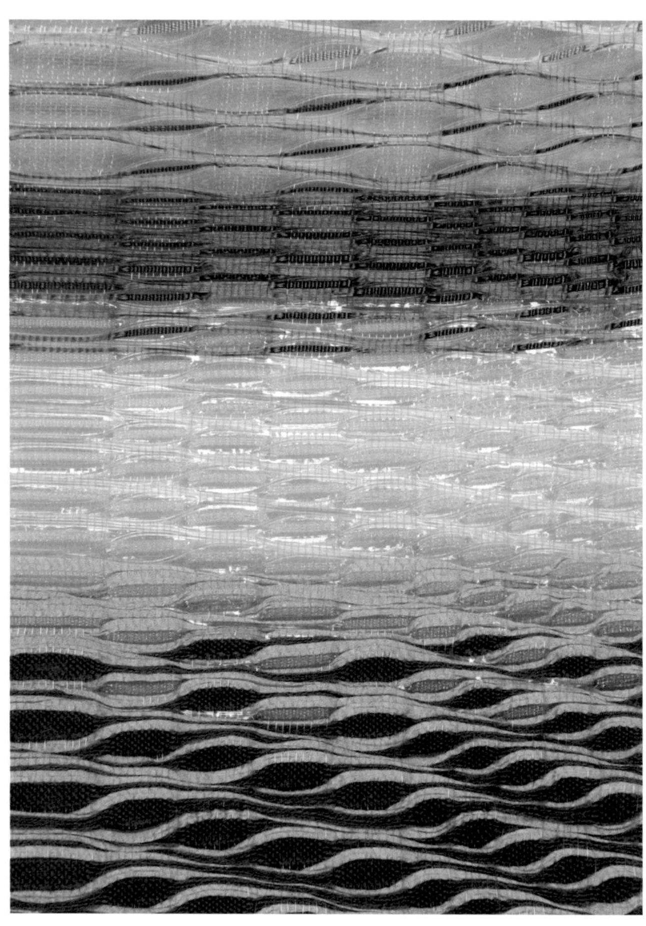

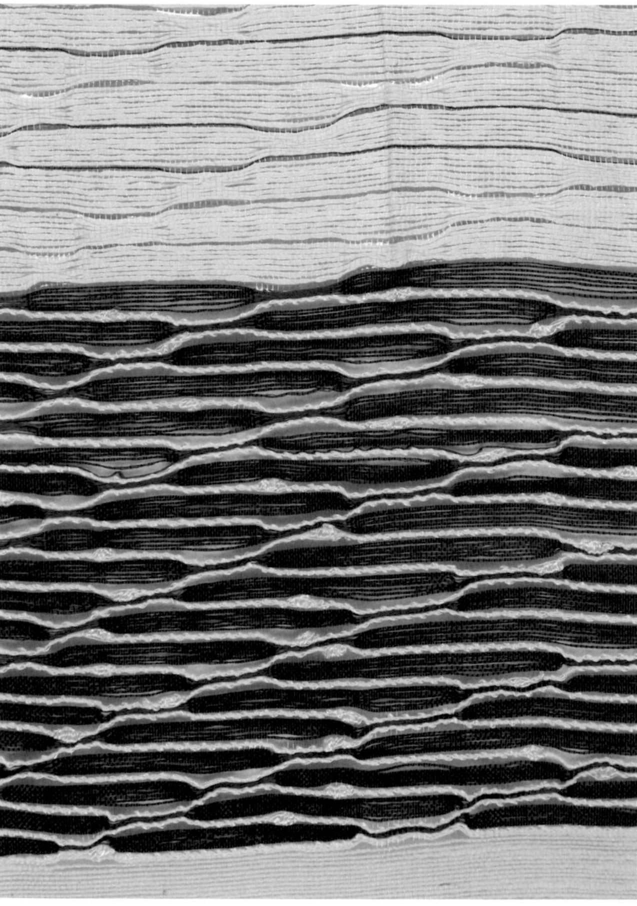

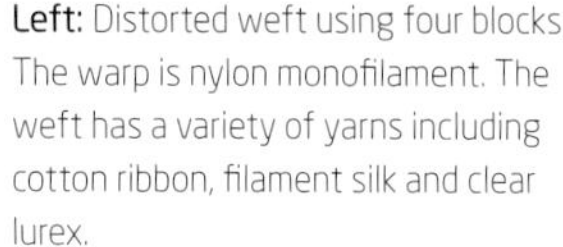

Left: Distorted weft using four blocks. The warp is nylon monofilament. The weft has a variety of yarns including cotton ribbon, filament silk and clear lurex.

Top right: Distorted weft using four blocks. The warp is nylon monofilament. The weft has a variety of yarns including cotton ribbon, filament silk and viscose slub.

Bottom right: Distorted weft using four blocks. The warp is nylon monofilament and the weft has a variety of yarns including filament silk, polyurethane and viscose slub.

6. Threading plan over 8 shafts: 2 blocks

Shaft																
8												X				X
7											X				X	
6										X				X		
5									X				X			
4				X				X								
3			X				X									
2		X				X										
1	X				X											

------------repeat------------ ------------repeat------------

Lifting plan examples: threading plan 6

Lifting sequence									1 x 3 twill blocks
8	X		X					X	One repeat
7	X		X				X		
6	X		X			X			
5	X		X		X				
4				X	X		X		One repeat
3			X		X		X		
2		X			X		X		
1	X				X		X		
	1	2	3	4	5	6	7	8	Shaft

Lifting sequence									3 x 1 twill blocks
8	X		X		X	X		X	One repeat
7	X		X		X		X	X	
6	X		X			X	X	X	
5	X		X		X	X	X		
4	X	X		X	X		X		One repeat
3	X		X	X	X		X		
2		X	X	X	X		X		
1	X	X	X		X		X		
	1	2	3	4	5	6	7	8	Shaft

The twills can be different in each section if you choose, or you can, of course, use plain weave as an alternative structure.

When weaving the distorted weft structure, there will naturally be a block at the fabric side edge (selvedge) that is formed by floating ends. The weft yarn will not be trapped in by these floats, and will only be caught down when it reaches the first plain- or twill-weave block. This is a natural occurrence in the structure, and will not detract from the overall design.

EXAMPLES OF DISTORTED WEFT FABRICS

Plain-weave distorted weft over two blocks. The warp uses wire for one block and nylon monofilament for the other. The weft yarn is lurex and filament silk.

Distorted weft on two blocks, each using eight shafts. A 1 x 7 twill has been used in the distorted weft and is set against a plain-weave section. The warp and weft are in spun silk.

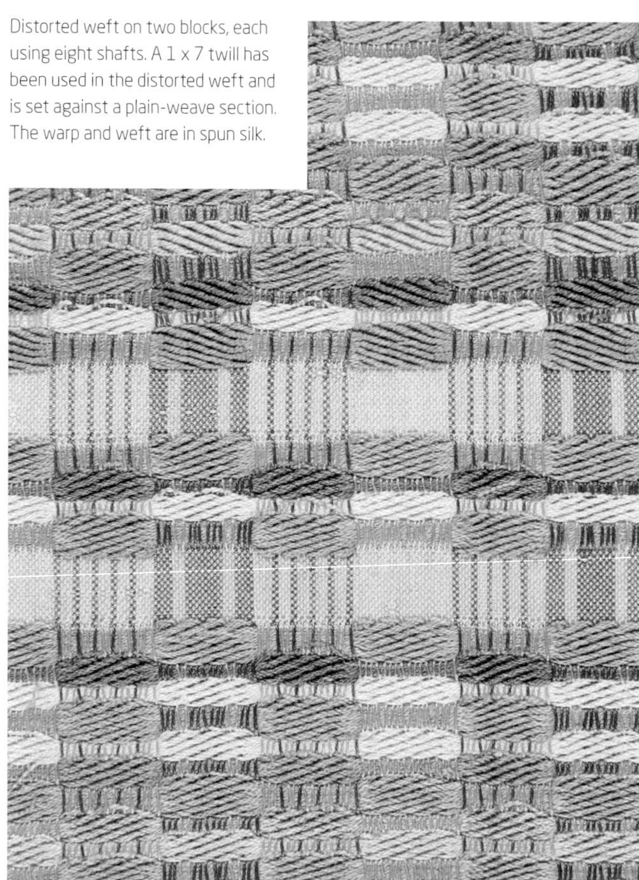

Distorted weft on two blocks, each using eight shafts. The distortion is set against a variety of other weaves including twill, plain weave and crêpe.

A twill weave has been used in the distorted weft blocks, and is set against plain weave. Cotton warp and weft.

Distorted weft on two blocks, one over two shafts and the other over four. It has a cotton warp and various weft yarns including cotton slub, viscose and wool.

Distorted weft blocks using twills set against a 1 x 7 twill and plain weave.

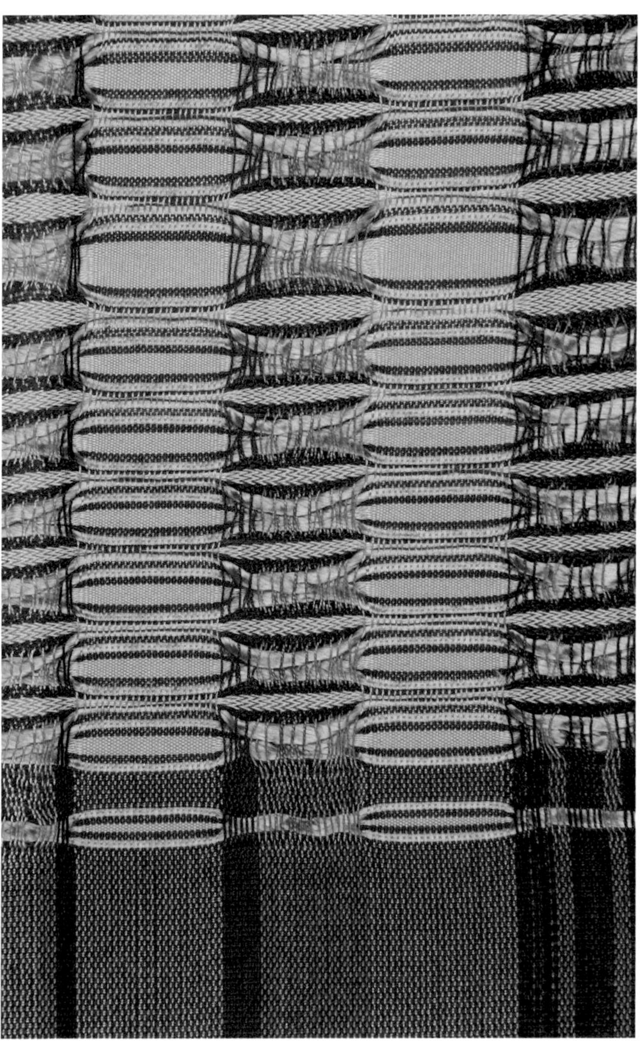

Distorted weft on two blocks, one over two shafts and the other over four. It has a cotton warp and weft with viscose to accentuate the curve.

GROUPED WARP DISTORTIONS

These are formed by groups of floating warp ends being packed together by the firmness of the adjacent plain-weave area. The distortion occurs where the groups fan out again into plain weave. Several groups of ends can be combined to make a repeat pattern.

Grouped warp distortions

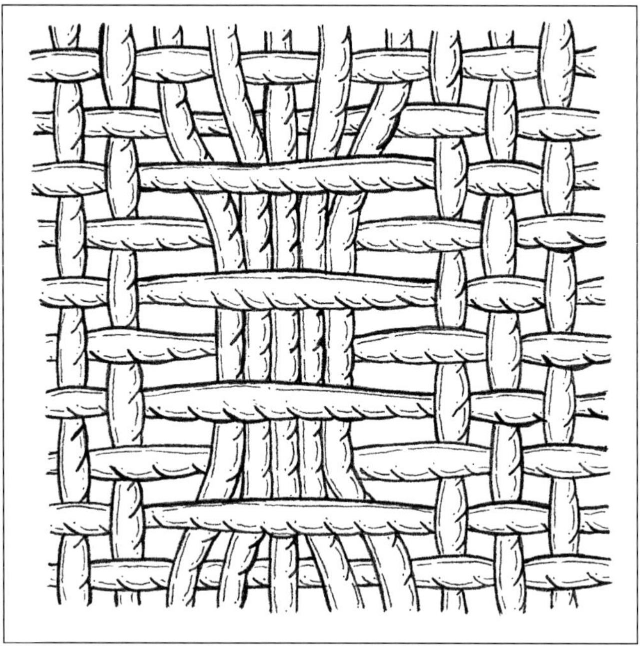

Threading plan over 4 shafts

Shaft																				
4							X		X								X		X	
3						X		X		X						X		X		X
2	X		X		X						X		X		X					
1		X		X								X		X						

Lifting plan

Lifting sequence					
10	X			X	One repeat distortion 2
9	X		X		
8	X			X	
7	X		X		
6		X	X		One repeat distortion 1
5	X		X		
4		X	X		
	X		X		
2		X	X		Shaft
1	X		X		
	1	2	3	4	Shaft

Try using a section of plain-weave picks between each distortion block to help frame the distorted areas.

SINGLE-END DISTORTIONS

Single warp or weft threads can be made to form a zigzag pattern across the width of a cloth or down the length. Additional warp threads are required in both cases, and will normally be wound as a separate warp to the ground cloth, and placed on a second beam. This is because the additional threads will be woven at a different rate to the ground cloth, and may also be considerably thicker to give a more pronounced effect.

HORIZONTAL ZIGZAGS

The extra warp ends will be used to trap down additional weft threads. The weft pick distortion offers more flexibility than the warp end, as you can change the type of weft feature yarn used as you weave. The zigzag pattern is clearly visible as you work.

Extra weft single-end distortion

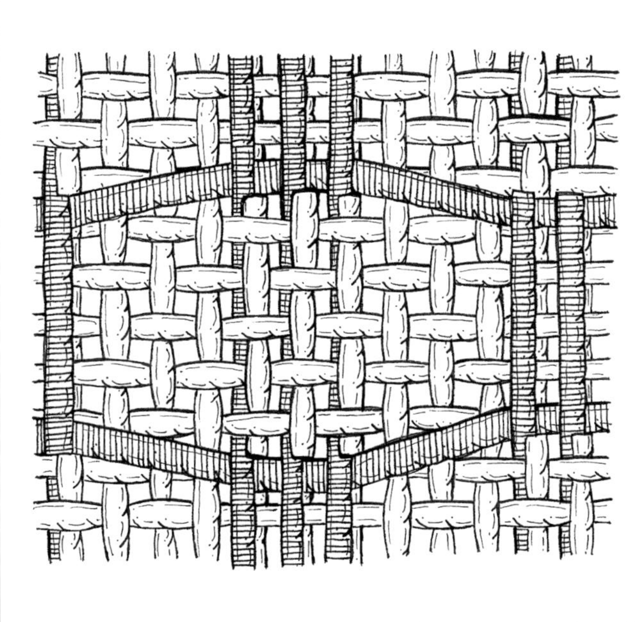

REED PLAN

When denting, the additional ends will be accommodated in the same dent as the previous ground thread. For example: if you have two ends of yarn per dent to form the base cloth, then where an additional thread occurs in the threading plan, it will make three. On your point paper, you can colour in the squares below the threading plan to indicate how many threads are in each dent in the reed. You can use this simple but effective method whenever you have additional warp ends.

FEATURE THE ADDITIONAL WARP THREADS

The additional warp threads are there to add value as well as perform a function, so use contrasting texture, thickness and colour to accentuate the feature. Alternatively, when producing a horizontal zigzag, you could use a nylon monofilament yarn, which is relatively invisible, to trap your weft. The line will be uninterrupted and will therefore appear to float on top of the base cloth.

Threading plan (ground ends = X, extra ends = 0)

Shaft																		
6																		0
5									0									
4				X				X					X				X	
3			X				X					X				X		
2		X				X					X				X			
1	X				X					X				X				
Reed plan	■	■			■	■				■	■			■	■			
			■	■			■	■	■			■	■			■	■	■

In this example, since the base cloth is formed by threading the warp over four shafts, you could use a combination of plain and twill weaves to give contrast and variety in the ground.

Lifting plan

Lifting sequence							
10					X	X	Insert feature yarn
9		X		X		X	Repeat 6-9
8	X		X			X	
7		X		X		X	
6	X		X			X	
5					X	X	Insert feature yarn
4	X		X		X		Repeat 1-4
3		X		X	X		
2	X		X		X		
1		X		X	X		
	1	2	3	4	5	6	Shaft

Cotton twill ground with black polyurethane yarn trapped by additional cotton threads.

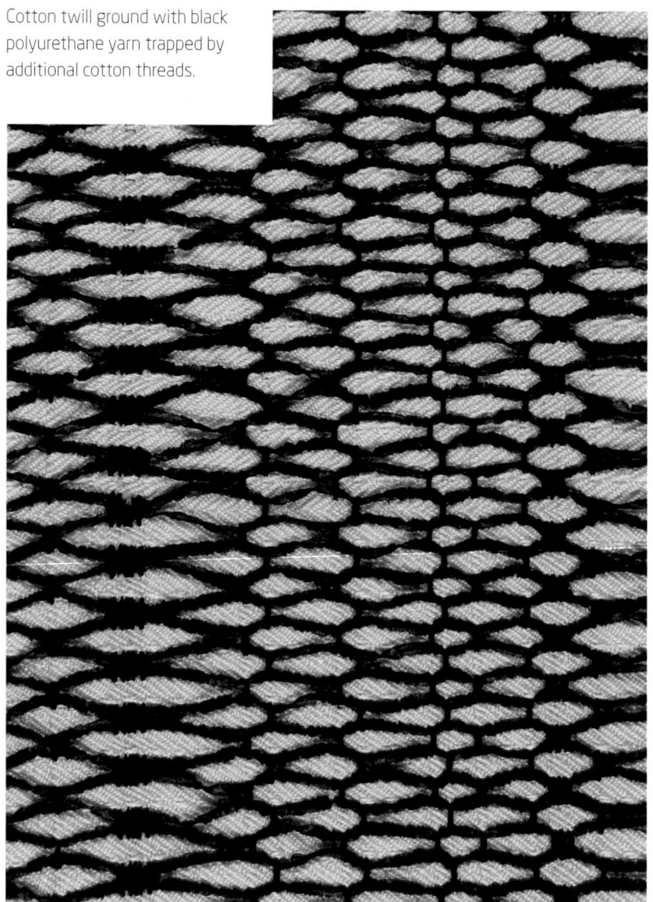

Cotton and wool twill ground with polyurethane and nylon raffia yarn.

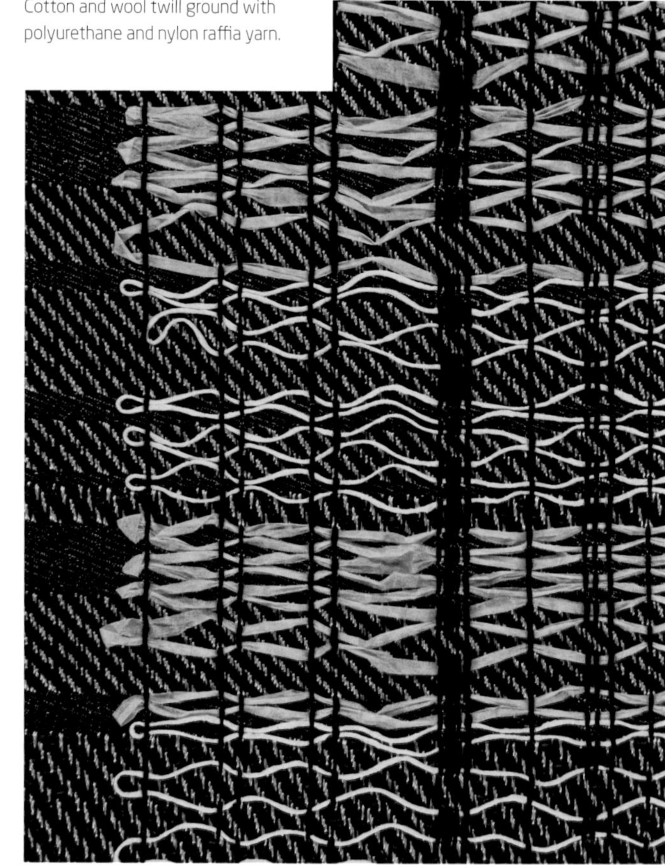

EXAMPLES OF EXTRA-WEFT SINGLE-END DISTORTIONS

Spun silk warp, with a cotton slub yarn being trapped by additional silk threads.

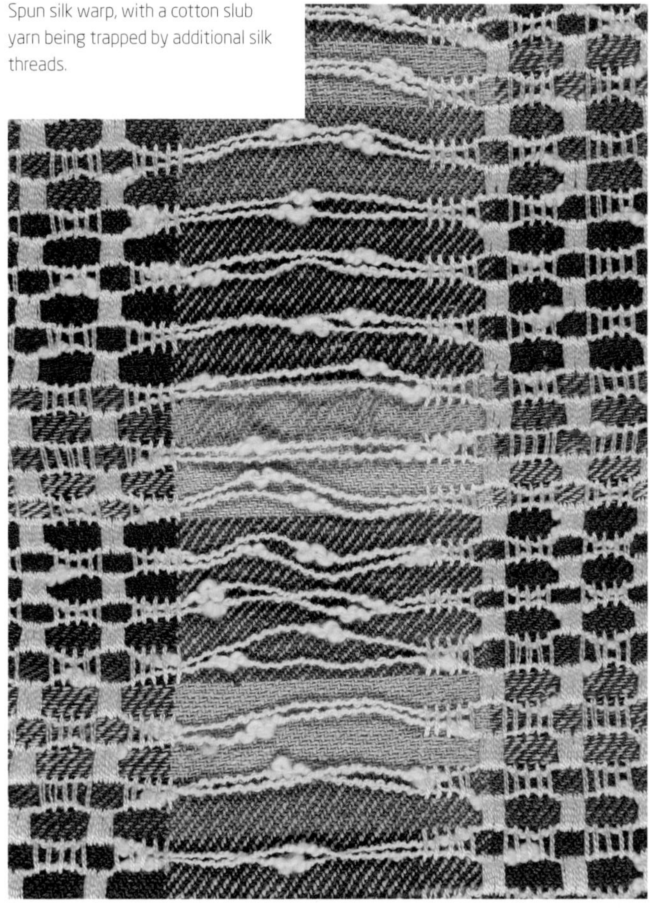

Spun silk plain-weave ground with a wool loop being trapped by additional silk threads.

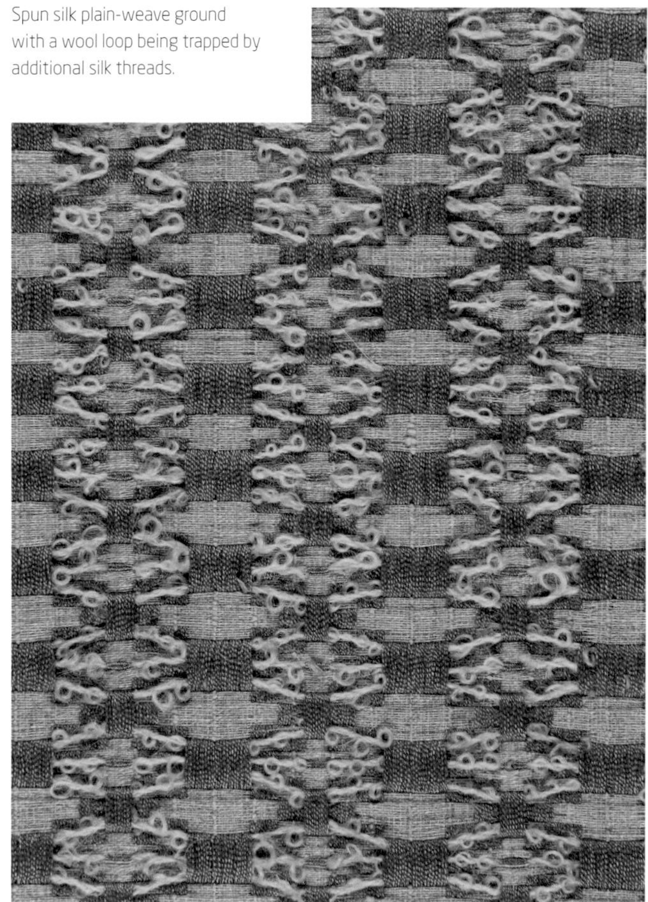

Spun silk twill ground with a knitted nylon tape being trapped by additional silk threads.

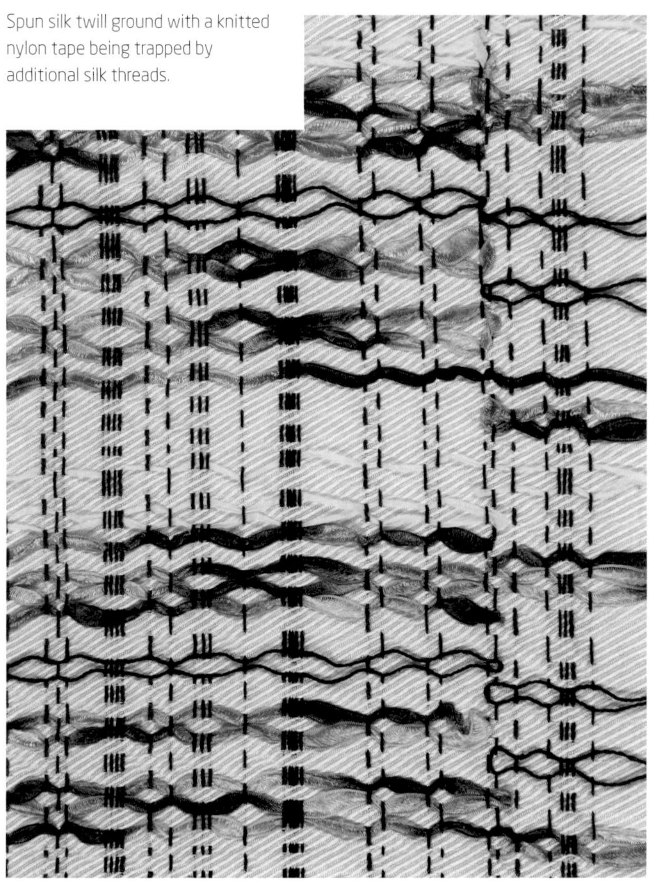

Cotton twill ground with a cotton string and polyurethane yarn being trapped by additional linen and polyurethane threads.

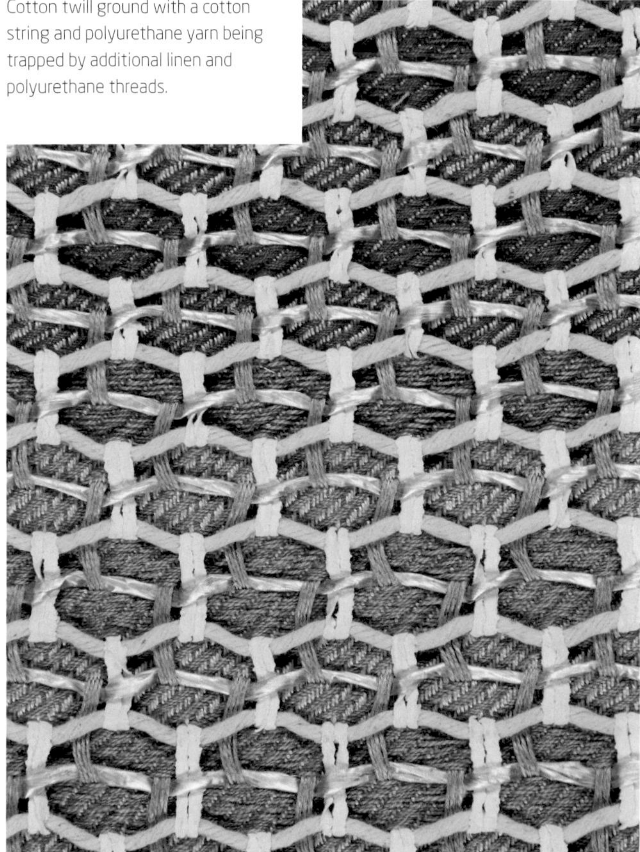

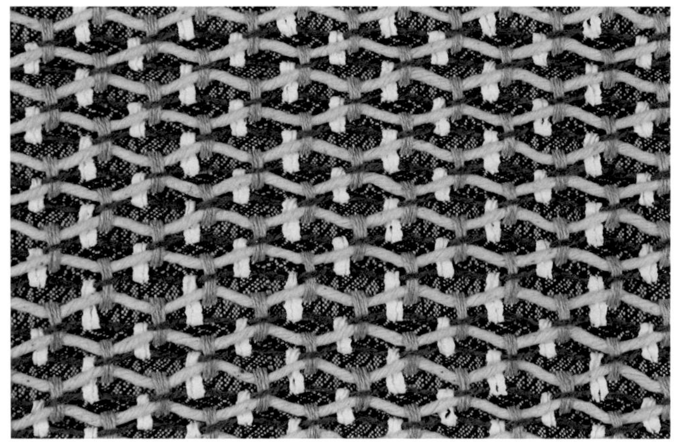

Cotton twill ground with a cotton string and linen yarn being trapped by additional linen and polyurethane threads.

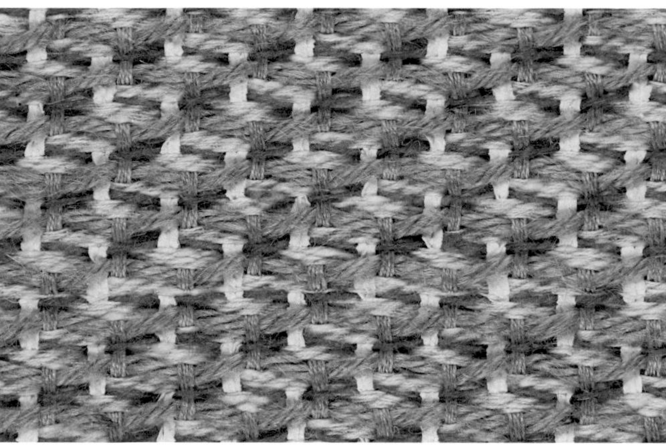

Cotton twill ground with a linen string being trapped by additional linen and polyurethane threads.

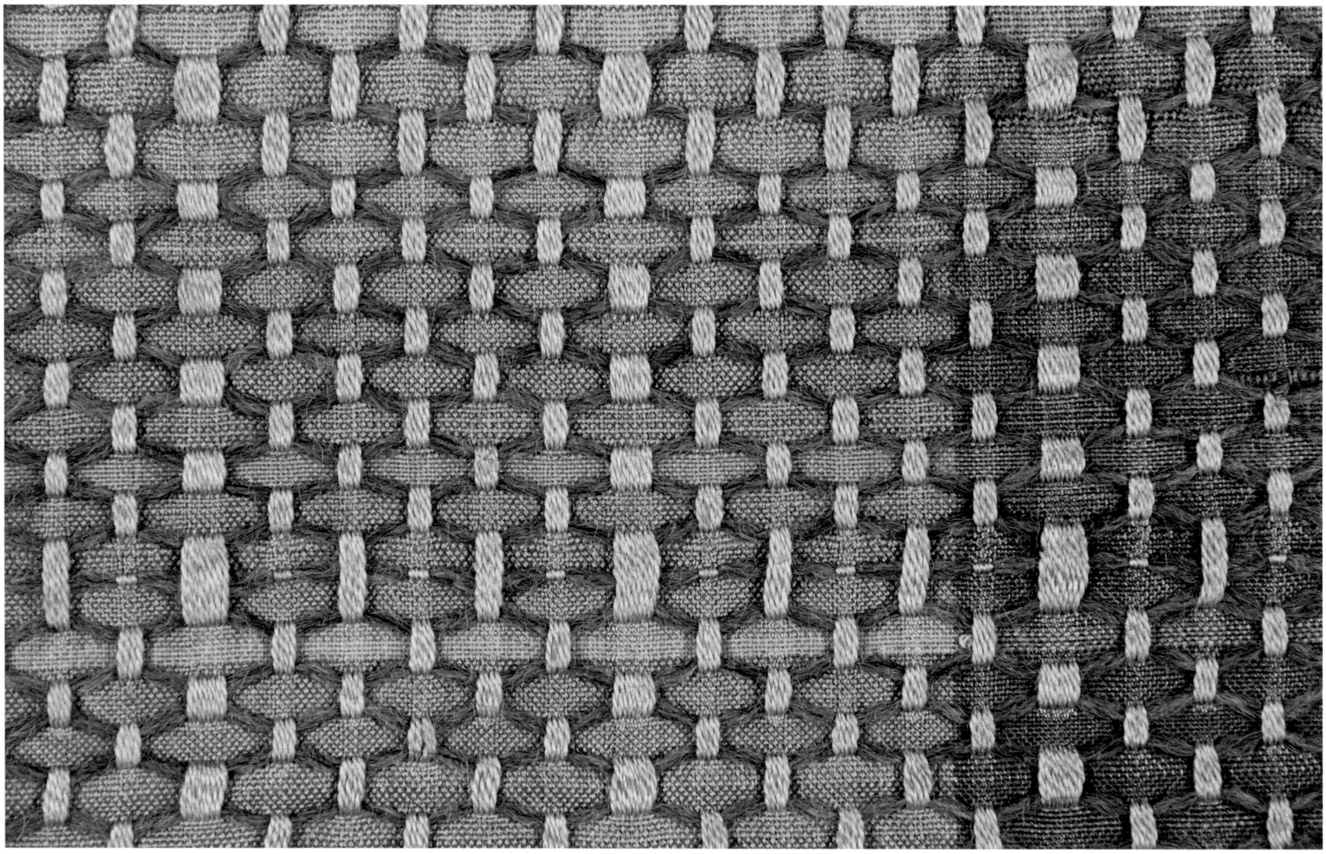

Spun silk plain-weave ground with a wool yarn being trapped by additional spun silk threads.

VERTICAL ZIGZAGS

Feature warp threads are also used to create this effect. The distortion is created by the placing of weft floats over the additional ends. Due to the tensioning of the warp, the effect becomes more apparent when the cloth is removed from the loom, when the ground weave comes off tension and contracts a little.

Threading plan (ground ends = X, extra ends = O)

Shaft																
5					O								O			
4							X				X					
3			X												X	
2		X		X					X					X		X
1	X					X		X		X		X				
Reed plan	■	■				■	■			■	■				■	■
			■	■	■			■	■			■	■	■		

Lifting plan

10	X		X		X	
9		X		X	X	
8	X		X		X	
7		X		X	X	
6	X					
5		X		X	X	
4	X		X		X	
3		X		X	X	
2	X		X		X	
1		X				
	1	2	3	4	5	Shaft

Single warp end distortions

CREATING A DIAGONAL LINE ACROSS THE WEAVE

It is possible to achieve a diagonal line rather than a parallel line with the weft yarn by altering the angle of the reed. Normally, the reed is parallel to the fell (edge) of the cloth, beating the weft into place horizontally across the cloth. If you have a loom on which you can change the position of the sley (batten/beater) with a series of pivot points – either two, three or four – then the angle can be altered. The more positions, the more dramatic the effect.

This technique can be used with any weave structure.

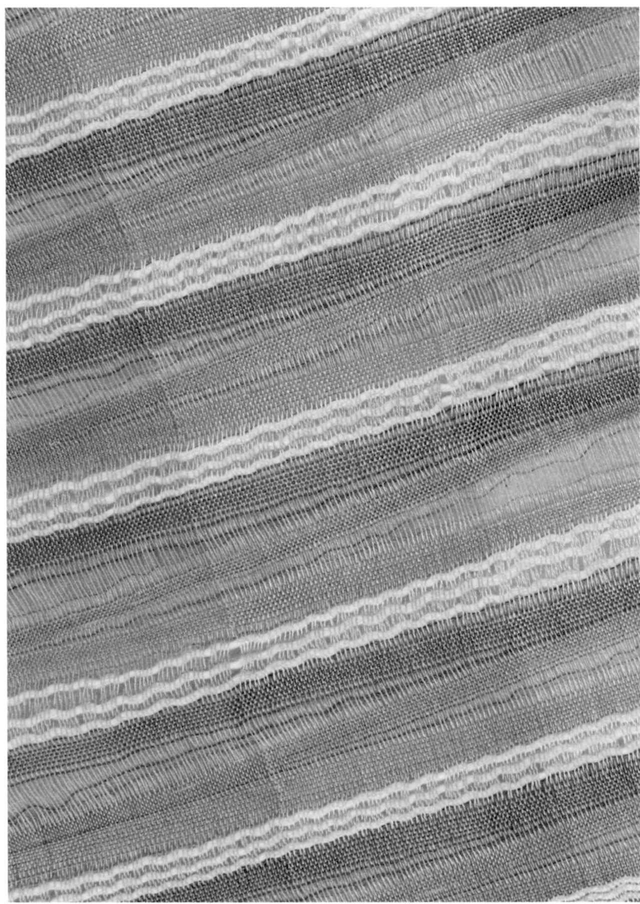

Plain weave fabric in cotton using the angled batten technique.

Diagram of how the weft yarn lies at an angle when the batten is angled

STEP 1

Start with the sley in corresponding positions, with the pair of pivot points farthest from the fell of the cloth. Weave a few picks in this position.

STEP 2

On the left, move the sley one position forward and weave a few picks in this position.

STEP 3

Move one position forward on the left, weaving a few picks each time, until you are in the position nearest to the fell of the cloth.

STEP 4

Now move one position forward at a time on the right, weaving a few picks each time until the sley is once again parallel, and in the positions nearest to the fell of the cloth.

STEP 5

Now move one position backwards on the left.

STEP 6

Reverse on the right-hand side until the sley is once again in a parallel position farthest away from the fell of the cloth. Repeat the process. A zigzag line will be visible across the width of the cloth.

There will naturally be very dense areas contrasting with very loose areas caused by the angle of the sley beating down the weft picks. The diagonal line can be enhanced by using a feature yarn of a different colour, thickness or texture at the points where the angle is most acute. The diagonal line will be more acute in a narrow cloth as the angle achieved will be greater. The wider the cloth sample, the shallower the angle.

EXAMPLES OF FABRIC SAMPLES IN VARIOUS STRUCTURES USING ANGLED SLEY TECHNIQUE

Nylon monofilament and spun silk warp and weft in a distorted weft structure.

Nylon monofilament and spun silk warp in a distorted weft structure and a spun silk weft.

Cotton warp and weft in plain weave and twill using the angled batten technique.

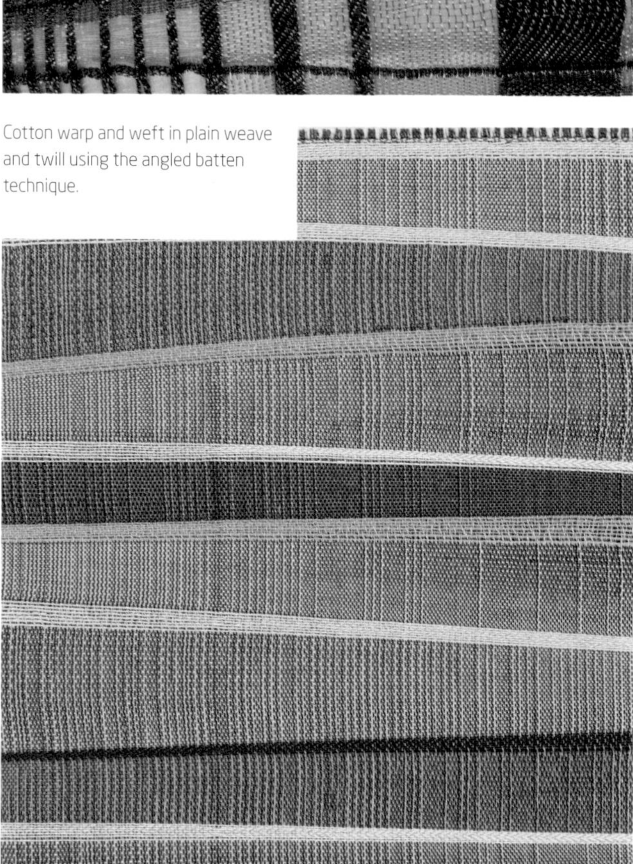

Spun silk warp and weft patterned ground using the angled batten technique.

Spun silk warp with plain weave and distorted weft ground using the angled batten technique.

Spun silk warp with a patterned ground using the angled batten technique.

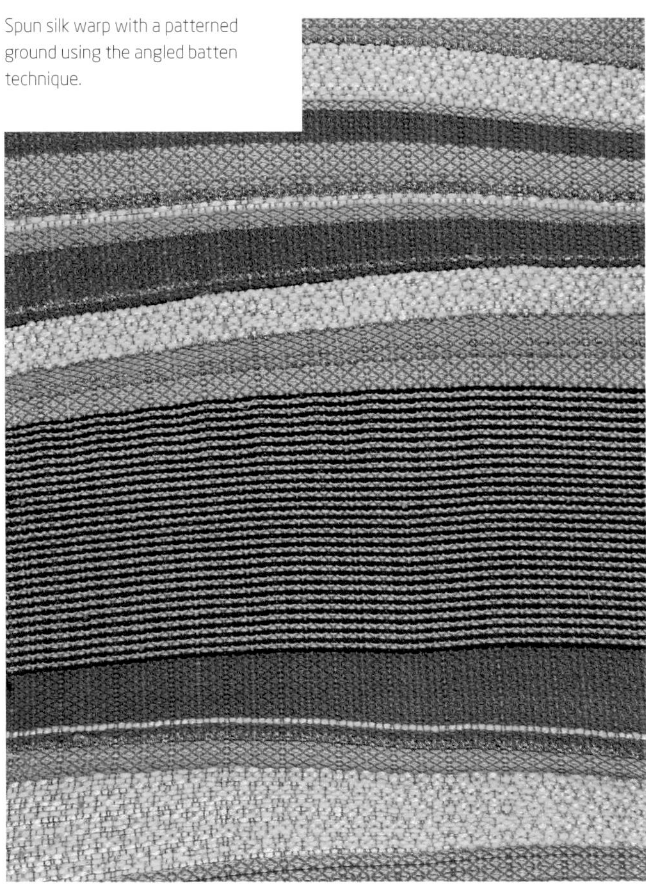

Cotton warp and weft plain-weave double cloth using the angled batten technique.

6
TEXTURED WEAVES

TEXTURED WEAVES

There are many ways to add texture to your weave designs, the simplest being by contrasting yarn types – thick against thin or hairy against smooth. Alternatively, you can use one of several weave structures to create really dramatic textural effects in your weaving. Honeycomb, mock leno, seersucker, corded cloths, pile constructions and crêpes exaggerate the surface texture of the fabric, and add a three-dimensional character.

HONEYCOMB (WAFFLE)

The name given to this weave is very apt as it resembles the structure in a honeycomb or a waffle. It is created by arranging warp and weft floats in a diamond formation. A course of plain weave outlining the diamond formation pins down the floats. Ridges are formed along the longest vertical and horizontal floats, which give four sides of a square. Once the fabric is removed from the loom, the floats contract, forcing the centre inward and forming a three-dimensional hollow that is known as a 'cell'.

Any type or thickness of yarn can be used to create the honeycomb structure. The scale of the cells can be varied by using a fine or a thick yarn in the warp. The thicker the yarn and the more shafts used, the more dramatic and large-scale the effect. Using a fine yarn over multiple shafts gives the cloth a spongy texture, and if a springy or lively yarn is used – this may be a wool that contracts more readily than a stable yarn, such as cotton or silk, or an over-twisted yarn – then this will increase the shrinkage to give deeper cells.

Yarns of contrasting colour, thickness or texture can be introduced to the honeycomb weave at strategic points to accentuate the form and enhance the shape of the cell. A feature yarn should be threaded in the warp on shaft 1 (which, when woven, will be the longest warp float), and introduced in the weft at the longest weft float in the lifting plan sequence.

All honeycomb weaves are woven on a point draft threading plan (see p.47). The smallest repeat is over four shafts, but this does not produce a very pronounced effect. Ideally, more shafts should be used to give an effective texture.

Diagram of 6-shaft honeycomb weave structure

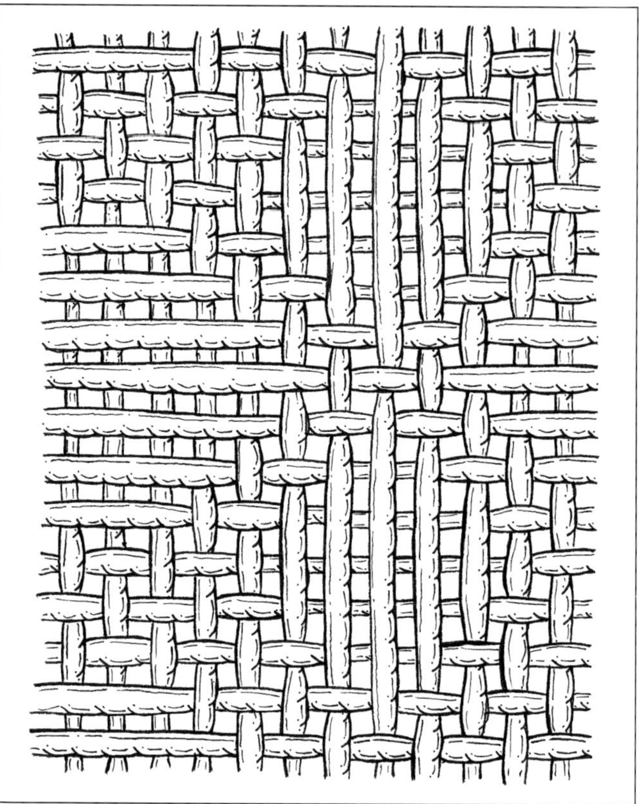

Top and bottom: Honeycomb on eight shafts.
Left: Scarf using a honeycomb structure.

Honeycomb weave over 4 shafts: 6-end repeat

Threading												
4				X						X		
3			X		X				X		X	
2		X				X		X				X
1	X						X					

Lifting plan				
		X		
	X		X	
	X	X		X
	X		X	
		X		
	X			
Shaft	1	2	3	4

Design

Honeycomb weave over 6 shafts: 10-end repeat

Threading										
6						X				
5					X		X			
4				X				X		
3			X						X	
2		X								X
1	X									

Lifting plan						
		X				
	X		X			
	X	X		X		
	X	X	X		X	
	X	X	X	X		X
	X	X	X		X	
	X	X		X		
	X		X			
		X				
	X					
Shaft	1	2	3	4	5	6

Design

The cloth construction in the six- and eight-shaft examples are based on a single-stitch diamond weave – diagonal stitching lines pinning down the warp and weft floats.

Honeycomb weave over 8 shafts: 10-end repeat

Threading														
8								X						
7							X		X					
6						X				X				
5					X						X			
4				X								X		
3			X										X	
2		X												X
1	X													

Lifting plan								
		X						
	X		X					
	X	X		X				
	X	X	X		X			
	X	X	X	X		X		
	X	X	X	X	X		X	
	X	X	X	X	X	X		X
	X	X	X	X	X		X	
	X	X	X	X		X		
	X	X	X		X			
	X	X		X				
	X		X					
		X						
	X							
Shaft	1	2	3	4	5	6	7	8

Design

Honeycomb weave over 12 shafts: 22-end repeat

Threading																						
12												X										
11											X		X									
10										X				X								
9									X						X							
8								X								X						
7							X										X					
6						X												X				
5					X														X			
4				X																X		
3			X																		X	
2		X																				X
1	X																					

A single stitching end can be used in the 12-shaft example, but if the floats are excessively long for practicality, then two stitching ends can be used, as in Lifting plan 2.

Lifting plan 1: 12 shafts

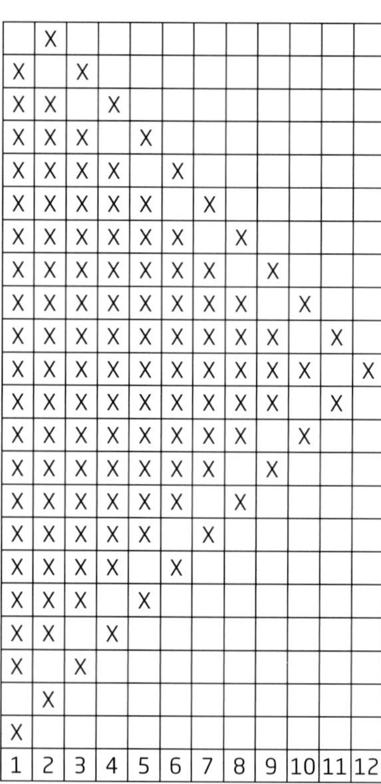

	X										
X		X									
X	X		X								
X	X	X		X							
X	X	X	X		X						
X	X	X	X	X		X					
X	X	X	X	X	X		X				
X	X	X	X	X	X	X		X			
X	X	X	X	X	X	X	X		X		
X	X	X	X	X	X	X	X	X		X	
X	X	X	X	X	X	X	X	X	X		X
X	X	X	X	X	X	X	X	X		X	
X	X	X	X	X	X	X	X		X		
X	X	X	X	X	X	X		X			
X	X	X	X	X	X		X				
X	X	X	X	X		X					
X	X	X	X		X						
X	X	X		X							
X	X		X								
X		X									
	X										
X											
1	2	3	4	5	6	7	8	9	10	11	12

Lifting plan 2: 12 shafts

	X		X								
X		X		X							
X	X		X		X						
X	X	X		X		X					
X	X	X	X		X		X				
X	X	X	X	X		X		X			
X	X	X	X	X	X		X		X		
X	X	X	X	X	X	X		X		X	
X	X	X	X	X	X	X	X		X		X
X	X	X	X	X	X	X	X	X		X	
X	X	X	X	X	X	X	X	X	X		X
X	X	X	X	X	X	X	X	X		X	
X	X	X	X	X	X	X	X		X		X
X	X	X	X	X	X	X		X		X	
X	X	X	X	X	X		X		X		
X	X	X	X	X		X		X			
X	X	X	X		X		X				
X	X	X		X		X					
X	X		X		X						
X		X		X							
	X		X								
X		X									
	X										
X											
1	2	3	4	5	6	7	8	9	10	11	12

EXAMPLES OF HONEYCOMB WEAVES

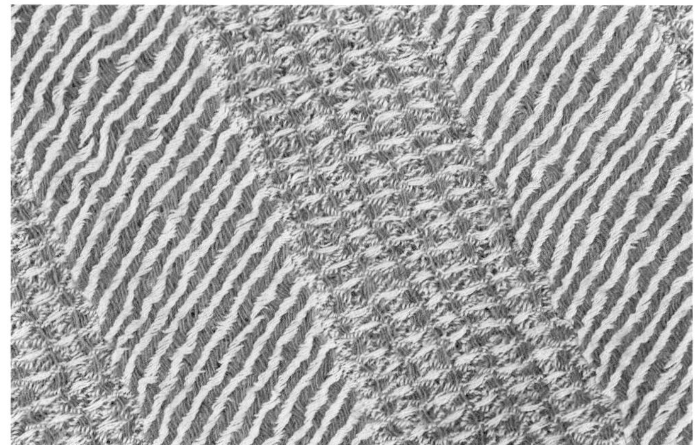

Honeycomb with twill weave.

Six-shaft honeycomb used with a plain weave in a distorted weft structure. The plain-weave block is on two shafts

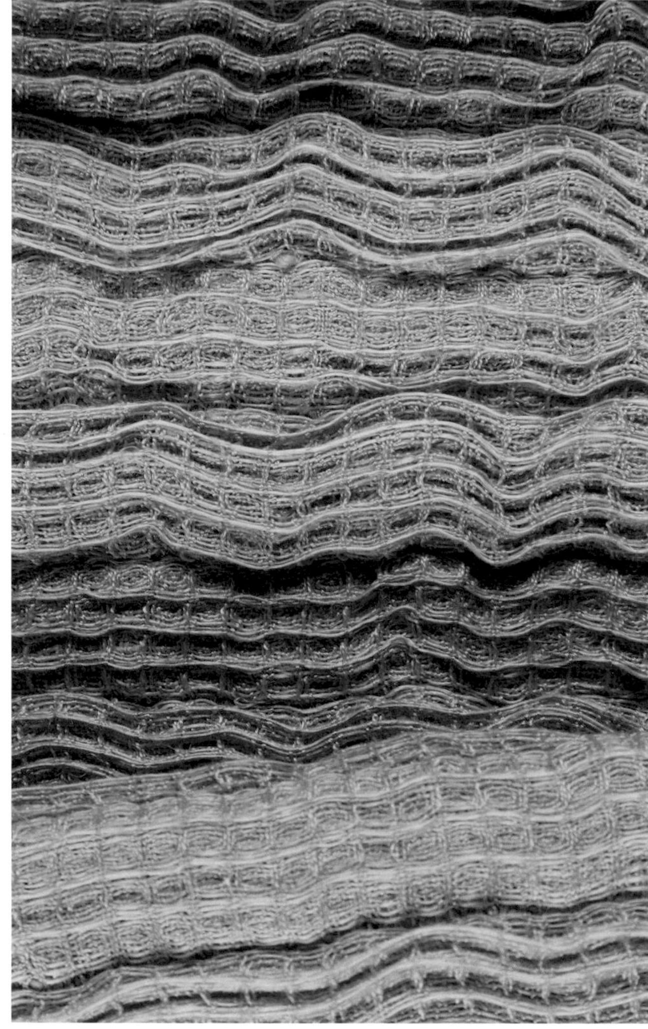

An eight-shaft honeycomb with high-twist wool in the warp to accentuate the shrinkage, and a linen weft.

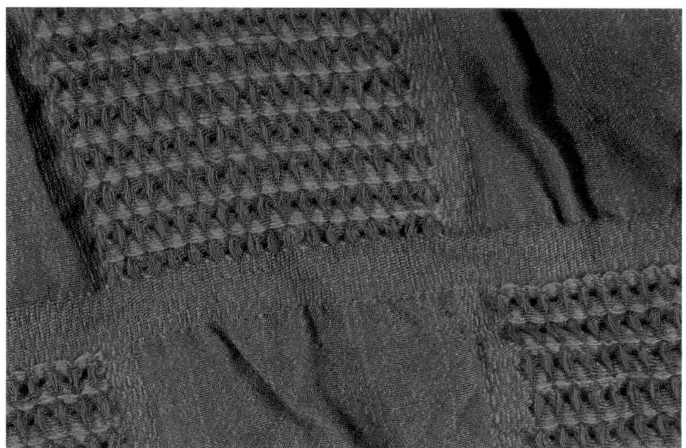

An eight-shaft honeycomb against plain weave and twill. Cotton and wool.

BRIGHTON HONEYCOMB

The texture of the weave in a Brighton honeycomb is less regular than that in the traditional honeycomb. It requires a straight draft, with the smallest repeat unit being over eight shafts. Increases in the size of the units must be in multiples of four – i.e. 8, 12, 16 shafts – for the structure to repeat correctly. Each diamond area contains four smaller diamonds, consisting of two with weft floats and two with warp floats. The longest floats form ridges that, through their contraction, force down the centres of the squares on either side. The formation in the eight-shaft weave is less defined.

Brighton honeycomb over 8 shafts

Threading																	Lifting plan								
8								X								X			X	X	X	X	X		X
7							X								X			X		X	X	X		X	
6						X								X					X		X		X		
5					X								X							X		X			
4				X								X									X		X		
3			X								X									X	X	X		X	
2		X								X									X	X	X	X	X		X
1	X								X									x	X	X	X	X		x	
																	Shaft	1	2	3	4	5	6	7	8
Design																									

Brighton honeycomb over 12 shafts

Threading													Lifting plan												
12												X			X	X	X	X	X		X	X	X		X
11											X			X		X	X	X				X		X	
10										X					X		X						X		
9									X							X		X				X			
4								X							X	X	X		X		X		X		
8							X							X	X	X	X	X		X		X	X	X	
6						X									X	X	X		X		X	X	X	X	X
5					X											X		X		X		X	X	X	
4				X													X				X		X		
3			X													X						X		X	
2		X													X		X				X	X	X		X
1	X													X		X	X	X		X	X	X	X	X	
													Shaft	1	2	3	4	5	6	7	8	5	6	7	8
Design																									

Brighton honeycomb over 16 shafts

Threading																	Lifting plan																
16																X			X	X	X	X	X	X	X		X	X	X	X	X		
15															X			X		X	X	X	X	X				X	X	X		X	
14														X					X		X	X	X						X		X		
13													X							X		X								X			
12												X									X		X						X				
11											X									X	X	X		X				X		X			
10										X									X	X	X	X	X		X		X		X	X	X		
9									X									X	X	X	X	X	X	X		X		X	X	X	X	X	
4								X											X	X	X	X	X		X		X	X	X	X	X	X	
8							X													X	X	X		X		X	X	X	X	X	X	X	
6						X															X		X				X		X	X	X		
5					X																	X						X		X			
4				X																	X								X		X		
3			X																	X		X						X	X	X		X	
2		X																	X		X	X	X				X	X	X	X	X		
1	X																	X		X	X	X	X	X		X	X	X	X	X	X	X	
																	Shaft	1	2	3	4	5	6	7	8	9	10	11	12	13	14	15	16
Design																																	
1																																	
2																																	
3																																	
4																																	
5																																	
6																																	
7																																	
8																																	
9																																	
10																																	
11																																	
12																																	
13																																	
14																																	
15																																	
16																																	

Regular honeycomb: 16-end repeat lifting plan

	X														X
X		X												X	
X	X		X										X		X
X	X	X		X								X		X	X
X	X	X	X		X						X		X	X	X
X	X	X	X	X		X				X		X	X	X	X
X	X	X	X	X	X		X		X		X	X	X	X	X
X	X	X	X	X	X	X		X		X	X	X	X	X	X
X	X	X	X	X	X		X		X		X	X	X	X	X
X	X	X	X	X		X				X		X	X	X	X
X	X	X	X		X						X		X	X	X
X	X	X		X								X		X	X
X	X		X										X		X
X		X												X	
	X														X
X															

MOCK LENO

Mock leno cloth is also known as 'imitation gauze', and is created by grouping together small units of alternating warp and weft floats. A unit is formed of three, four or five ends that work together as a small group to form the mock leno structure. Two units on separate pairs of shafts are needed to achieve the effect, so a minimum of four shafts are used to produce a mock leno design. The weave results in a slightly perforated cloth, giving a lacy effect to your fabric design. The open effect is caused partly by the method of denting in the reed and partly by the weave.

THE REED

The lacy appearance of the cloth can be emphasized if the warp threads in each unit in the threading plan are placed together in one dent of the reed, i.e. three ends per dent in a three-end unit, four ends in a four-end unit and so on. More obvious perforations are created if you leave one dent empty on either side of each unit.

Diagram of a 3-end mock leno structure

Example 1: 3-end units over 4 shafts. One unit is on shafts 1 and 2, the other on shafts 3 and 4. The denting is 3 ends per dent.

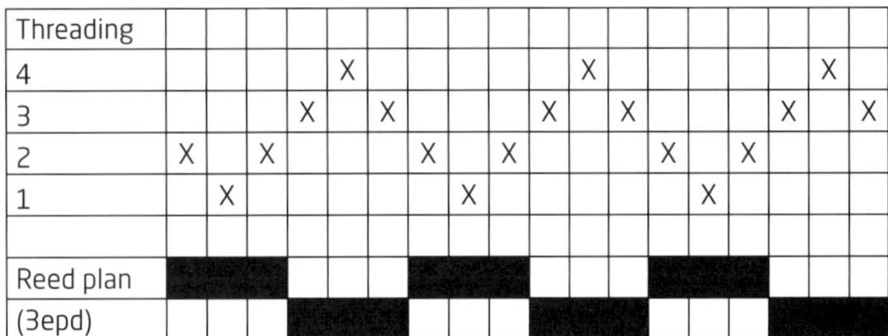

Threading																		
4					X						X						X	
3				X		X				X		X				X		X
2	X		X				X		X				X		X			
1		X						X						X				
Reed plan	■	■	■				■	■	■				■	■	■			
(3epd)				■	■	■				■	■	■				■	■	■

Example 2: To emphasize the perforated effect, you can leave an empty dent between each unit - indicated on the point paper by a blank square left between each unit in the threading plan, and an empty square in the reed plan.

Threading															
4						X								X	
3					X		X						X		X
2	X		X						X		X				
1		X								X					
Reed plan	■	■	■		■	■	■		■	■	■		■	■	■
(3epd miss1)															

The mock leno effect can be used as an all-over design or, if used with plain weave, you can create vertical stripes or blocks of mock leno, which will emphasize the contrast between the lacy effect and the closely woven plain weave. A minimum four shafts are required to achieve the effect, and the more shafts you have available, the more complex your placements and designs can be.

CALCULATING THE SIZE OF REED FOR MOCK LENO

Once you have established the ends per cm/inch of your yarn – calculate it for a plain weave – consideration needs to be given to what reed you intend to use to achieve the desired result of perforations and to retain a good sett to the cloth.

The yarn is 14epcm and the mock leno is in three-end units

Use a reed with 48 dents per 10cm and put three ends per dent. (Example 1)

For a more pronounced effect, use a reed with 96 dents per 10cm and put three ends per dent and leave the next empty. (Example 2)

The yarn is 36epi and the mock leno is in three-end units

Use a 12's reed at three ends per dent:

3 × 12 = 36 (Example 1)

If you want to exaggerate the effect, use a 24's reed with three ends and put three ends per dent and leave the next empty. (Example 2)

CALCULATING THE SIZE OF REED FOR MOCK LENO WITH PLAIN WEAVE

Once you have established the ends per cm/inch of your yarn – calculate it for the plain weave – consideration needs to be given to what reed you need to use to achieve the desired perforations and a good plain-weave sett.

The yarn is 14epcm and the mock leno is in three-end units

Use a reed with 48 dents per 10cm and put three ends per dent. (Example 3)

Use a reed with 96 dents per 10cm and put three ends in a dent and leave one empty in the mock leno section. In the plain weave section, put two ends per dent and one end in the next to achieve 14epcm. (Example 4)

The yarn is 36epi and the mock leno is in three-end units

Use a 12's reed at ends ends per dent. (Example 3)

Use a 24's reed at three ends per dent and leave one empty in the mock leno section. In the plain weave section, put two ends in one dent and one end in the next dent to achieve 36epi:

12 × 2 + 12 × 1= 36 (Example 4)

If you leave an extra dent between each mock leno unit, a vertical line will be visible when using plain weave across the width of the fabric. This is caused by the empty dents in the mock leno units.

Example 3: 3-end units over 4 shafts with plain weave (X = mock leno units, O = plain-weave section)

Threading																		
4								X						X				
3	O		O		O		X		X				X		X			
2		O		O		O				X		X				X		X
1											X						X	
Reed plan	■	■	■				■	■	■				■	■	■			
				■	■	■				■	■	■				■	■	■

Three-end mock leno in wool.

Example 4: 3-end units over 4 shafts with plain weave (X = mock leno units, O = plain-weave section). An empty dent is left between each mock leno unit.

Threading																						
4									X								X					
3	O		O		O			X		X						X		X				
2		O		O		O						X		X						X		X
1													X								X	
Reed plan	■	■		■	■			■	■	■		■	■	■		■	■	■		■	■	■
			■			■																

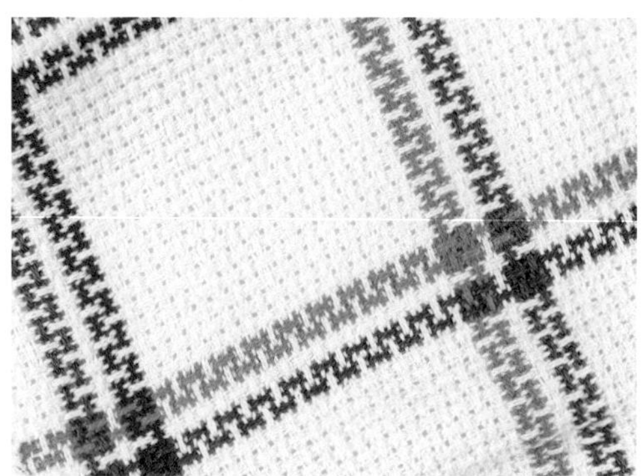

Three-end mock leno in cotton.

Mock leno over 4 shafts

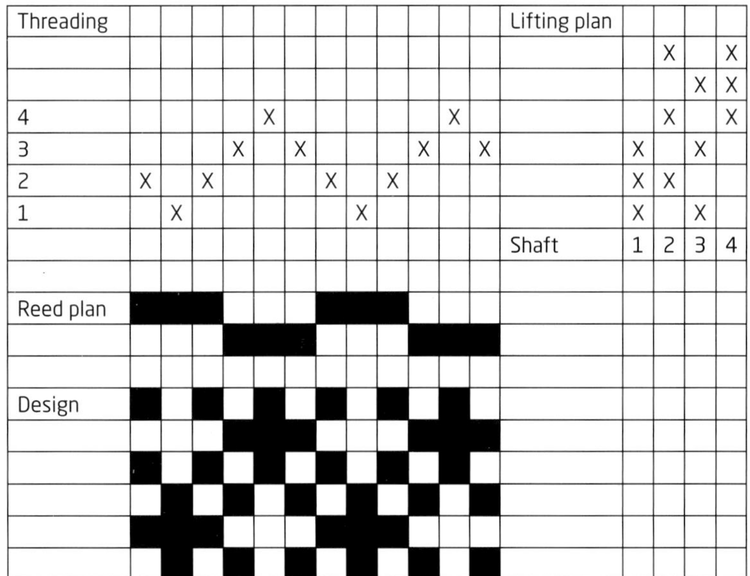

Threading													Lifting plan				
															X		X
																X	X
4					X						X				X		X
3				X		X				X		X		X		X	
2	X		X				X		X					X	X		
1		X						X						X		X	
													Shaft	1	2	3	4
Reed plan	■	■	■				■	■	■								
				■	■	■				■	■	■					
Design	■		■		■		■		■		■						
				■	■	■				■	■	■					
	■		■		■		■		■		■						
		■		■		■		■		■		■					
	■	■	■				■	■	■								
		■		■		■		■		■		■					

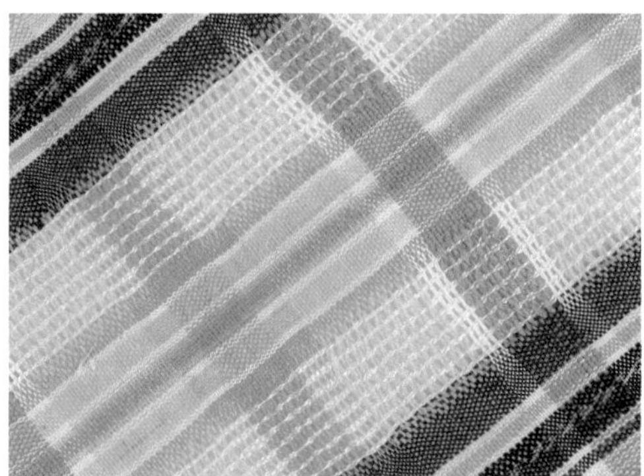

Three-end mock leno in plain weave.

Mock leno over 4 shafts

Threading													Lifting plan				
															X		X
													Plain weave	x		X	
															X		X
																X	X
4								X							X		X
3	O		O		O		X		X					X		X	
2		O		O		O				X		X		X	X		
1											X		Mock leno	X		X	
													Shaft	1	2	3	4

---------repeat--------- ---------repeat---------

Reed plan	■	■	■				■	■	■			
				■	■	■				■	■	■
Design												
		■		■		■		■		■		■
Plain	■		■		■		■		■		■	
		■		■		■		■		■		■
	■		■		■		■	■	■			
		■		■		■		■		■		■
	■		■		■		■		■		■	
Mock leno		■		■		■				■	■	■
and plain	■		■		■		■		■		■	

EXAMPLES OF MOCK LENO WITH PLAIN WEAVE

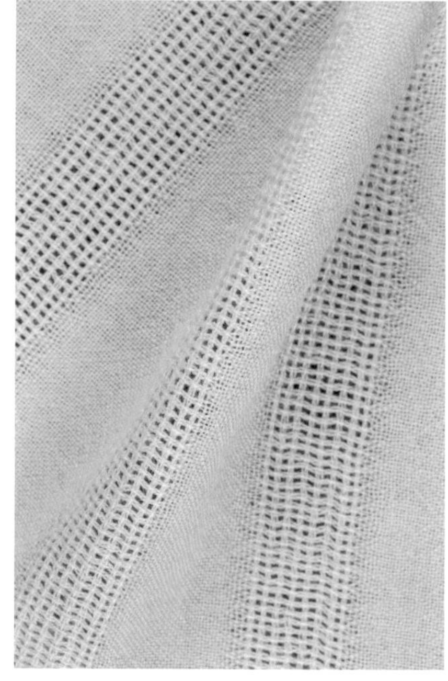

Three-end mock leno structure against plain weave forming a vertical strip.

Three-end mock leno structure against plain weave forming squares.

Detail of three-end mock leno structure against plain weave forming squares.

Diagram of 5-end mock leno structure

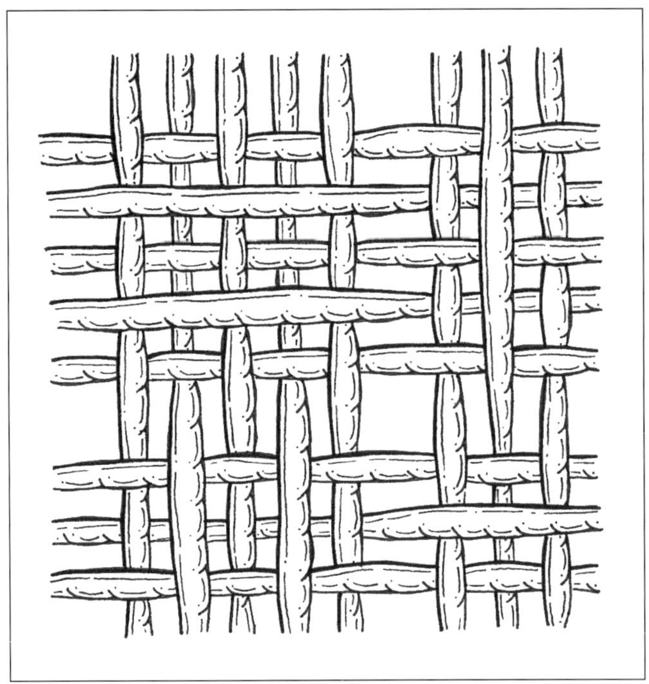

Threading plan over 4 shafts: 5-end units of mock leno

Threading											Lifting plan				
													X		X
														X	X
													X		X
														X	X
													X		X
4							X		X			X		X	
3						X		X		X		X	X	X	
2	X		X		X							X		X	
1		X		X								X	X		
											Mock leno	X		X	
Reed plan	■	■	■	■	■						Shaft	1	2	3	4
						■	■	■	■	■					

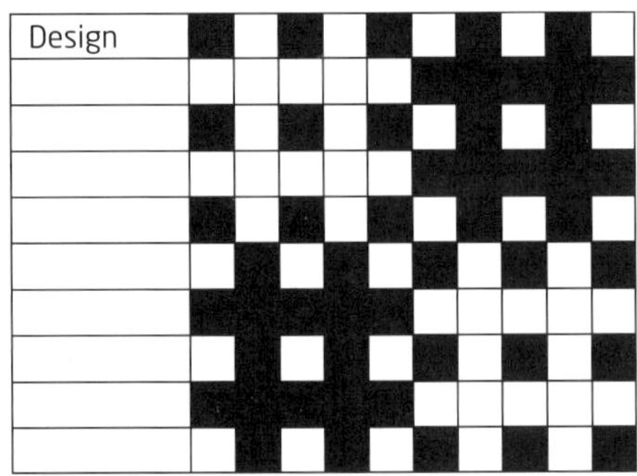

Threading plan over 4 shafts: 4-end units of mock leno

Threading									Lifting plan				
											X		X
												X	X
												X	X
											X		X
4		X	X							X		X	
3	X			X						X	X		
2					X			X		X	X		
1						X	X			X		X	
									Shaft	1	2	3	4
Reed plan	■	■	■	■									
					■	■	■	■					
Design		■	■		■			■					
	■	■	■	■									
	■	■	■	■									
		■	■		■			■					
	■			■		■	■						
					■	■	■	■					
					■	■	■	■					
	■			■		■	■						

The second and third picks in the lifting plan are identical, as are the sixth and seventh. This means that the weft yarn will shoot through unless you hold the weft in place while weaving pick three and seven. To give a neater finish, hook the weft yarn around the warp thread at the edge of the cloth.

EXAMPLES OF FOUR-END MOCK LENO

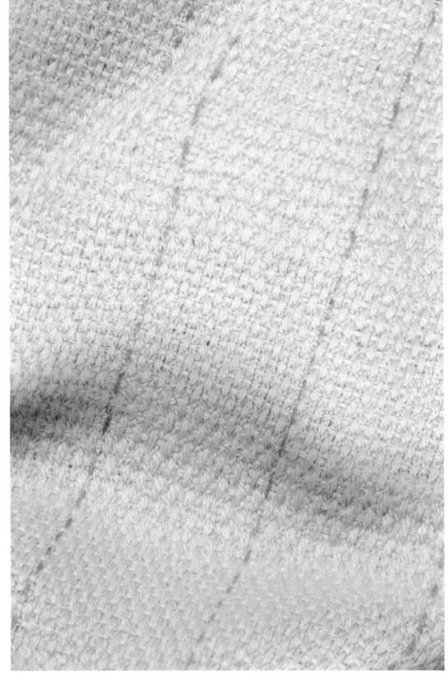

All-over three-end mock leno.

Three-end mock leno against a twill weave.

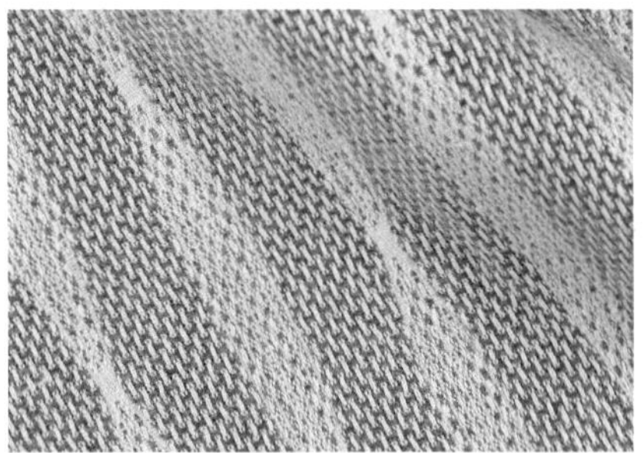

Four-end mock leno used as a ground weave in a double-cloth fabric.

CREATING PATTERNS WITH MOCK LENO

A more complex pattern formation can be achieved if there are more shafts available. Four shafts are needed for each mock leno section, which each have the two units required to create the mock leno design.

The following examples show how you can use the mock leno effect against plain weave, or as an all-over design.

Mock over 12 shafts: 3-end units over three 4-shaft sections

Threading																		
12																	X	
11																X		X
10													X		X			
9														X				
8											X							
7										X		X						
6							X		X									
5								X										
4					X													
3				X		X												
2	X		X															
1		X																

---------repeat--------- ---------repeat--------- ---------repeat---------

Reed plan	■	■	■				■	■	■				■	■	■			
				■	■	■				■	■	■				■	■	■

Design 1: A narrow diagonal line of mock leno against plain weave

Lifting plan (Design 1)													
18		X		X		X		X		X		X	Repeat 13-18
17	X		X		X		X				X	X	
16		X		X		X		X		X		X	
15	X		X		X		X		X		X		
14		X		X		X		X	X	X			
13	X		X		X		X		X		X		
12		X		X		X		X		X	X		Repeat 7-12
11	X		X				X	X	X		X		
10		X		X		X		X		X		X	
9	X		X		X		X		X		X		
8		X		X	X	X		X				X	
7	X		X		X		X		X		X		
6		X		X		X		X		X		X	Repeat 1-6
5			X	X	X		X		X		X		
4		X		X		X		X		X		X	
3	X		X		X		X		X		X		
2	X	X				X		X		X		X	
1	X		X		X		X		X		X		
	1	2	3	4	5	6	7	8	9	10	11	12	

PATTERN COMBINATIONS

The threading plan using 12 shafts is in blocks of four, so why not try experimenting with other basic four-shaft weaves to create interesting and exciting combinations of weaves in your fabric designs. They can be used to produce a horizontal pattern, or try contrasting structures side by side.

1 × 3 twill

3 × 1 twill

2 × 2 twill

Distorted weft

Extra weft floats

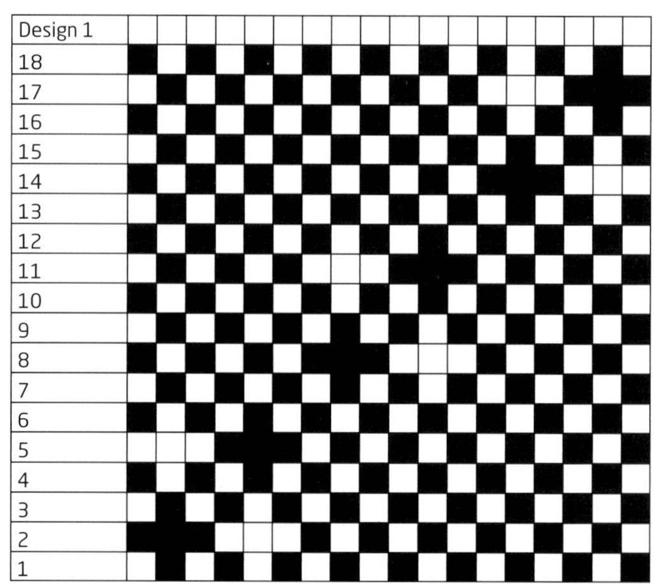

Design 2: A broad diagonal line of mock leno against plain weave

Lifting plan (Design 2)													
18		X		X		X		X		X		X	Repeat 13-18
17			X	X	X		X				X	X	
16		X		X		X		X		X		X	
15	X		X		X		X		X		X		
14	X	X				X		X	X	X			
13	X		X		X		X		X		X		
12		X		X		X		X		X		X	Repeat 7-12
11	X		X				X	X			X	X	
10		X		X		X		X		X		X	
9	X		X		X		X		X		X		
8		X		X	X	X			X	X			
7	X		X		X		X		X		X		
6		X		X		X		X		X		X	Repeat 1-6
5			X	X			X	X	X		X		
4		X		X		X		X		X		X	
3	X		X		X		X		X		X		
2	X	X			X	X				X		X	
1	X		X		X		X		X		X		
	1	2	3	4	5	6	7	8	9	10	11	12	

Design 2
18
17
16
15
14
13
12
11
10
9
8
7
6
5
4
3
2
1

Design 3: All-over mock leno

Lifting plan (Design 3)													
6		X		X		X		X		X		X	Repeat 1-6
5			X	X			X	X			X	X	
4		X		X		X		X		X		X	
3	X		X		X		X		X		X		
2	X	X			X	X		X	X	X			
1	X		X		X		X		X		X		
	1	2	3	4	5	6	7	8	9	10	11	12	

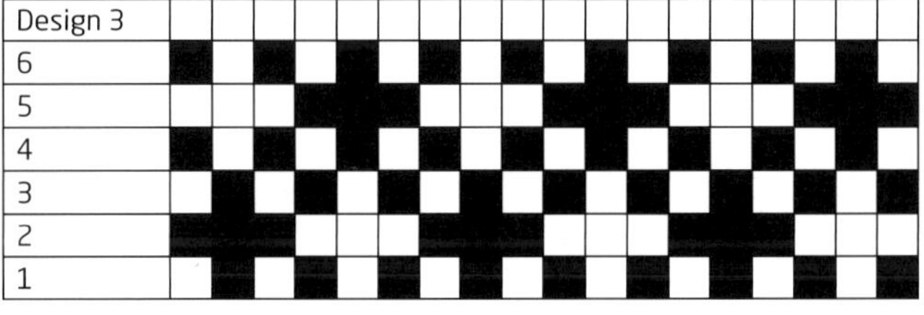

Design 4: Horizontal bands of mock leno and plain weave or reverse twill

Lifting plan (Design 4)													
12	X			X	X			X	X			X	Repeat 9-18
11			X	X			X	X			X	X	
10		X	X			X	X			X	X		
9	X	X			X	X			X	X			
8		X		X		X		X		X		X	Repeat 7-8
7	X		X		X		X		X		X		Rlain weave
6		X		X		X		X		X		X	Repeat 1-6
5			X	X			X	X			X	X	
4		X		X		X		X		X		X	
3	X		X		X		X		X		X		
2	X	X			X	X			X	X			
1	X		X		X		X		X		X		
	1	2	3	4	5	6	7	8	9	10	11	12	

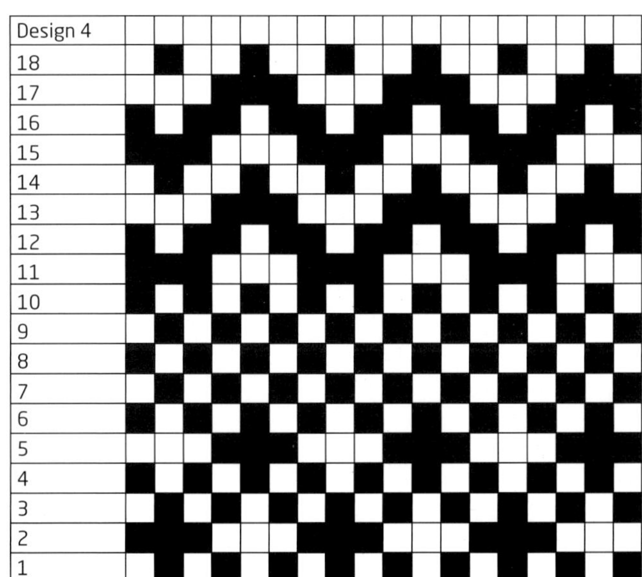

SEERSUCKER

A seersucker or crinkle cloth features distinctive puckered areas in contrast to stable areas within the finished fabric. These are normally formed as vertical stripes, although horizontal bands or blocks are possible too, depending on the technique that you use.

There are several ways of producing seersucker:

- In the weave itself, using contrasting tensions in the warp.
- By using a combination of stable yarns with yarns that, after undergoing wet finishing, will shrink when removed from the loom.
- By using stable yarns with elasticated yarns.

Cotton seersucker created by varying the warp tension. A 2 x 2 twill is used in the taut section and plain weave in the loose section.

TENSIONED SEERSUCKER

The most stable seersuckers are made from firmly woven cloths. Two warp beams are essential, as the bands of yarn need to be tensioned differently to achieve the effect. The 'ground' ends are firmly tensioned, and the 'crimping' ends are lightly tensioned.

- The width of the alternating bands of tightly tensioned and crimped ends need to be determined before making your warp.
- When preparing your warps, make sure that the crimped warp is 30 per cent longer than the taut warp as there will be more take-up in the slack strips.
- The yarn used in the warp must be strong enough to undergo heavy beating of the weft yarn by the batten, enabling the seersucker to be held down firmly.
- Remember to keep the selvedge tightly tensioned – a loose edge will be messy and difficult to control.
- Narrow bands are effective and easier to control than broad bands – but this should not be a restrictive rule to follow.

A plain-weave structure is normally used, as it holds the weft firmly and does not disguise the effect of the puckering. In theory you can produce a tensioned seersucker on two shafts, but you will be restricted in the thickness of the yarn that you can use.

When using four shafts, the threading plan is normally a straight draft from shafts 1 to 4, but if the thickness of yarn allows, then you can thread each band on a block draft, two shafts per block.

If six shafts are available, then the puckering warp can be threaded on two shafts and the tight warp on the remaining four, allowing you to produce a wider variety of structures and weave combinations.

THREADING PLANS

In Threading plans 1, 2 and 3, following, X indicates where the ends in the warp are tensioned tightly, and O indicates the slack ends.

Plan 1																					
4				X				X				O				O			X		X
3			X				X				O				O			X		X	
2		X				X				O				O					X		X
1	X				X				O				O					X		X	
																	Shaft	1	2	3	4

-------------repeat------------- -------------repeat-------------

Plan 2																					
4										O		O		O		O			X		X
3									O		O		O		O			X		X	
2		X		X		X		X											X		X
1	X		X		X		X											X		X	
																	Shaft	1	2	3	4

-------------repeat------------- -------------repeat-------------

Plan 3																		
6										O		O						
5									O		O							
4				X				X						X			X		X
3			X				X									X	X	X	
2		X				X									X	X			X
1	X				X									X	X			X	
													Shaft	1	2	3	4	5	6

---------repeat--------- ---------repeat---------

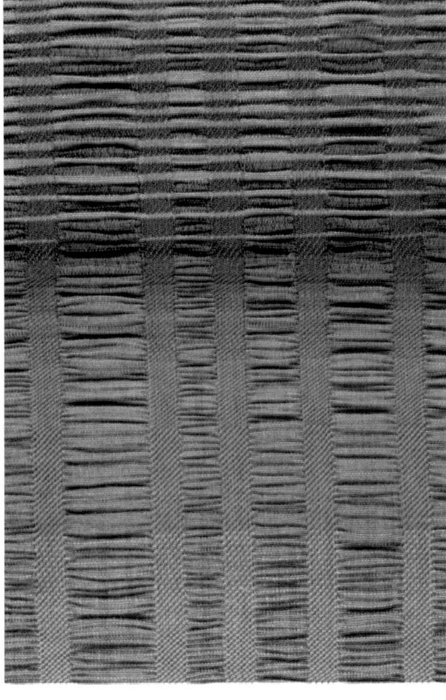

Examples of cotton seersucker created by varying the warp tension.

MINI PLEATS

Using Threading plans 2 or 3, which are block drafts, you can also produce simple or mini pleats in the slack bands by weaving these strips independently of the tight bands. You must use a block draft to produce mini pleats because it allows you to isolate and weave the different sections independently.

With the tension tight on both beams, use plain weave to create a firm cloth.

Keep the tension tight, and only weave the strips on shafts 3 and 4 (Plan 2) or shafts 5 and 6 (Plan 3). If you use one shuttle across the complete width of the warp, then floats will occur, crossing the sections that are not being woven. If you want independent pleats with neat edges, then use an individual bobbin for each pleat section. The process is longer, but each pleat could be a different colour.

Once you have woven a sufficient amount to allow you to produce the pleat, slacken off the beam holding the warp threads in this section. Then, with this section of the warp still slack, pull the batten toward the fell (horizontal edge) of the cloth.

With the tension still off the pleated section, weave across the whole warp using plain weave. This will anchor the pleats to the taut sections. Once the pleat is held down firmly enough, you can replace the tension and repeat.

If you put back the tension too soon – too few weft picks to hold the pleat – then the pleat will pull out.

Sequence for mini pleats: 4 shafts

Plan 2																					
																	Plain weave - slack tension		X		X
																		X		X	
																					X
																	Weave pleats - tight tension			X	
4										X		X		X		X					
3									X		X		X		X						
2		X		X		X		X											X		X
1	X		X		X		X										Plain weave - tight tension	X		X	
																	Shaft	1	2	3	4

-------------repeat------------- -------------repeat-------------

Sequence for mini pleats: 6 shafts

Plan 3													Plain weave - slack tension						
															X		X		
														X		X			
6										X		X							X
5									X		X		Weave pleats - tight tension					X	
4				X				X											
3			X				X												
2		X				X									X		X		X
1	X				X								Plain weave - tight tension	X		X		X	
													Shaft	1	2	3	4	5	6

---------repeat--------- ---------repeat---------

SHRINKING-YARN SEERSUCKER

You can achieve very effective seersuckers by using yarns of different shrinkage, such as wool against cotton or silk. The fabric is formed using strips of alternating shrinking and stable yarn. It is advisable to use two beams as the wool yarn is much springier than the cotton or silk, which will cause tension problems when weaving if using only one beam.

The effect is created only once the fabric is removed from the loom and wet finished, either by hand or machine washing. The wool will relax and shrink and the cotton or silk will remain stable. The result is a puckered appearance in the cotton area. If you use a washing machine to finish your fabric, begin on a gentle programme first so that you can assess the rate of shrinkage. If it does not shrink enough, put it through a longer cycle. It is not just the temperature of the water that will shrink or felt the wool, but the length of time for which it is agitated. Remember that if you start on a hot long wash there is no going back.

You can use as few as two shafts to create the effect, or follow the plans shown for the tensioned seersucker over four or six shafts. When planning your fabric, remember that it will shrink when finished, so compensate by producing longer and wider sample designs.

It is not necessary to have the stable yarn at the outside edges of your fabric. If you use wool for the selvedge it will shrink and contain the seersucker sections. If you use the stable yarn on the selvedge, when the wool shrinks you will achieve a frilly edge.

Design possibilities

- Use fine yarns of equal thickness to create a sophisticated lightweight fabric.
- Use a fine, stable yarn as the base cloth, divided by much thicker wool ends to give contrast.
- Use a stable yarn in the weft to create a vertical seersucker.
- Alternate bands of wool and a stable yarn in the weft will result in 'blisters' of cotton surrounded by wool, forming a check pattern.

ELASTICATED SEERSUCKER

An elasticated or high-twist yarn will naturally contract after it is used under tension, either in the warp or in the weft. A high-twist yarn is one that has been spun very tightly in manufacture, resulting in a lively nature that makes the thread curl back on itself.

When these yarns are used in a warp, they are under constant tension, and will naturally contract when the weaving is removed from the loom and allowed to relax. The effect can be increased either with steam from an iron or by light washing.

You will need a loom with two beams if using an elasticated yarn contrasting with a stable yarn in the warp. Any of the threading plans shown for the tensioned seersucker can be used, and provided the yarns are of a suitable thickness, then you can achieve the effect using only two shafts.

This method of creating a seersucker means you have less control over the results – but you do get an instant pucker.

Design possibilities

- Use alternating bands of elasticated and stable yarn in the warp. Remember that the elastic will shrink considerably, so compensate by making your warps 50 per cent longer than you would normally. You will have a vertical seersucker.
- Use bands of stable yarn and bands of elasticated yarns in the weft as well as the warp to create a 'blister' effect when the yarn shrinks.
- Set up the loom with one warp in a stable yarn. Use alternating bands of elastic and stable yarn to create a horizontal seersucker. Remember that when using elastic yarn in the weft, the width of the cloth will reduce considerably when taken off the loom.

CRÊPE WEAVES

All crêpe weaves have a non-directional weave construction with no prominent effect, such as in a twill weave. A crêpe fabric can be created using adaptations to traditional weaves such as twill, sateen or plain weave. The effect produced can be one of a confused textural pattern, or a small-scale all-over repeat pattern.

Simple crêpe weaves can be achieved by:

- Adding extra stitching points to a traditional weave.
- Adding or eliminating stitching points on a plain weave.
- Combining two basic weave structures.
- Rotating a basic weave pattern.

In the lifting plans that follow, X indicates the base weave and O indicates additional lifts. All of the examples are based on a straight draft over eight shafts.

Threading plan over 8 shafts

Shaft															
8								X							
7							X								
6						X									
5					X										
4				X											
3			X												
2		X													
1	X														

Crêpe weave based on a 4-end sateen with added stitching points

Design A									Lifting plan A			X	O	O		X	
										O	O		X				X
											X				X	O	
										X		O	O	X			
										O		X				X	O
													X	O	O		X
											X	O			X		
										X				X		O	O
									Shaft	1	2	3	4	5	6	7	8

Crêpe weave based on a plain weave with added stitching points

Design B									Lifting plan B		X		X	O	X		X
										X		X		X		X	
											X		X		X		X
										X		X		X		X	
											X	O	X		X		X
										X		X		X		X	
											X		X		X		X
										X	O	X		X		X	
									Shaft	1	2	3	4	5	6	7	8

Crêpe weave based on a plain weave with added stitching points

Design C	Lifting plan C								
		O		X		O		X	
			O		X		O		X
			X	O			X	O	
		X			O				O
		O		X		O		X	
			O		X		O		X
			X	O			X	O	
		X			O	X			O
	Shaft	1	2	3	4	5	6	7	8
	4-end			X				X	
	sateen				X				X
			X				X		
		X				X			
	Shaft	1	2	3	4	5	6	7	8
	1 x 3 twill	O				O			
			O				O		
				O				O	
					O				O
	Shaft	1	2	3	4	5	6	7	8

Crêpe weave formed by rotating a 4-end weave pattern

Design D	Lifting plan D	X		X				X	X
		X	X		X		X	X	
			X		X	X			X
				X			X	X	
			X	**X**			X		
		X			**X**	X		X	
			X	**X**		X		X	X
		X	**X**				X		X
	Shaft	1	2	3	4	5	6	7	8

Bold X = basic pattern, which is then rotated in the adjacent squares

There are many alternatives – you can create your own patterns quite easily by starting with the basic weave structure on point paper, adding extra stiching points or a different weave, or rotating a four-end weave, and seeing what happens. Draw out the design on point paper first to see how the pattern works.

Additional pattern examples over 8 shafts (black squares indicate that the shaft is lifting)

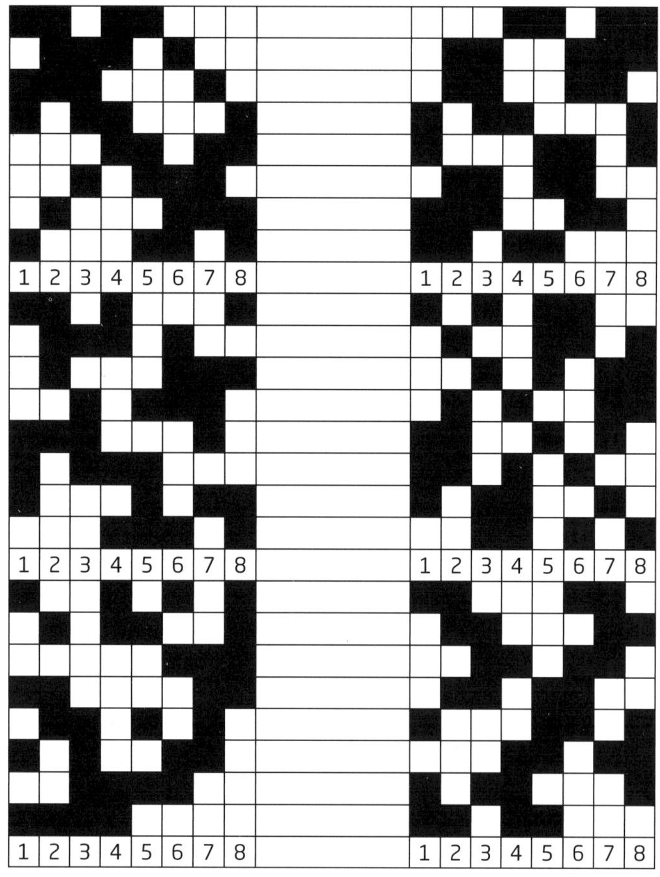

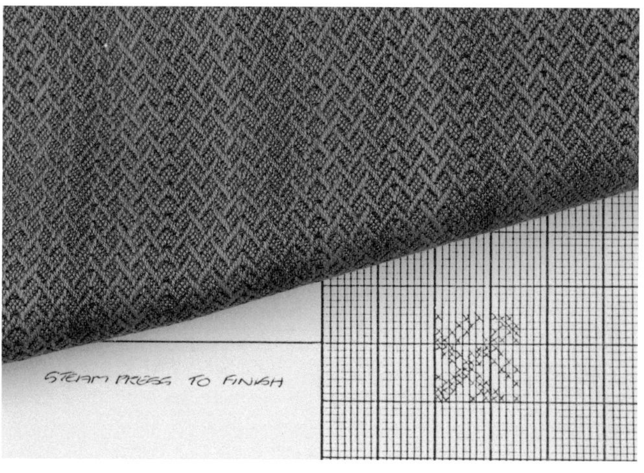

Above: A crêpe weave over 12 shafts with lifting plan.

Threading plan over 6 shafts

Shaft													
6						X							
5					X								
4				X									
3			X										
2		X											
1	X												

Crêpe weave over 6 shafts

Design							Lifting plan		X	X	X		
									X		X	X	X
								X	X				X
								X				X	X
								X	X	X		X	
										X	X	X	
							Shaft	1	2	3	4	5	6

Additional patterns over 6 shafts (black squares indicate that the shaft is lifting)

Six ends, six picks, crêpe, blue warp, orange weft.

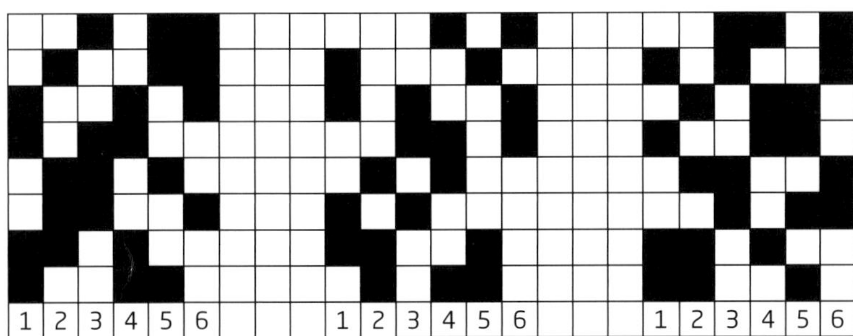

Six ends, eight picks, crêpe, blue warp, orange weft.

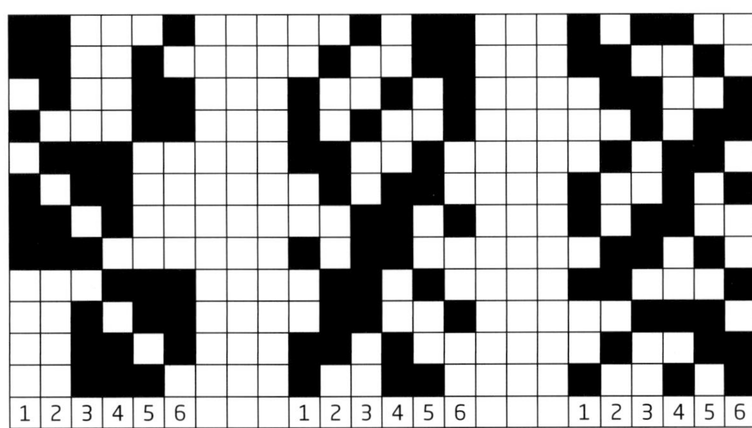

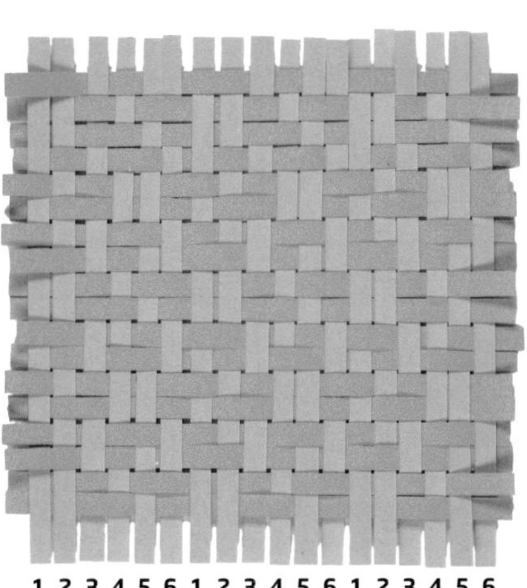

Six ends, eight picks, crêpe, blue warp, orange weft.

CORDED CLOTHS

As the name suggests, corded cloths are textured weaves that characteristically have ribs formed on the surface of the cloth, either in vertical, horizontal or undulating lines. The ribs are created by short floats on the reverse of a ground fabric that contract when the cloth is removed from the loom. These structures are known as **Bedford cords**. In the most basic form, a Bedford cord can be produced using four shafts, but more effective structures will use six, eight or more shafts.

Similar in construction to a Bedford cord, a **corduroy** fabric also relies on floats to create the structure, the difference being that the weft floats are cut to achieve a pile.

VERTICAL BEDFORD CORD

These have very clearly defined vertical ribs, which are separated by two or four warp ends, known as **cutting lines**. The ribs are woven in either plain weave or 2 × 1 twill, while each cutting line is formed by a two-end or four-end unit of plain weave.

The threading plan is in blocks. When weaving, the first two picks float under the first block – or rib – and weave through the second block – or rib. The second pair of picks weave through the first block and float under the second. You can also create the effect by alternating **pick and pick**.

Elasticated yarn is used to pull the ribs of the bedford cord together for greater prominence.

Diagram of how the additional floating weft sits on the reverse of the cloth

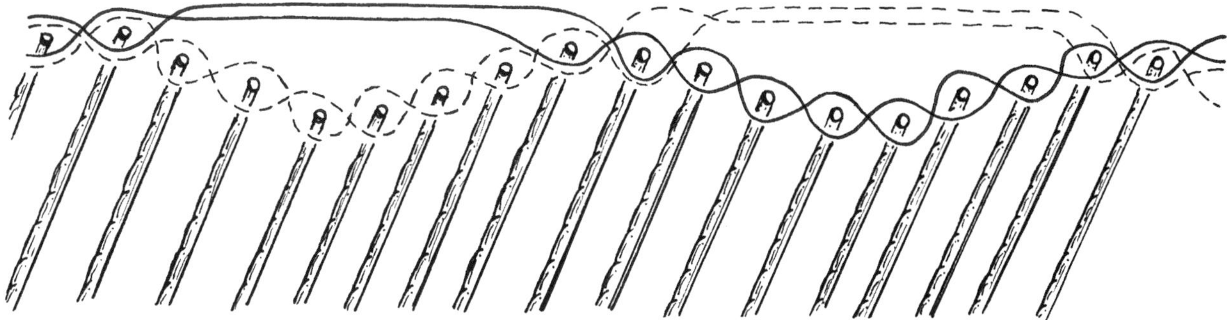

The contraction of the floats when the cloth is taken from the loom pulls up the ground cloth into a rib, and a depression is formed where the alternating floats cross the cutting line. The width of each rib is generally limited to a maximum of 2cm (3/4in) or less because the weft contraction is not sufficient to pull a wider area of ground cloth together. Weft yarns that naturally contract – such as wool, which has a natural elasticity – or 'lively', over-spun yarns, will increase the shrinkage of the weft floats when the fabric is removed from the loom.

STITCHING ENDS ON A SEPARATE BEAM

As with the Bedford cord structure, if there is an additional beam available on your loom, it is advisable to wind the stitching ends onto a separate beam from the ground sections. The stitching ends are woven as a plain weave throughout, so the take-up is greater in these sections.

Bedford cord formed by using an elasticated yarn to pull the ribs together.

The ribs can be enhanced to great effect by using thicker **wadding ends** in the warp. These additional threads will need to be wound onto a separate beam as their only function is to lie flat, trapped in place by the weft floats. Consequently there is no yarn take-up, so they need tensioning independently of the ground yarn. They will need to be allocated their own shaft, and will also pass through the same reed as the ground ends. The wadding ends should be of a much greater thickness to the ground ends, and a fine reed will rub and weaken them. Select a more open reed to avoid any problems when weaving. When denting, the additional ends will be accommodated in the same dent as the previous ground thread.

MINIMIZING VERTICAL LINES

If you are using a wider-spaced reed, reed marks may appear in your cloth – vertical lines formed by the thicker wire intersections. These lines will become less obvious once the fabric is removed from the loom and allowed to relax with a blast of steam from an iron or a gentle wash.

Bedford cord over 4 shafts

													Lifting plan 1		X	X	X
													Pair of floats	X		X	X
														X	X	X	X
														X	X	X	
														1	2	3	4
Threading																	
4								X		X		X	Lifting plan 2		X	X	X
3							X		X		X			X	X		X
2		X		X		X								X		X	X
1	X		X		X									X	X	X	
													Shaft	1	2	3	4

-------repeat------- -------repeat-------

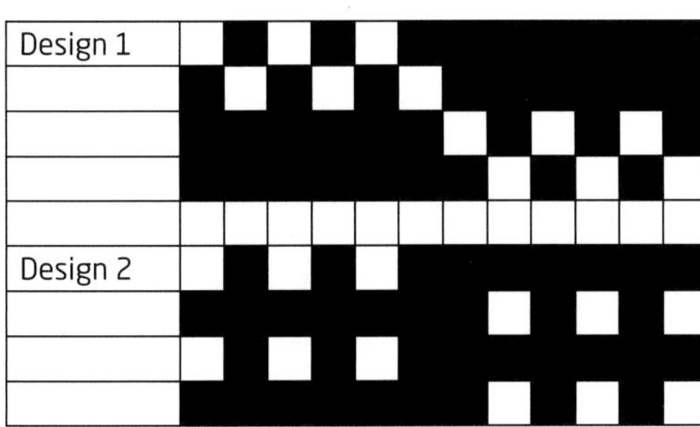

Bedford cord over 6 shafts (threads in bold X form the cutting line)

Threading																							
6												X		X		X							
5											X		X		X								
4				X		X		X									Lifting plan		X		X	X	X
3			X		X		X											X		X		X	X
2		**X**								**X**									X	X	X		X
1	**X**								**X**									X		X	X	X	
																	Shaft	1	2	3	4	5	6

------------repeat------------ ------------repeat------------

Design

Bedford cord over 8 shafts (threads in bold X form the cutting line)

																Lifting plan		X	X		X	X	X	X
																	X			X	X	X	X	X
																		X	X	X	X	X		X
Threading																	X		X	X	X		X	X
8												X			X			X	X	X		X	X	X
7											X			X			X		X		X	X	X	X
6										X			X					X	X	X	X	X	X	
5					X			X									X		X	X	X	X		X
4				X			X											X		X	X	X	X	X
3			X			X											X		X	X		X	X	X
2		**X**								**X**								X	X	X	X		X	X
1	**X**								**X**								X		X	X	X	X	X	
																Shaft	1	2	3	4	5	6	7	8

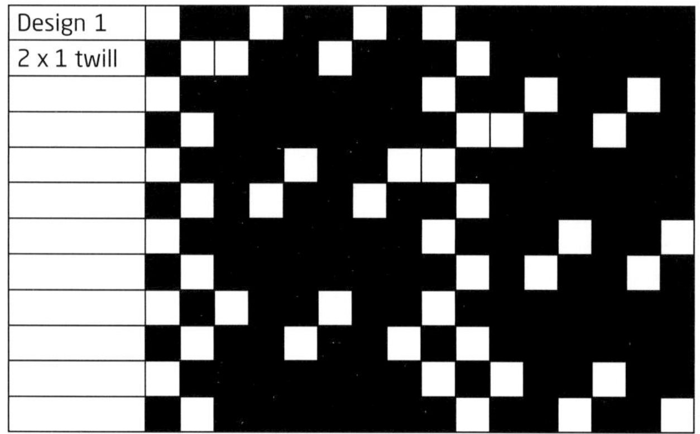

SEPARATE BEAM FOR CUTTING LINE

When producing a Bedford cord, it is advisable to wind the threads used as the cutting line onto a separate beam from the rib sections. The cutting-line ends are woven as a plain weave throughout; therefore the take-up is greater than in the rib sections, which are woven less frequently.

Bedford cord over 8 shafts using wadding ends (threads in bold X form the cutting line; threads in bold O are the wadding ends)

Shaft																	**O**			**O**
8																				
7							**O**			**O**						X			X	
6															X			X		
5																				
4						X		X												
3					X		X													
2		**X**		**X**								**X**		**X**						
1	**X**		**X**								**X**		**X**							

----------------repeat----------------   ----------------repeat----------------

Reed plan	■	■	■	■							■	■	■	■						
					■	■	■	■	■	■					■	■	■	■	■	■

Lifting plans for Bedford cord with wadding ends

A												B							
													X			X	X		X
												X		X		X	X	X	X
													X	X	X		X	X	
												X		X	X	X		X	X
	X		X	X	X		X						X		X	X	X		X
		X		X	X		X					X		X		X	X	X	X
	X	X	X		X	X							X	X	X		X	X	
X		X	X	X		X						X		X	X	X		X	X
1	2	3	4	5	6	7	8					1	2	3	4	5	6	7	8

Design A		■		■		■			■			■		■	■	■	■	■	■	■
2	■		■		■			■			■		■		■	■	■	■	■	■
3		■		■	■	■	■	■	■	■		■		■		■			■	
4	■		■		■	■	■	■	■	■	■		■		■			■		
5																				
6																				
Design B		■		■		■			■			■		■	■	■	■	■	■	■
8	■		■		■		■	■		■	■		■		■	■	■	■	■	■
9		■		■	■	■	■	■	■	■		■		■		■			■	
10	■		■		■	■	■	■	■	■	■		■		■		■	■		■
11		■		■		■			■			■		■	■	■	■	■	■	■
12	■		■		■		■	■		■	■		■		■	■	■	■	■	■
13		■		■	■	■	■	■	■	■		■		■		■			■	
14	■		■		■	■	■	■	■	■	■		■		■		■	■		■
	1	2	1	2	3	4	7	3	4	7	1	2	1	2	5	6	8	5	6	8

Plan A: Bedford cord.
Plan B: Bedford cord with wadding picks woven into the ground cloth.

DIAGONAL BEDFORD CORD

A diagonal rib will use at least eight shafts. There are no independent stiching ends because the ground ends take on a different role as the rib progresses diagonally through the pattern.

																			D		X		X		X		X
																				X	X	X	X	X	X		X
																				X		X		X		X	
																				X	X	X	X	X	X	X	
																			C		X		X		X		X
																				X	X	X	X		X	X	X
																				X		X		X		X	
																				X	X	X	X	X		X	X
Shaft																			B		X		X		X		X
8														X		X				X	X		X	X	X	X	X
7													X		X					X		X		X		X	
6										X		X								X	X	X		X	X	X	X
5									X		X																
4						X		X											A		X		X		X		X
3					X		X														X	X	X	X	X	X	X
2		X		X																X		X		X		X	
1	X		X																	X		X	X	X	X	X	X
																				1	2	3	4	5	6	7	8

The lifting plan progresses in repeats of four – Plans A, B, C and D. Work through the whole plan once for a shallow diagonal line, or repeat each section of four to create a steeper line. To make the line undulate, increase and decrease the repeat in each section gradually: A × 2, B × 3, C × 4, D × 5, A × 4, B × 3, C × 2, D × 3, A × 4, B × 5, C × 4, D × 3.

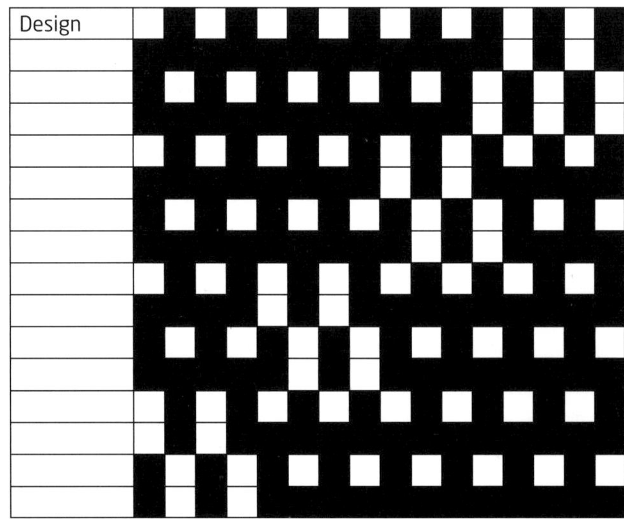

Diagonal cord over 12 shafts: straight draft

													Lifting plan		X		X		X		X		X		X
															X	X	X	X	X	X	X	X	X		X
														X		X		X		X		X		X	
														X		X	X	X	X	X	X	X	X	X	
															X		X		X		X		X		X
														X	X	X	X	X	X	X	X		X		X
														X		X		X		X		X		X	
														X	X	X	X	X	X	X	X	X		X	
															X		X		X		X		X		X
														X	X	X	X	X	X		X		X	X	X
														X		X		X		X		X		X	
Threading														X	X	X	X	X	X	X		X		X	X
12												X			X		X		X		X		X		X
11											X			X	X	X	X		X		X	X	X	X	X
10										X				X		X		X		X		X		X	
9									X					X	X	X		X	X		X	X	X	X	X
8								X						X		X		X		X		X		X	
7							X							X	X		X		X	X	X	X	X	X	X
6						X								X		X		X		X		X		X	
5					X									X	X	X		X		X	X	X	X	X	X
4				X											X		X		X		X		X		X
3			X												X		X	X	X	X	X	X	X	X	X
2		X												X		X		X		X		X		X	
1	X													X		X		X	X	X	X	X	X	X	X
													Shaft	1	2	3	4	5	6	7	8	9	10	11	12

Design

HORIZONTAL BEDFORD CORD

Horizontal Bedford cords are woven differently to vertical and diagonal Bedford cords. Ribs that run horizontally across the cloth are sometimes called 'welts'. Two warps are needed to produce the effect – a backing warp and a face warp – and each should be wound onto separate beams. The backing warp forms the floats on the reverse of the cloth, which should be more openly sett than the face cloth, and should be highly tensioned. The ribs will not become apparent until the weaving is removed from the loom, and the backing warp floats allowed to relax.

The face cloth can be woven in a variety of structures such as plain weave, twill or sateen. When denting, the additional ends will be accommodated in the same dent as the previous ground thread. The addition of wadding picks will enhance the indentation of the rib.

Horizontal Beford cord showing face and back. The ground cloth is a point draft over six shafts and the additional warp ends are on two shafts .

CHOOSING YARNS FOR THE ADDITIONAL WARP

It is advisable to use a finer yarn in the face warp than that in the backing warp, or the same thickness for both. If the face is heavier than the backing warp, then the floats will have little chance of pulling the ribs together.

- If a stable yarn such as cotton is used as the additional warp, it will need to be strong and highly tensioned. The height of the rib will be limited because the longer the float, the less likely it is to pull the ribs together. The resulting welt will be a soft ripple. Using a wadding pick will greatly enhance the effect.
- A strong wool yarn under high tension during weaving will naturally shrink when removed from the loom, due to its natural elasticity. The ribs will be more pronounced.
- A wool yarn that shrinks or felts during a wet finish will result in very pronounced ribs.

Horizontal Bedford cord over 6 shafts: threading plan (X = ground ends, O = additional warp ends)

Shaft													Lifting plans						
6						O						O							
5			O						O				C	X	X	X	X		
4					X						X								
3				X						X			B		X		X		
2		X						X						X		X			
1	X	X					X												
													A		X		X		X
Reed plan	■	■	■				■	■	■					X		X		X	
				■	■	■				■	■	■	Shaft	1	2	3	4	5	6

REED PLAN

There are two warps: one ground warp and an additional warp used to create floats on the back of the fabric, or to hold wadding picks in place. When denting the warps, the additional warp threads are included in the same dent as the previous two ground ends. They are there to form the rib, not as an integral part of the face cloth.

LIFTING PLANS

Lifting plan A: Both warps woven together – backing ends held firmly. Repeat twice or more depending on the space required between ribs.

Lifting plan B: Face warp woven as plain weave, backing ends float on the reverse – repeat until the rib is the desired size.

Lifting plan C: Insert wadding pick here.

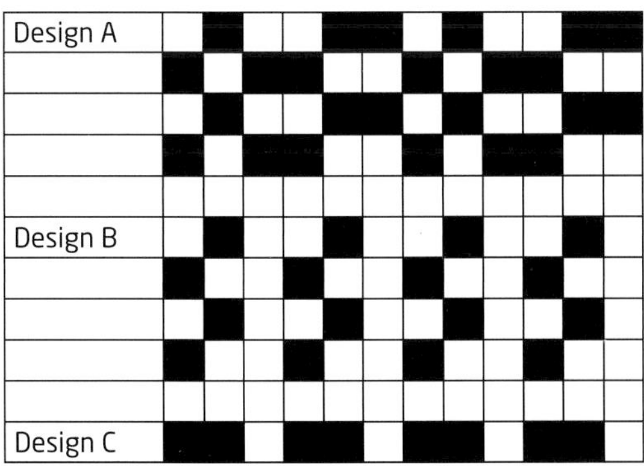

You could try using four-shaft twills instead of plain weave, or a combination of structures for additional surface interest on the rib.

WAVED BEDFORD CORDS

You can create a wavy line across the width of the fabric by weaving the backing warp ends into the ground cloth in a diamond shape or a zigzag pattern. The backing warp 'stitches' the shape into the ground cloth, and then floats on the reverse until the next pattern is formed. The wadding picks are forced into the spaces around the shapes. It is important to keep a good tension on the backing warp in order to achieve a pronounced effect.

The majority of shafts will be used by the backing warp in order for the shapes to be created. A minimum of six shafts are required, using four shafts for the pattern and two for the face cloth.

Threading plan 1: waved Bedford cord over 6 shafts

Shaft																		
6												O						
5									O						O			
4						O												O
3			O															
2		X			X			X			X			X			X	
1	X			X			X			X			X			X		
Reed plan	■	■	■				■	■	■				■	■	■			
				■	■	■				■	■	■				■	■	■

Threading plan 2: waved Bedford cord over 6 shafts

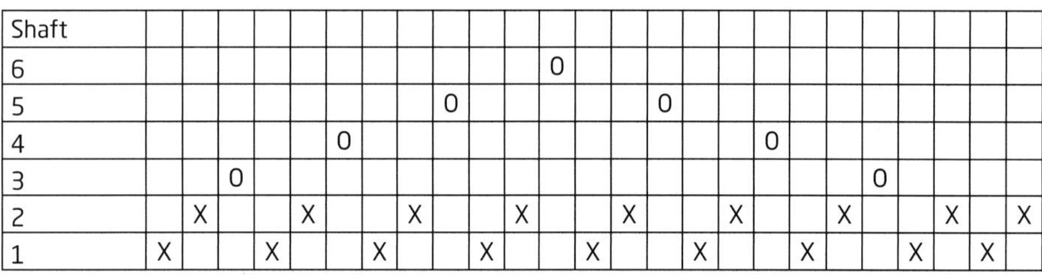

Shaft																									
6												O													
5									O						O										
4						O												O							
3			O																		O				
2		X			X			X			X			X			X			X			X		X
1	X			X			X			X			X			X			X			X		X	

---------------------repeat--------------------- ---------------------repeat---------------------

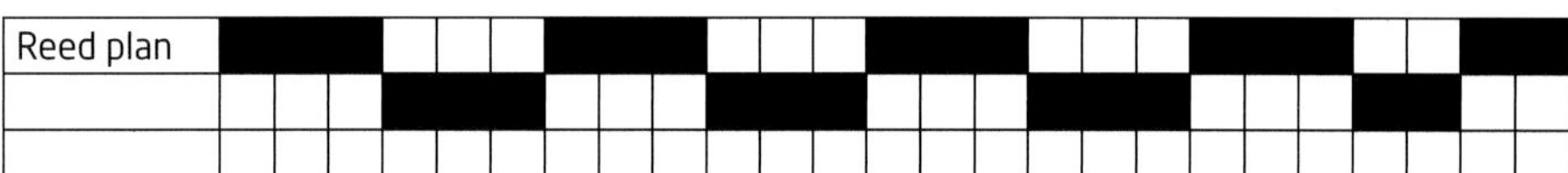

Reed plan	■	■	■				■	■	■				■	■	■				■	■	■			■	■
				■	■	■				■	■	■				■	■	■				■	■		

A								B	X	X					Wadding pick
										X					
									X						
										X					
									X		X				
										X					
									X		X	X			
										X					
									X		X	X	X		
										X					
									X		X	X	X	X	
										X					
									X		X	X	X		
										X					
									X		X	X			
										X					
									X		X				
X	X					Wadding pick				X					
	X								X						
X									X	X					Wadding pick
	X									X					
X					X				X					X	
	X									X					
X				X	X				X				X	X	
	X									X					
X			X	X	X				X			X	X	X	
	X									X					
X		X	X	X	X				X		X	X	X	X	
	X									X					
X		X	X	X					X			X	X	X	
	X									X					
X		X	X						X				X	X	
	X									X					
X		X							X					X	
1	2	3	4	5	6				1	2	3	4	5	6	

EXAMPLES OF WAVED BEDFORD CORD

Left: A waved Bedford cord showing the face of the cloth. The ground warp is wool and the backing ends are cotton.

Right: A waved Bedford cord showing the reverse of the cloth. The wadding picks are formed of thick cotton.

CORDUROY

This is a fabric similar in construction to Bedford cord, the difference being that the weft floats are cut to achieve a pile. The pile picks must be bound into the ground cloth securely by 'stitching' ends – at least two or four ends for stability in a plain-weave formation. The pile forms vertical cords, and is generally woven in a 2:1 ratio – two float picks to one ground pick, but this rule can be flexible, and is dependent on the thickness of the yarn used.

- Thick float pick and fine ground pick – 1:1 ratio or 1:2 ratio (2 ground picks) if the float pick is considerably thicker.
- Equal thickness in float and ground picks – 2:1 or 3:1 ratio.

The yarn used for the pile picks needs to be of a certain type – one that will naturally 'burst' when cut. Filament yarns in silk, viscose or cotton of any thickness are ideal, as the individual threads making up the yarn are not twisted or spun to hold them securely.

Four shafts are needed to produce corduroy with a plain-weave ground, and six or more if you intend to use twill weaves in the ground cloth. Diagonal lines can be achieved if 12 or more shafts are available.

Diagram of cut and uncut floats to form corduroy

Handwoven corduroy with a cotton ground and a viscose filament yarn used to create the cut corduroy

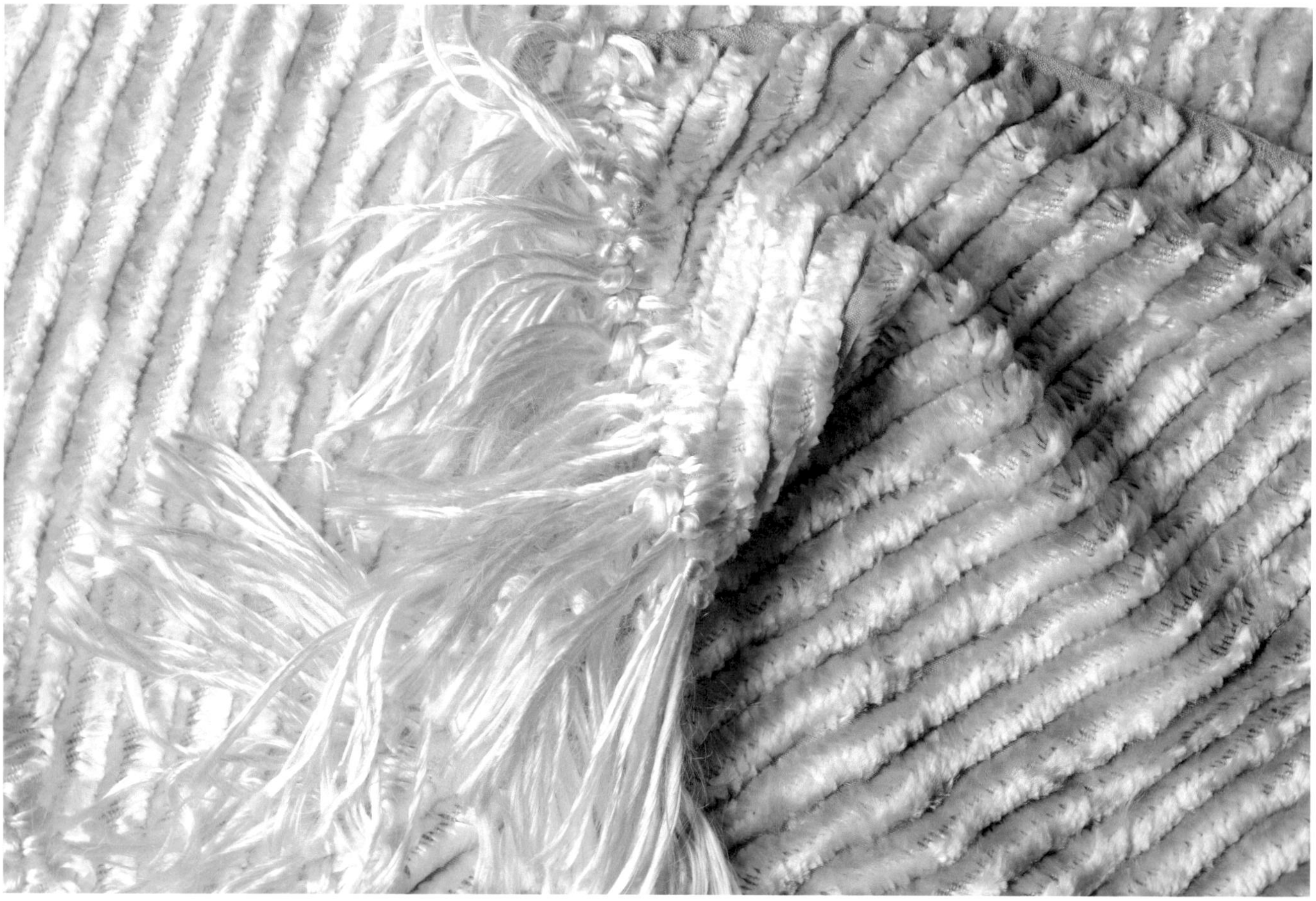

FINISHING

In order to be able to cut the floats, their width needs to be sufficient to allow you to insert small, very sharp scissors underneath them. This procedure can be carried out either on or off the loom, taking care not to cut through the ground cloth. Great care must also be taken to prevent the floats from being pulled out of the ground cloth when cutting.

- If the float is too small, then the yarn may be pulled from the ground by the action of the scissors.
- If a float pick is not bound into the ground sufficiently, it can easily be pulled out during the cutting process.
- Use very sharp scissors – a blunt pair will just pull on the floats.
- If a float is over-long it will be floppy rather than stand proud of the rib.

Once the floats are cut, the fabric should be blasted with a steam iron to encourage the cut floats to burst. This procedure opens out the yarn, giving a plush finish, and ensures that the ends are held more firmly in the ground fabric, which relaxes and shrinks slightly after being under tension on the loom.

Threading plan for corduroy over 4 shafts (threads in bold X form the stitching ends)

Shaft												
4						X		X		X		X
3					X		X		X		X	
2		**X**		**X**								
1	**X**		**X**									

-------------repeat-------------

Lifting plans

Design A		■		■									Plan A		X		
		■		■		■		■		■		■			X		X
	■		■											X			
	■		■		■		■		■		■			X		X	
													Shaft	1	2	3	4
Design B		■		■									Plan B		X		
	■		■											X			
		■		■		■		■		■		■			X		X
		■		■										X			
	■		■												X		
		■		■		■		■		■		■		X		X	
													Shaft	1	2	3	4
Design C		■		■									Plan C		X		
	■		■											X			
		■		■											X		
		■		■		■		■		■		■			X		X
	■		■											X			
		■		■											X		
	■		■											X			
	■		■		■		■		■		■			X		X	
													Shaft	1	2	3	4

Plan A: Pick and pick – 1:1 ratio plain weave and float. A finer yarn can be used for the ground and a thicker one for the float.

Plan B: One ground pick to two float picks. Equal thickness of yarn can be used, or a slightly thicker float yarn to give a richer pile.

Plan C: One ground pick to three float picks. Equal thickness of yarn can be used, or a slightly thicker float yarn to give a richer pile.

Threading plan for corduroy over 6 shafts (threads in bold X form the stitching ends)

Shaft								X				X
6								X				X
5							X				X	
4						X				X		
3					X				X			
2		**X**		**X**								
1	**X**		**X**									

--------------repeat--------------

Lifting plans

Design D	Plan D					
			X				
			X	X			X
		X					
		X				X	X
			X				
			X		X	X	
		X					
		X		X	X		
	Shaft	1	2	3	4	5	6

Design E	Plan E		X				
		X					
			X	X			X
		X					
			X				
		X				X	X
			X				
		X					
			X		X	X	
		X					
			X				
		X		X	X		
	Shaft	1	2	3	4	5	6

Plan D: A 2 x 2 twill-weave ground. Pick and pick – 1:1 ratio. A finer yarn can be used for the ground and a thicker one for the float.

Plan E: A 2 x 2 twill-weave ground. One ground pick to two float picks. Equal thickness of yarn can be used, or a slightly thicker float yarn to give a richer pile.

Threading plan for diagonal corduroy over 12 shafts

Shaft												
12												X
11											X	
10										X		
9									X			
8								X				
7							X					
6						X						
5					X							
4				X								
3			X									
2		X										
1	X											

---------------------repeat---------------------

Threading		X										X
	X		X									
		X		X		X		X		X		X
	X										X	
		X										X
	X		X		X		X		X		X	
										X		X
	X										X	
		X		X		X		X		X		X
									X		X	
										X		X
	X		X		X		X		X		X	
								X		X		
									X		X	
		X		X		X		X		X		X
							X		X			
								X		X		
	X		X		X		X		X		X	
						X		X				
							X		X			
		X		X		X		X		X		X
					X		X					
						X		X				
	X		X		X		X		X		X	
				X		X						
					X		X					
		X		X		X		X		X		X
			X		X							
				X		X						
	X		X		X		X		X		X	
		X		X								
			X		X							
		X		X		X		X		X		X
	X		X									
		X		X								
	X		X		X		X		X		X	
Shaft	1	2	3	4	5	6	7	8	9	10	11	12

7
EXTRA WARP AND WEFT PATTERNING

EXTRA WARP AND WEFT PATTERNING

These techniques allow you to add ornament to your fabric design by creating patterns, figures and shapes on the surface of a firmly woven ground cloth, either by using additional warp or weft threads – or both – without compromising the strength of the basic structure. So, if you pull out the extra warp or weft threads, there will be a complete ground weave remaining.

Using extra warp and weft techniques – sometimes known as supplementary warp and weft – opens up exciting possibilities when designing your woven fabric. By using very few shafts and clever use of colour, you can produce really rich, elaborate fabrics, and with more shafts at your disposal you can create complex, image-based motifs or all-over patterns.

The basis of the structure, whether the pattern is created by additional warp or weft, is that you will have a collection of threads sitting on the surface of your base, or ground cloth, that are pinned down at prescribed intervals to create the desired shape or pattern. The remaining floats lie beneath the surface on the reverse of the fabric.

When using this technique, the extra warp or weft threads can be in a contrasting colour, thickness or texture – or all three, depending on the effect required – to the yarn chosen for the ground cloth. As the pattern threads are additional to the basic structure, they can be used in varying proportions, and at any point within the design.

In both extra warp and extra weft, the more shafts you have at your disposal, then the greater the opportunity of producing a more recognizable shape to your motif. Stylized flowers, insects, birds and animals, architecture and complex patterning can be achieved. The possibilities are endless – just use your imagination with the equipment available.

COMPARISONS BETWEEN EXTRA WARP AND WEFT PATTERNING

Extra warp:

- You have to make two warps, so there is twice the amount of setting up.
- Once you have decided on the type of yarn you want to use for the extra warp, it stays the same throughout the weaving, as does the colour. If you wish, you can tie in different ends during weaving or dip-dye the extra warp to give variety.
- You can vary the proportion of the shapes by the way in which you thread the additional ends, creating small- or larger-scale motifs.
- Once the loom is prepared, only one set of weft threads are used, making it quicker to weave than an extra-weft construction.

Extra weft:

- An extra-weft structure requires only one warp, so it takes less time to set up the loom.
- The extra threads are introduced through the weft, so you can change the colour and type at will throughout the weave.
- You are restricted to the scale of the pattern because it is dictated by the thickness of the warp yarn – the more ends per cm/inch, the smaller the shape. To increase the scale you can use a stepped threading plan, but the shapes will be more angular.
- The weaving takes longer as there will be one pick for the ground cloth, and one or two for the extra-weft patterning.

PINNING DOWN THE FLOATS

Remember that when you are weaving, the extra warp or weft yarn that is floating on the surface is under tension, and will appear as a straight line. Once the cloth is taken from the loom, the yarn will relax and move, giving a less defined shape. While you are weaving, make sure that the floats forming your pattern are not over-long, and are pinned down into the fabric at regular intervals to avoid this.

EXTRA-WARP PATTERNING

- You can use as few as four shafts to create a basic pattern: two shafts for the ground and two for the extra warp.
- The scale of the design can be varied by allocating more shafts for the extra warp, or by threading multiple ends in sequence on each shaft.
- For a stronger contrast, the extra warp yarn can be thicker than the ground warp to give maximum impact. For a subtle contrast, use the same thickness of yarn.
- While the ground warp can be threaded over as few as two shafts, this will limit you to a plain-weave structure, but will free up more shafts for pattern potential.
- Consider the ground cloth – it will be more or less visible in different designs. Is it a single colour and there just to carry the extra warp pattern, or can it be striped to add interest and complexity to the overall effect?
- When denting, the additional ends will be accommodated in the same dent as the previous ground thread.
- The extra warp threads can be used to trap extra weft threads to produce additional interest.

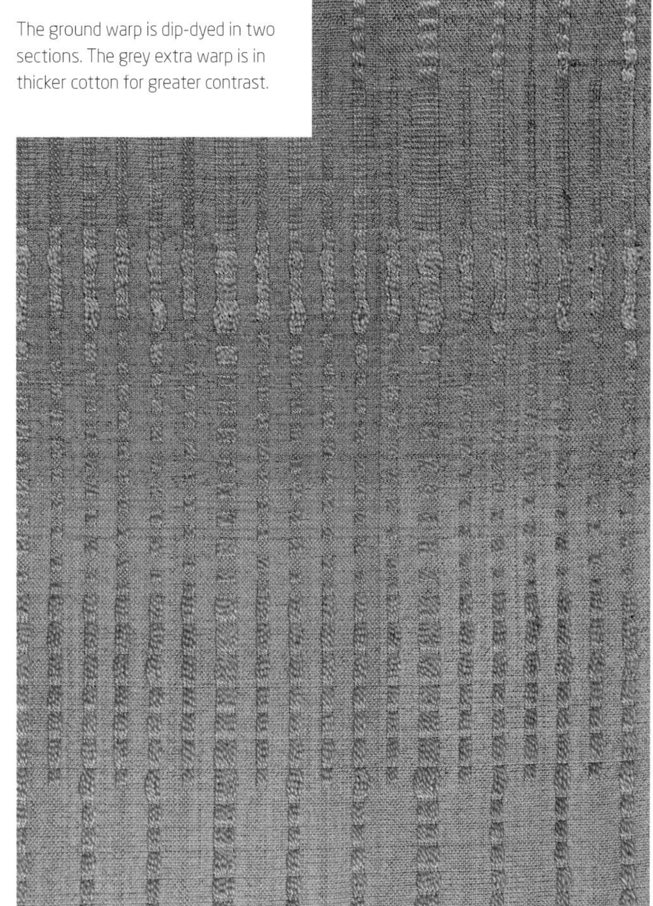

The ground warp is dip-dyed in two sections. The grey extra warp is in thicker cotton for greater contrast.

Cotton ground with cotton extra warp blocks.

Cotton ground in twill and plain weave with cotton extra warp blocks.

Diagram of single extra warp

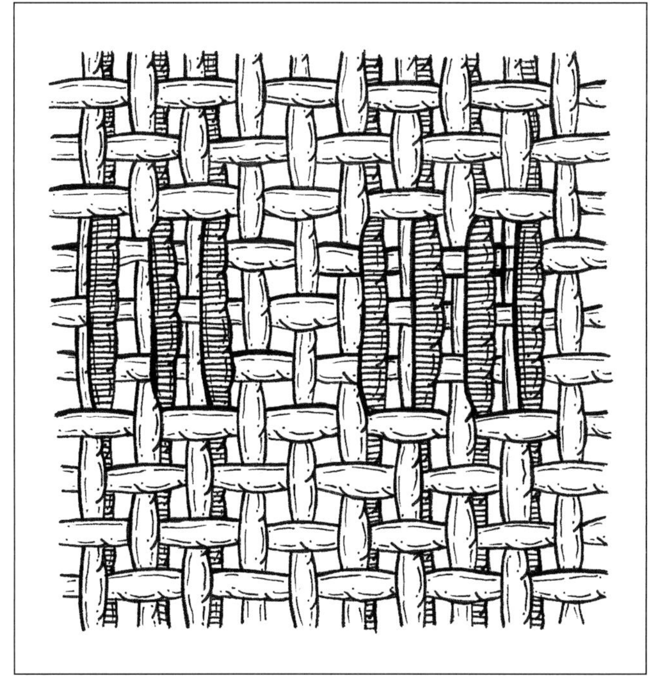

Extra-warp examples over 4 shafts (X = ground, O = extra warp)

1. Groups of ends on shafts 3 and 4 to form a spot motif (ground and extra warp ends are equal epc/epi)

Threading																
4														O		O
3						O		O								
2		X		X			X			X		X			X	
1	X		X		X				X		X		X			

----repeat---- ----repeat---- ----repeat---- ----repeat----

Reed plan			■	■					■	■			■	■	■	■
	■	■			■	■	■	■			■	■				

All reed plans are based on two ends per dent of ground yarn.

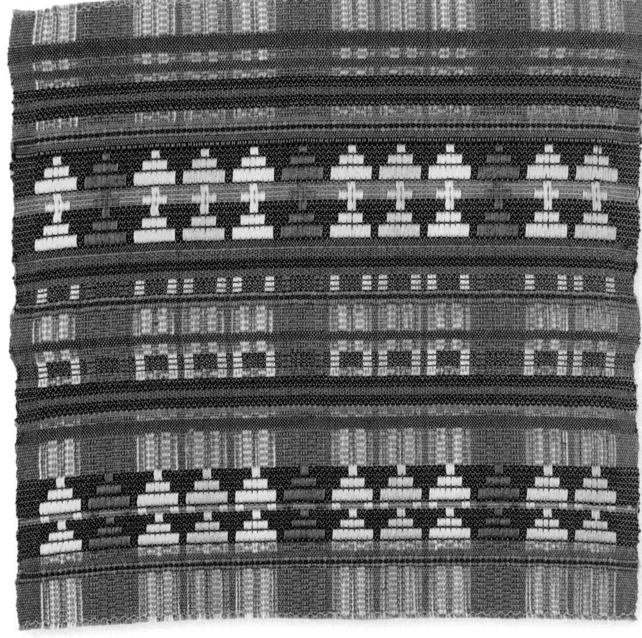

Left: Cotton ground on 3 shafts and cotton extra warp on 3 shafts forming a variety of simple patterns.

Lifting plan examples: extra-warp threading plan 1

A						B						C						D				
																				X	X	Extra
							X						X	X	X							
						X						X			X				X		X	Repeat
	X						X		X				X	X	X			X			X	
X		X	X			X			X			X			X				X		X	
	X						X		X				X	X	X			X			X	
X		X	X			X			X			X			X							
	X	X	X				X						X	X						X	X	Extra
X		X	X			X						X		X	X							
	X	X	X				X	X					X	X					X	X		Repeat
X		X	X			X		X				X		X	X			X		X		
	X						X	X					X	X					X	X		
X		X	X			X		X				X		X	X			X		X		
1	2	3	4			1	2	3	4			1	2	3	4			1	2	3	4	

Instructions adjacent to Plan D apply to Plan D only.

Plan A: Small blocks floating on the surface at the same time.
Plan B: Small blocks staggered.
Plan C: Staggered blocks – floats woven into the ground cloth.
Plan D: Extra weft yarn trapped by extra warp ends to form a zigzag pattern on the surface of the cloth – single-end distortions.

For all of the lifting plan examples, repeat sections as necessary to achieve the desired proportions.

2. Groups of ends on shafts 3 and 4 to form a fancy stripe (ground and extra warp ends are equal epc/epi)

Threading																
4										O		O				
3						O		O						O		O
2		X		X			X				X				X	
1	X		X		X				X				X			

----repeat---- ----repeat---- ----repeat---- ----repeat----

Reed plan			■	■					■	■	■	■				
	■	■			■	■	■	■					■	■	■	■

Lifting plan examples: extra-warp threading plan 2

E						F						G						H			
							X		X												
						X															
							X	X					X		X						X
						X			X			X			X				X		
							X						X		X						X
						X		X				X			X			X			
	X		X				X	X	X				X		X						X
X			X			X		X	X			X			X				X		
	X		X				X	X	X				X	X							X
X			X			X			X			X			X			X			
	X		X				X	X					X	X						X	
X			X			X		X	X			X		X					X		
	X	X					X	X	X				X	X						X	
X		X				X			X			X		X				X			
	X	X					X	X					X	X						X	
X		X				X		X	X			X		X					X		
	X	X					X	X	X				X		X					X	
X		X				X		X				X		X				X			
1	2	3	4			1	2	3	4			1	2	3	4			1	2	3	4

Plan E: Small blocks floating on the surface at the same time.
Plan F: Graduated stripe.
Plan G: Staggered blocks – floats woven into the ground cloth.
Plan H: Extra weft yarn trapped by extra warp ends to form contrasting blocks.

Threading												
4									O			O
3			O			O						
2		X			X			X			X	
1	X			X			X			X		

---------repeat-------- ---------repeat--------

Reed plan												
				■	■	■				■	■	■
	■	■	■				■	■	■			

Lifting plan examples: extra-warp threading plan 3 A, B, C, E, F, G, H

When using the lifting plans, repeat sections as necessary to achieve the desired proportions.

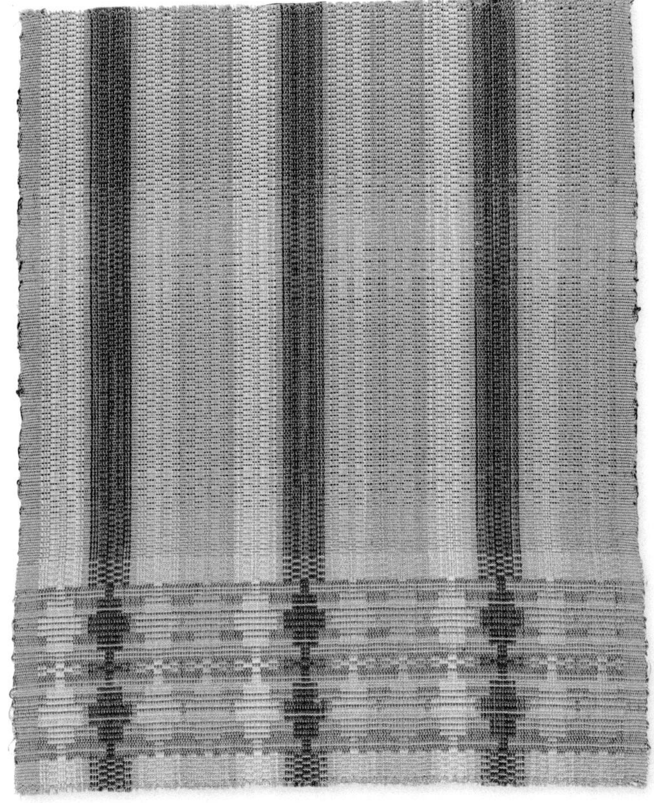

Cotton ground on three shafts and cotton extra warp on three shafts. The simple pattern forms a border and the extra warp is then firmly woven into the ground to form a stripe.

EXAMPLES OF SIMPLE EXTRA-WARP BLOCKS

Silk extra warp forming simple blocks forming a decorative stripe on a twill and plain-weave silk ground.

The ground warp is a clear nylon monofilament and the extra warp is a smoke-coloured nylon monofilament. When the weaving is removed from the loom, the longer extra warp floats are forced out due to the slight shrinkage of the ground weave.

The ground cloth is silk and is threaded over eight shafts. The extra warp is in a heavier-weight silk to heighten the contrast to the ground.

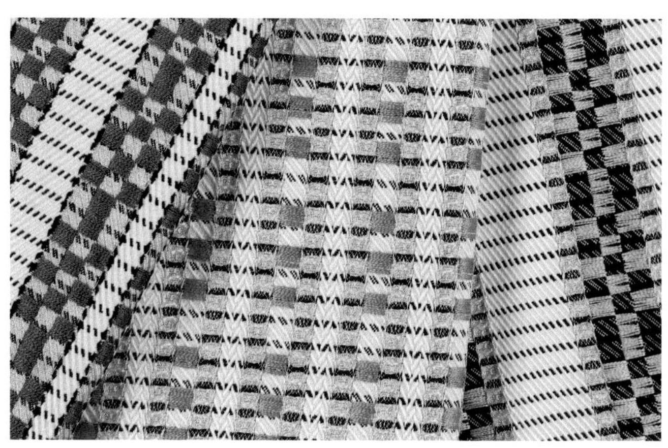

Collection of designs. The ground cloth is silk and is threaded over eight shafts. The extra warp is in a heavier-weight silk to heighten the contrast to the ground.

The ground warp is cotton and the extra warp is wool. This shows the reverse of the design. The fabric is lightly washed when taken from the loom and the wool shrinks.

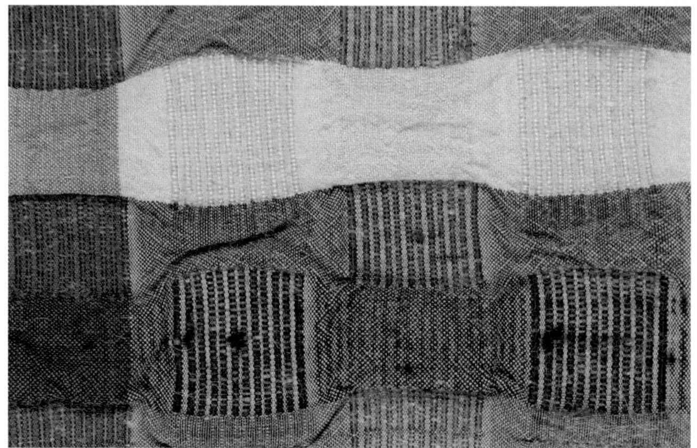

Basic four shaft double cloth structure for the gorund cloth and extra warp threads in black.

The ground cloth is threaded over two blocks using six shafts each. The extra warp is viscose floss, which is woven into the ground then floated on the surface. The floats are cut when the weaving is removed from the loom.

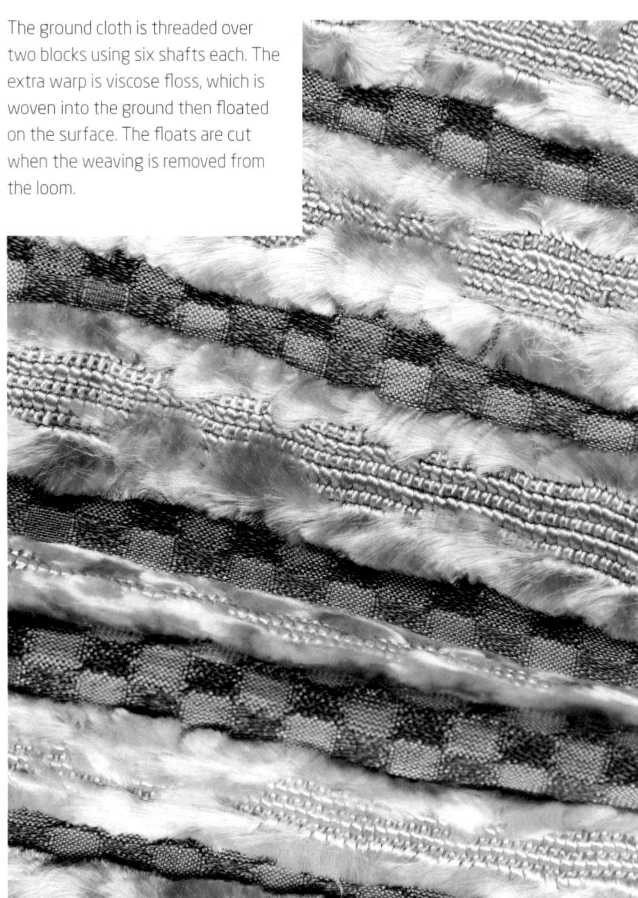

The ground cloth is clear lurex and filament silk, and the extra warp is wool. Weave the warps together then float the wool. The wool shrinks when the weaving is washed casuing the ground to pucker. This shows the face of the design.

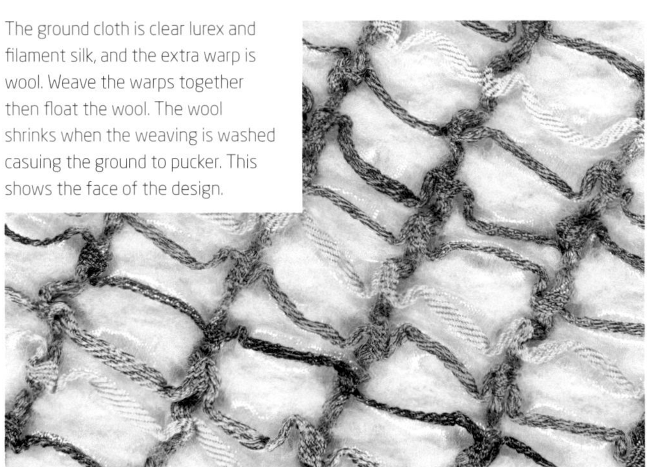

Reverse view of the design to the left.

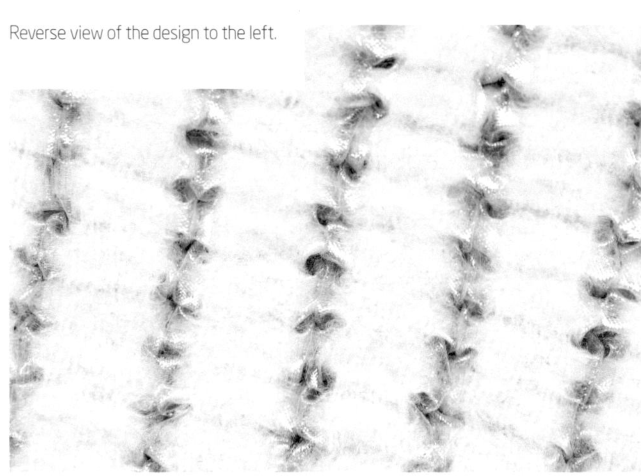

The ground cloth is clear lurex and filament silk, and the extra warp is wool. Weave the warps together then float the wool. The wool shrinks when the weaving is washed causing the ground to pucker. This shows the face of the design.

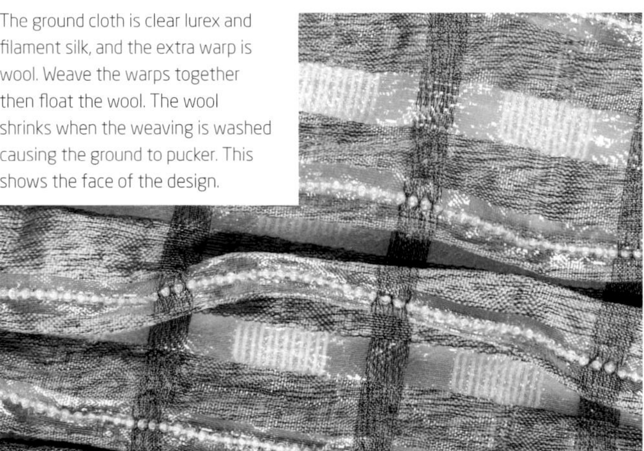

Reverse view of the design to the left.

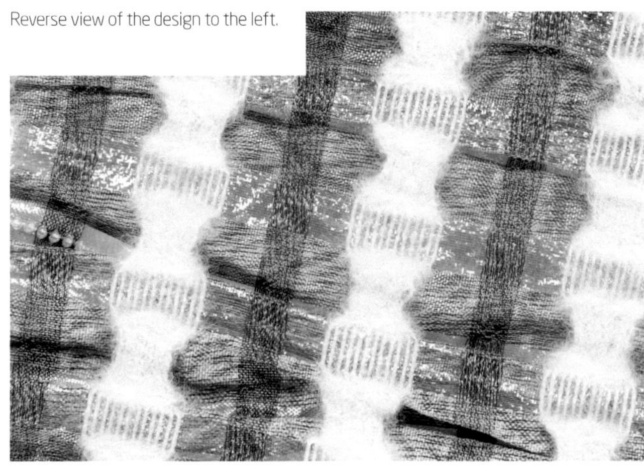

4. Extra warp ends over 4 shafts in a point draft: individual motifs (ground and extra warp ends are equal epc/epi)

Threading																			
6												O							
5										O				O					
4								O								O			
3						O												O	
2		X		X			X				X				X				X
1	X		X		X				X				X				X		

----repeat----

Reed plan			■	■					■	■	■	■					■	■	■
	■	■			■	■	■	■					■	■	■	■			

Lifting plan examples: extra-warp threading plan 4

I									J							K					
									X												
								X													
	X								X				X				X	X			X
X								X				X				X		X			X
	X								X		X		X				X			X	X
X					X			X		X		X	X			X				X	X
	X			X	X				X		X	X	X				X		X	X	X
X			X	X	X			X		X	X	X	X			X			X	X	X
	X	X	X	X					X		X	X	X				X	X	X	X	X
X			X	X	X			X		X		X	X			X		X	X	X	
	X			X	X				X		X						X	X	X		
X					X			X				X				X		X	X		
1	2	3	4	5	6			1	2	3	4	5	6			1	2	3	4	5	6

Lifting plan examples: extra-warp threading plan 4

L								M								N					
	X	X	X	X					X								X				
X		X	X	X	X			X								X		X			
	X	X	X	X					X								X	X	X		
X		X	X		X			X				X				X		X	X	X	
	X	X		X	X				X		X	X					X	X	X	X	X
X			X	X	X			X		X	X					X					
	X	X	X	X	X				X	X	X						X				X
X			X	X	X			X			X	X				X				X	X
	X	X		X	X				X			X	X				X		X	X	X
X		X	X		X			X					X			X		X	X	X	X
1	2	3	4	5	6			1	2	3	4	5	6			1	2	3	4	5	6

Plan I: Diamond.
Plan J: Diamond with stitched edges.
Plan K: Chevron.
Plan L: All-over diamond pattern – continuous stripe.
Plan M: Open diamond.
Plan N: Triangles.

5. Increase the scale of the motif by threading two consecutive ends per shaft. All-over pattern (ground and extra warp ends are equal epc/epi).

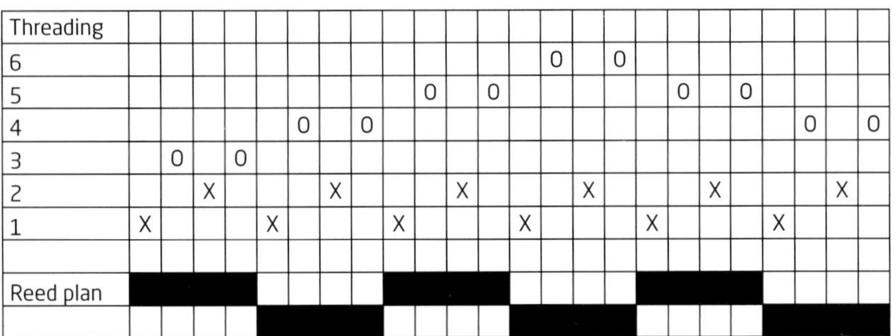

Threading																								
6														O		O								
5										O		O						O		O				
4						O		O														O		O
3		O		O																				
2			X				X				X				X				X				X	
1	X				X				X				X				X				X			
Reed plan	■	■	■	■					■	■	■	■					■	■	■	■				
					■	■	■	■					■	■	■	■					■	■	■	■

Lifting plan examples: extra-warp threading plan 5

O								P								Q					
	X								X												
X								X													
	X				X				X				X				X	X			X
X					X			X					X			X		X			X
	X			X	X				X			X	X				X	X			X
X				X	X			X				X	X			X				X	X
	X		X	X					X		X	X	X				X			X	X
X			X	X				X			X	X	X			X				X	X
	X	X	X						X	X	X	X					X		X	X	X
X		X	X					X		X	X	X				X			X	X	X
	X		X	X					X		X	X	X				X		X	X	
X			X	X				X			X	X	X			X		X	X	X	
	X			X	X				X			X	X				X	X	X	X	
X				X	X			X				X	X			X		X	X		
	X				X				X				X				X	X	X		
X					X			X					X			X		X	X		
1	2	3	4	5	6			1	2	3	4	5	6			1	2	3	4	5	6

Lifting plan examples: extra-warp threading plan 5

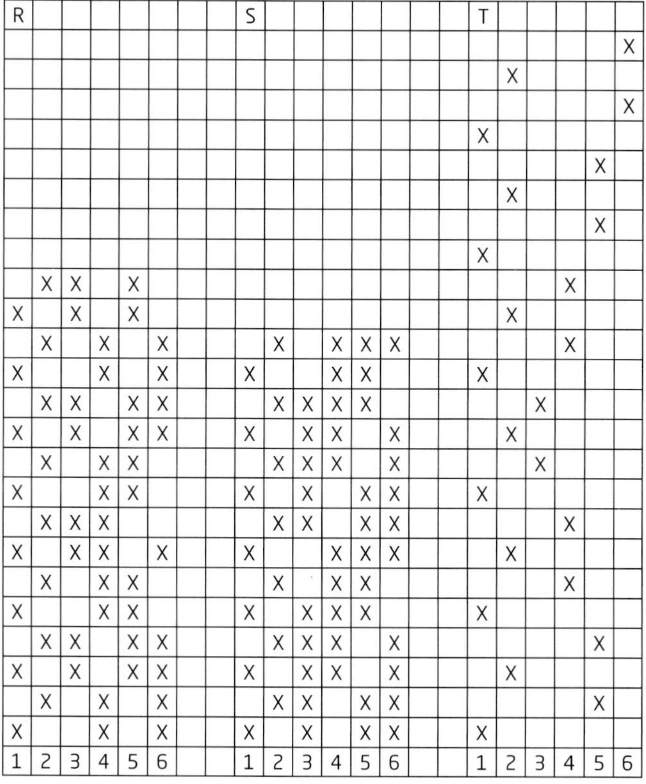

R								S								T					
																					X
																	X				
																					X
																X					
																				X	
																	X				
																				X	
																X					
	X	X		X															X		
X		X		X													X				
	X		X		X				X		X	X	X						X		
X			X		X			X			X	X				X					
	X	X		X	X				X	X	X	X						X			
X		X		X	X			X		X	X		X				X				
	X		X	X					X	X	X		X					X			
X			X	X				X		X		X	X			X					
	X	X	X						X	X		X	X						X		
X		X	X		X			X			X	X	X				X				
	X		X	X					X		X	X							X		
X			X	X				X		X	X	X				X					
	X	X		X	X				X	X	X		X							X	
X		X		X	X			X		X	X		X				X				
	X		X		X				X	X		X	X							X	
X			X		X			X		X		X	X			X					
1	2	3	4	5	6			1	2	3	4	5	6			1	2	3	4	5	6

Plan O: Outline diamond.
Plan P: Solid diamond.
Plan Q: Chevron.
Plan R: Diamond with plain weave.
Plan S: Solid chevron.
Plan T: Extra weft trapped by extra warp – diamond.

Instead of using single thick ends to create the contrast between the ground and the extra-warp patterns, you could try using two ends of a finer yarn together, which will give a softer effect. Create an exciting movement of colour by using different colour combinations for each pair – or keep them the same for a more solid effect.

6. Extra warp ends forming fancy stripes (2 extra warp ends to 1 ground)

Threading																								
6				O	O																			
5																O	O							
4													O	O					O	O				
3										O	O											O	O	
2		X				X		X				X						X						X
1	X		X				X		X						X						X			

-repeat- -------repeat------- -repeat- --------------------------------repeat--------------------------------

Reed plan																								
			■	■	■	■			■	■	■	■	■	■							■	■	■	■
	■	■					■	■							■	■	■	■	■	■				

Lifting plan examples: extra-warp threading plan 6

U								V								W					
																		X			X
																	X				
																		X			X
																X					
																				X	X
																X					
																		X			X
																	X				
																		X			X
																X					
																			X		X
																X					
	X	X							X	X									X		X
X		X			X			X		X	X						X				
	X	X	X		X				X	X	X	X							X		X
X		X	X		X			X		X	X					X					
	X		X	X	X				X	X			X							X	X
X			X	X				X				X	X				X				
	X	X	X		X				X		X	X	X							X	X
X		X	X		X			X		X	X	X	X			X					
	X	X			X				X		X	X	X					X			X
X		X			X			X				X	X				X				
	X			X					X	X								X			X
X				X	X			X		X	X					X					
	X		X	X	X				X	X	X	X								X	X
X			X	X	X			X		X	X						X				
	X	X	X		X				X	X			X							X	X
X		X	X					X				X	X			X					
	X		X	X	X				X		X	X	X						X		X
X			X	X	X			X		X	X	X	X				X				
	X			X	X				X		X	X	X						X		X
X				X	X			X				X	X			X					
1	2	3	4	5	6			1	2	3	4	5	6			1	2	3	4	5	6

Plan U: Solid diamonds – large. Continuous stripe.
Plan V: Solid diamonds – small. Block stripe.
Plan W: Extra weft trapped by extra warp – diamond and continuous stripe.

EXAMPLES OF EXTRA WARPS FORMING SIMPLE PATTERNS

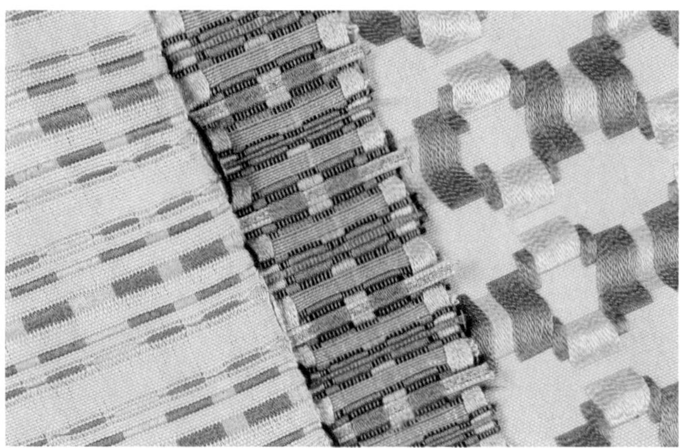

A collection of designs with a spun silk warp and weft and a spun silk extra warp forming a simple pattern.

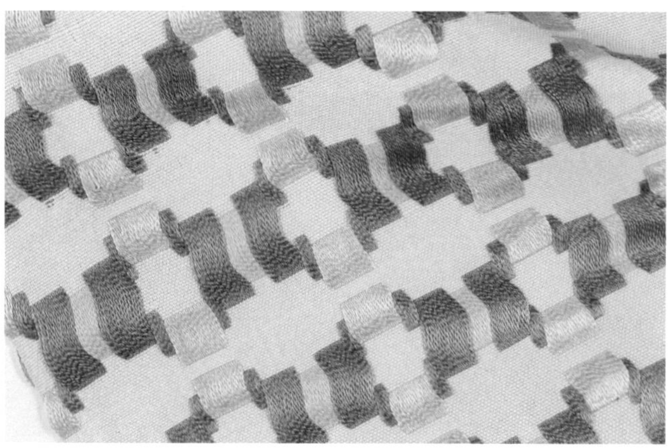

A spun silk warp and weft and a spun silk extra warp forming a simple pattern.

A spun silk and nylon monofilament ground warp with a spun silk extra warp. When the weaving is removed from the loom, the long floats relax and move out of position.

The ground warp is a spun silk on two shafts. The pattern is formed by a spun silk extra warp on four shafts.

The ground cloth is cotton and is threaded on two shafts. The extra warp is threaded over four shafts in a point draft/threading plan.

The ground warp is threaded over eight shafts and the extra warp over 16 shafts. Both warps are in spun silk.

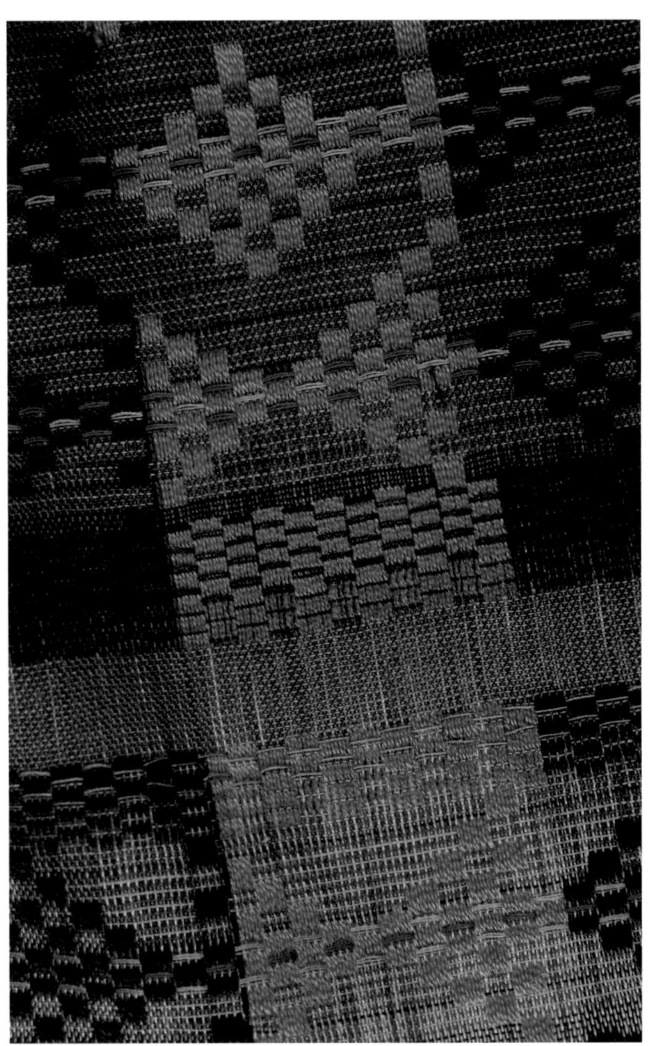

The extra warp is in cotton and is threaded over six shafts, and the ground is also cotton and is threaded on two shafts.

The ground warp is threaded over four shafts and is woven as a plain-weave and twill structure. The extra warp is also on four shafts and forms a diamond pattern. Both warps are cotton.

PROPORTIONS OF THE EXTRA-WARP PATTERNS

To achieve a pleasing shape, you need to calculate how many picks of weft yarn you need to use. If you are using the same thickness of yarn in warp and weft, then the number of picks should equal the number of ends beneath the pattern to give the same height and width to the shape. If you want the shape to have more height, either increase the length of the lifting plan, or use a thicker yarn. If you want the shape to be shorter, use a finer weft or shorten the lifting plan.

The ground warp is in spun silk woven in a plain-weave structure on two shafts. The extra warp is cotton chenille threaded over four shafts.

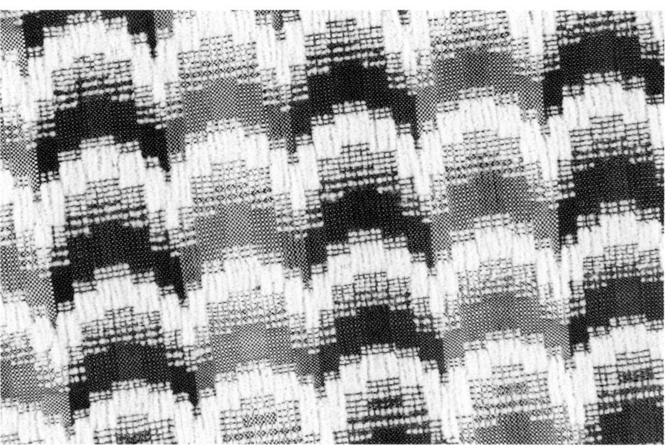

The ground warp is in spun silk woven in a plain-weave structure on two shafts. The extra warp is cotton chenille threaded over four shafts.

The ground warp is threaded over four shafts. The extra warp is also on four shafts. The face and back of the design are shown. The warp floats are clearly seen on the reverse of the fabric.

DOUBLE EXTRA WARPS

It is possible over relatively few shafts to achieve a more exciting combination of colours and textures by using two extra warps that interact with each other. It is preferable to use separate beams for each extra warp, but if you have only two warp beams at your disposal then you can wind both extra warps onto one beam, and the ground onto the other. You will need to wind the extra warps end and end when you make the warp.

WHEN MAKING A DOUBLE EXTRA WARP TO BE WOUND ON TO ONE BEAM, TAKE ONE END OF EXTRA WARP 1 AND ONE END OF EXTRA WARP 2 AND WIND THEM ON THE WARPING MILL OR FRAME AT THE SAME TIME. WHEN YOU THREAD THE WARP, THERE WILL BE TWO ENDS IN EACH CROSS – ONE FROM EACH EXTRA WARP. FOLLOW THE THREADING PLAN, ALTERNATING EACH COLOUR.

7. Double extra warps on 8 shafts (in the threading plan below, X = ground warp, O = extra warp 1, Z = extra warp 2)

Threading																								
8															Z			Z						
7									Z			Z									Z			Z
6			Z			Z																		
5														O			O							
4								O			O									O			O	
3		O			O																			
2				X						X						X						X		
1	X						X						X						X					

--repeat--

Reed plan																								
							■	■	■	■	■	■							■	■	■	■	■	■
	■	■	■	■	■	■							■	■	■	■	■	■						

The reed plan is based on two ends per dent of ground – total six ends per dent, including extra warp ends.

EXAMPLES OF DOUBLE EXTRA WARP

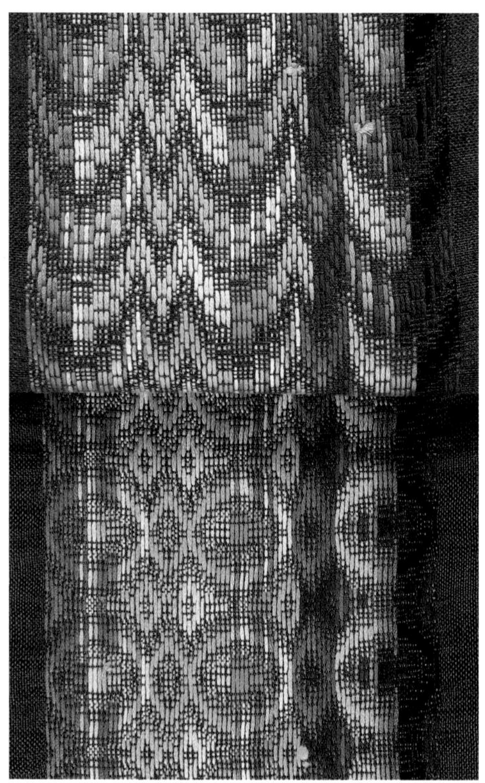

Left: The ground warp is in linen on four shafts, and the extra warps are cotton. Each extra warp is threaded over six shafts. This view shows the face of the design.

Right: The ground warp is in linen on four shafts, and the extra warps are cotton. Each extra warp is threaded over six shafts. This view shows the reverse of the design.

Lifting plan examples: extra-warp threading plan 7

X										Y										Z							
											X																
										X																	
											X						X										
										X							X										
											X					X	X										
										X						X	X										
											X				X	X	X				X				X	X	
										X					X	X	X			X					X	X	
											X				X	X					X				X	X	
										X					X	X				X		X				X	X
											X				X						X	X				X	X
										X					X					X		X				X	X
	X			X	X	X					X										X	X	X				X
X				X	X	X				X										X		X	X				X
	X			X	X	X					X			X							X	X	X				X
X			X	X	X					X				X						X			X	X	X		
	X		X	X	X						X		X	X							X		X	X	X		
X			X	X	X					X			X	X						X			X	X	X		
	X	X	X				X				X	X	X	X							X	X	X				X
X		X	X				X			X		X	X	X						X		X	X				X
	X	X	X				X				X	X	X								X	X	X				X
X		X				X	X			X		X	X							X		X				X	X
	X	X				X	X				X	X									X	X				X	X
X		X				X	X			X		X								X		X				X	X
1	2	3	4	5	6	7	8			1	2	3	4	5	6	7	8			1	2	3	4	5	6	7	8

Plan X: Zigzags – alternating extra warps. No ground visible.
Plan Y: Zigzags – alternating extra warps. Ground visible.
Plan Z: Interlocking diamond shapes. No ground visible.

HOW TO COPE WITH WARP FLOATS

There are several ways of dealing with the additional floats on the underside of the weaving.

1. The extra yarn at the back of the cloth will float freely until you bring it to the surface. This is acceptable if the ground is dense enough not to notice the floats, and if the cloth is to be used in situations that do not render them objectionable or impractical.

2. If the ground is lightweight or transparent, the floats will be visible from the face side. To avoid this, the extra floats can be woven into the ground securely around the pattern, and then cut away after the cloth is taken from the loom.

3. The additional threads can be 'stitched' into the underside of the ground cloth at regular intervals, and can be hidden to some extent by following the weave structure used in the ground. Twill structures are good for hiding the stitching points as they are based on floats. If you use a plain-weave ground structure, then the stitches will be visible, but can add to the overall effect.

4. The additional floats can be used to form smaller shapes, stripes or figures to give a fuller, more complex pattern. This will add density to the finished cloth.

Threading example for individual motif extra warp: Ground (X) on 4 shafts, extra warp (O) on 8 shafts

Shaft																				
12																				O
11																		O		
10																O				
9														O						
8												O								
7										O										
6								O												
5						O														
4				X							X								X	
3			X						X								X			
2		X					X								X					
1	X				X								X							

----Repeat----

Lifting plan example for lightweight or transparent cloth: extra warp floats woven into the ground as a plain weave before and after the pattern motif

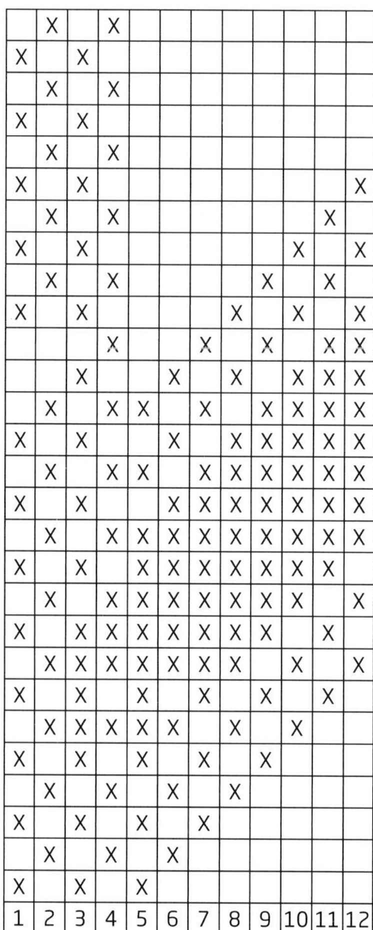

	X		X								
X		X									
	X		X								
X		X									
	X		X								
X		X									X
	X		X							X	
X		X							X		X
	X		X					X		X	
X		X					X		X		X
			X			X		X		X	X
		X			X		X		X	X	X
	X		X	X		X		X	X	X	X
X		X			X		X	X	X	X	X
	X		X	X		X	X	X	X	X	X
X		X			X	X	X	X	X	X	X
	X		X	X	X	X	X	X	X	X	X
X		X		X	X	X	X	X	X	X	
	X		X	X	X	X	X	X	X		X
X		X	X	X	X	X	X	X		X	
	X	X	X	X	X	X	X		X		X
X		X		X		X		X		X	
	X	X	X	X	X		X		X		
X		X		X		X		X			
	X		X		X		X				
X		X		X		X					
	X		X		X						
X		X		X							
1	2	3	4	5	6	7	8	9	10	11	12

Lifting plan example for floats being 'stitched' into the ground cloth

X			X				X				X
		X	X			X				X	
	X	X			X				X		
X	X			X		X	X	X	X	X	X
X			X			X	X	X	X	X	X
		X	X			X	X	X	X	X	X
	X	X			X	X	X	X	X	X	X
X	X			X		X	X	X	X	X	X
X			X			X	X	X	X	X	X
		X	X			X	X	X	X	X	X
	X	X			X				X		
X	X			X				X			
X			X				X				X
		X	X			X				X	
	X	X		X	X	X	X	X	X		
X	X			X	X	X	X	X	X		
X			X	X	X	X	X	X	X		X
		X	X	X	X	X	X	X	X	X	
	X	X	X	X	X	X	X	X	X		
X	X			X	X	X	X	X	X		
X			X	X	X	X	X	X	X		X
		X	X	X	X	X	X	X	X	X	
	X	X			X				X		
X	X			X				X			
1	2	3	4	5	6	7	8	9	10	11	12

Lifting plan example for floats being used to form smaller shapes or patterns

X			X		X					X	
		X	X	X		X			X		X
	X	X			X					X	
X	X			X			X	X			
X			X			X	X	X	X		
		X	X		X	X	X	X	X	X	
	X	X		X	X	X	X	X	X	X	X
X	X			X	X	X	X	X	X	X	X
X			X		X	X	X	X	X	X	
		X	X			X	X	X	X		
	X	X		X			X	X			X
X	X			X	X					X	X
X			X		X	X			X	X	
		X	X	X			X	X			X
	X	X			X	X			X	X	
X	X			X	X					X	X
X			X	X			X	X			X
		X	X			X	X	X	X		
	X	X			X	X	X	X	X	X	
X	X			X	X	X	X	X	X	X	X
X			X	X	X	X	X	X	X	X	X
		X	X		X	X	X	X	X	X	
	X	X				X	X	X	X		
X	X			X			X	X			X
1	2	3	4	5	6	7	8	9	10	11	12

EXAMPLES OF DESIGNS WITH CUT FLOATS

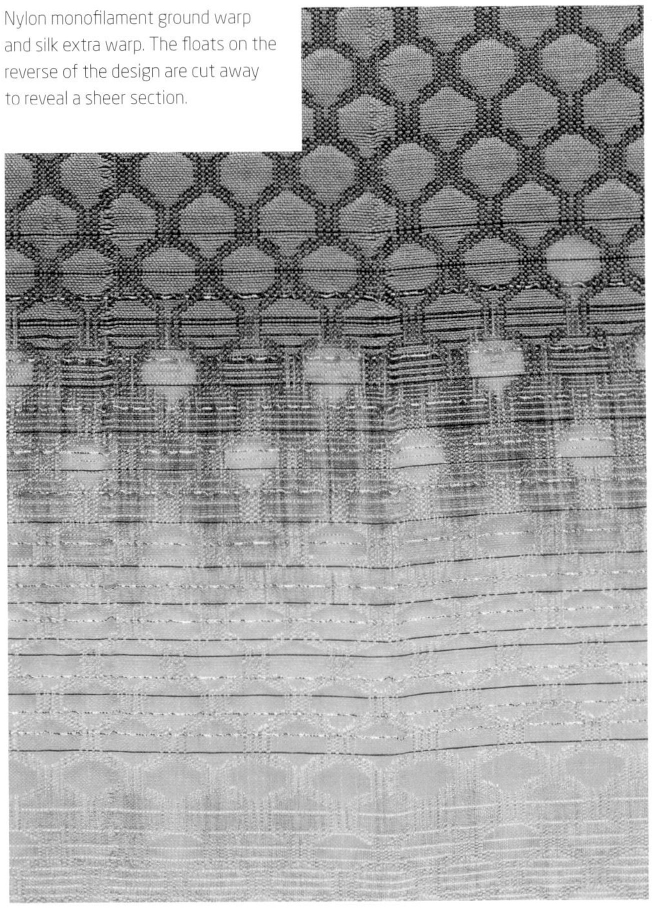

Nylon monofilament ground warp and silk extra warp. The floats on the reverse of the design are cut away to reveal a sheer section.

Nylon monofilament ground warp and silk extra warp. The floats on the reverse of the design are cut away to reveal a sheer section.

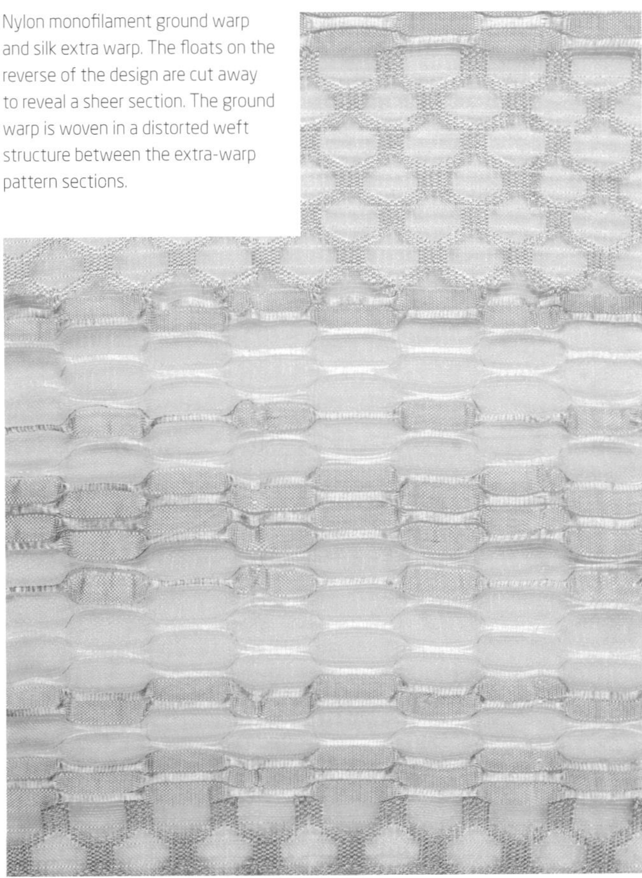

Nylon monofilament ground warp and silk extra warp. The floats on the reverse of the design are cut away to reveal a sheer section. The ground warp is woven in a distorted weft structure between the extra-warp pattern sections.

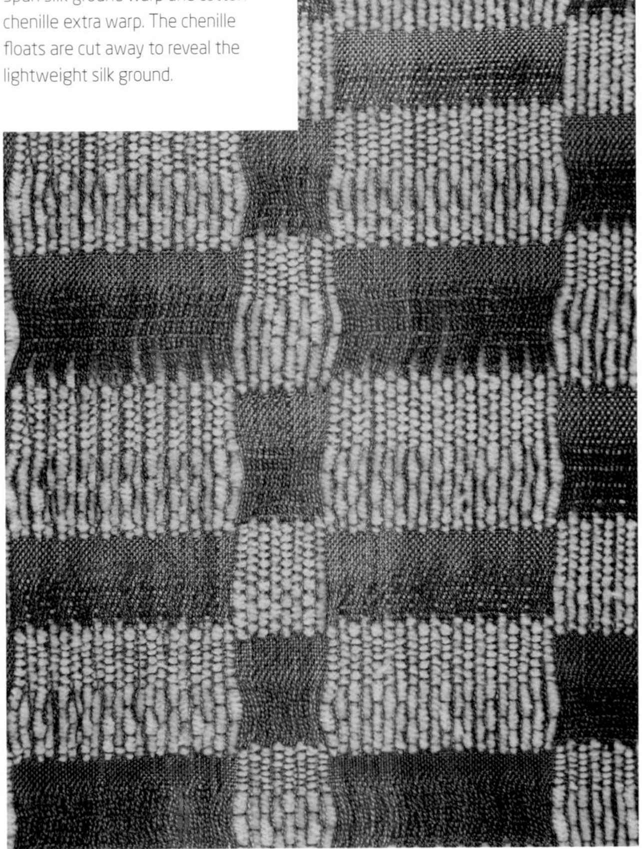

Spun silk ground warp and cotton chenille extra warp. The chenille floats are cut away to reveal the lightweight silk ground.

EXTRA-WEFT PATTERNING

- This is constructed using only one warp. However, two weft picks are required – one to create the ground cloth, and one to form the pattern.
- The ground pick and pattern pick alternate when creating the pattern.
- When creating the pattern, any yarn can be used in the weft, in any colour or texture, giving greater flexibility when designing.
- The greater the number of shafts, the more complex the pattern can be.
- The scale of the pattern or motif is dependent on the thickness of the warp yarn. The finer the yarn and the more ends per cm/inch, the smaller the design; the thicker the yarn and the fewer ends per cm/inch, the bigger the design.
- A basic extra weft can be produced on as few as four or six shafts.

Simple extra weft

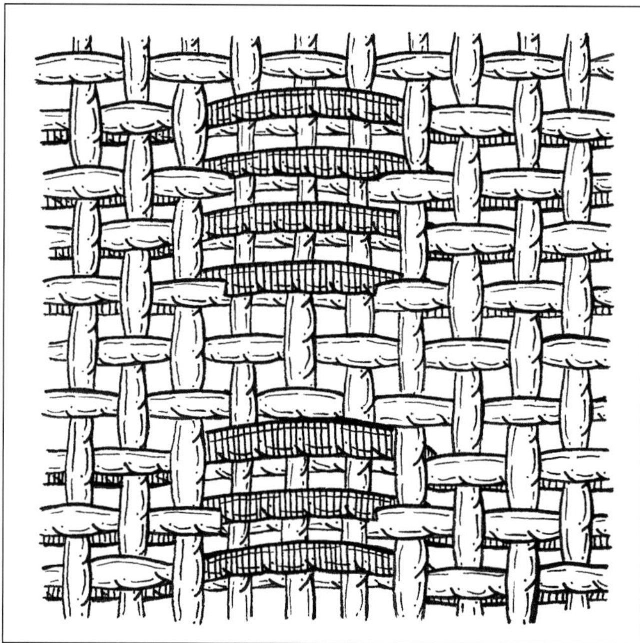

Extra-weft threading examples over 4 shafts

1. Block draft

Threading								
4						X		X
3					X		X	
2		X		X				
1	X		X					

----repeat---- ----repeat----

IMPROVISING EXTRA-WEFT PATTERNS

When weaving extra-weft patterns the proportion, quality and consistency of the shapes can change considerably through heavy or light beating down of the weft, and by the use of different thicknesses of weft yarn – so be prepared to experiment, analyse the outcomes and make changes to achieve the most pleasing effect.

In all lifting plan examples for extra-weft patterns, X = ground pick, O = extra weft pick

A						B						C						D						E			
	O								O				O	O	O			O	O		O					O	
	X		X				X		X				X		X				X		X				X		X
O								O				O		O	O			O	O	O					O		
X		X				X		X				X		X				X		X				X		X	
	O								O				O	O	O			O	O		O						O
	X		X				X		X				X		X				X		X				X		X
O								O				O						O	O	O				O			
X		X				X		X				X						X		X				X		X	
1	2	3	4			1	2	3	4			1	2	3	4			1	2	3	4			1	2	3	4

Plan A: Extra weft on surface floating over ends on shafts 3 and 4.
Plan B: Extra weft on surface floating over ends on shafts 1 and 2.
Plan C: Extra-weft floats on reverse. Plain-weave blocks through shafts 1 and 2.
Plan D: Extra-weft floats on reverse. Plain-weave blocks through shafts 3 and 4.
Plan E: Extra-weft floats alternating between blocks.

EXAMPLES OF SIMPLE EXTRA-WEFT BLOCKS

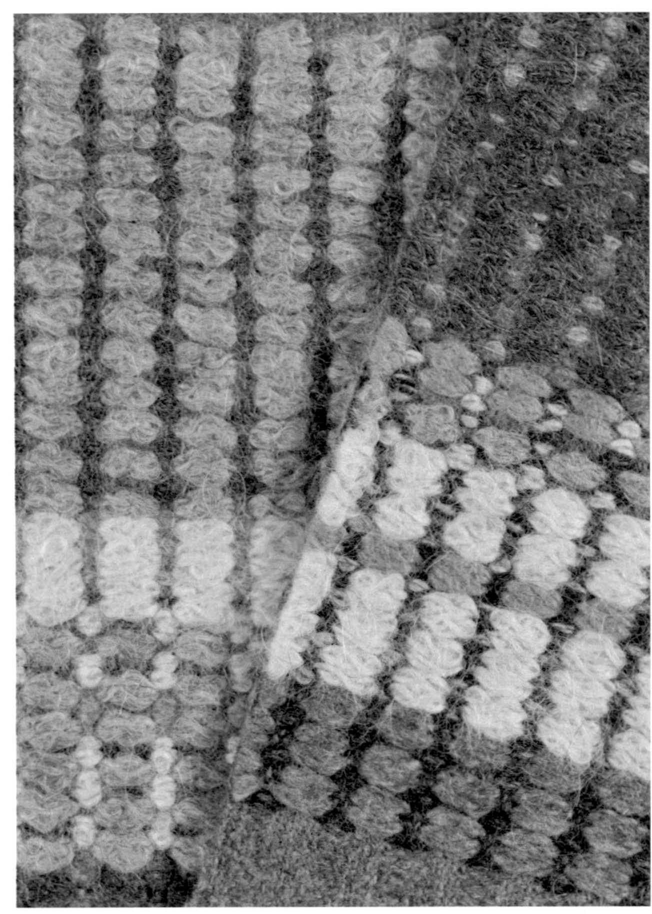

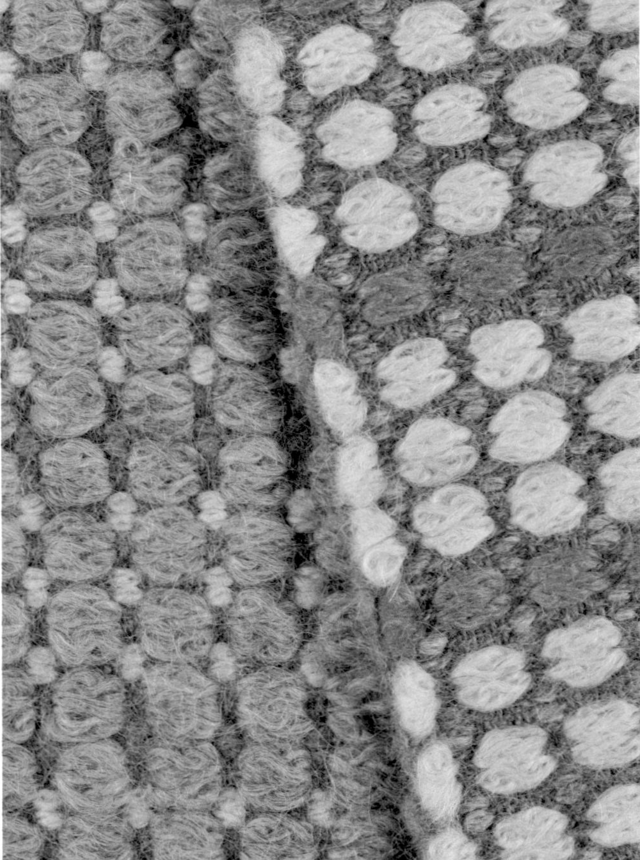

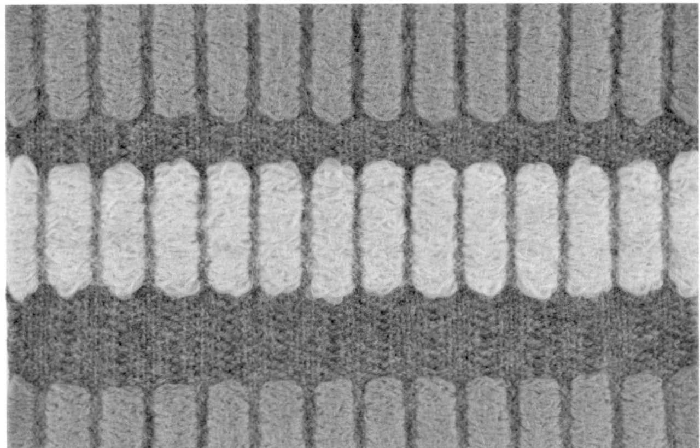

Top left: Simple extra-weft blocks in wool yarn for both warp and weft. A twill structure is used as the ground weave. Face and reverse of the design are shown.

Bottom left: Simple extra-weft blocks in wool yarn for both warp and weft. Face and reverse of the design are shown.

Top right: Simple extra-weft blocks in wool yarn for both warp and weft. Face and reverse of the design are shown.

Bottom right: Simple extra-weft blocks in wool yarn for both warp and weft. Face and reverse of the design are shown.

Nylon monofilament warp threaded in blocks. The ground weft is in nylon monofilament; the squares are formed using filament silk. The floats between the squares are cut away when the weaving is removed from the loom.

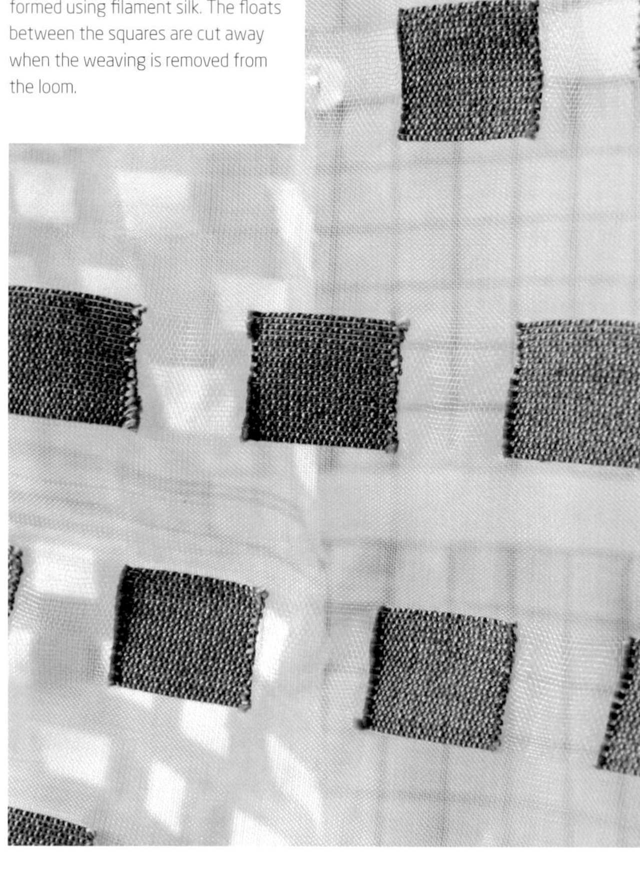

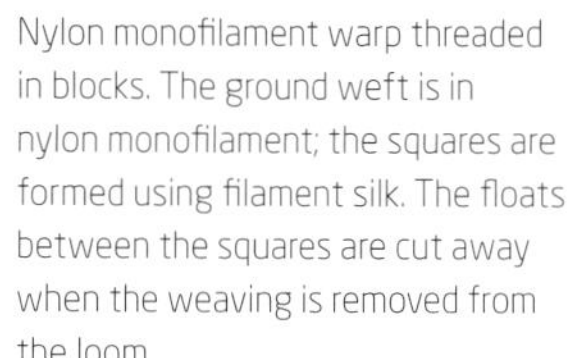

Nylon monofilament warp threaded in blocks. The ground weft is in nylon monofilament; the squares are formed using filament silk. The floats between the squares are cut away when the weaving is removed from the loom.

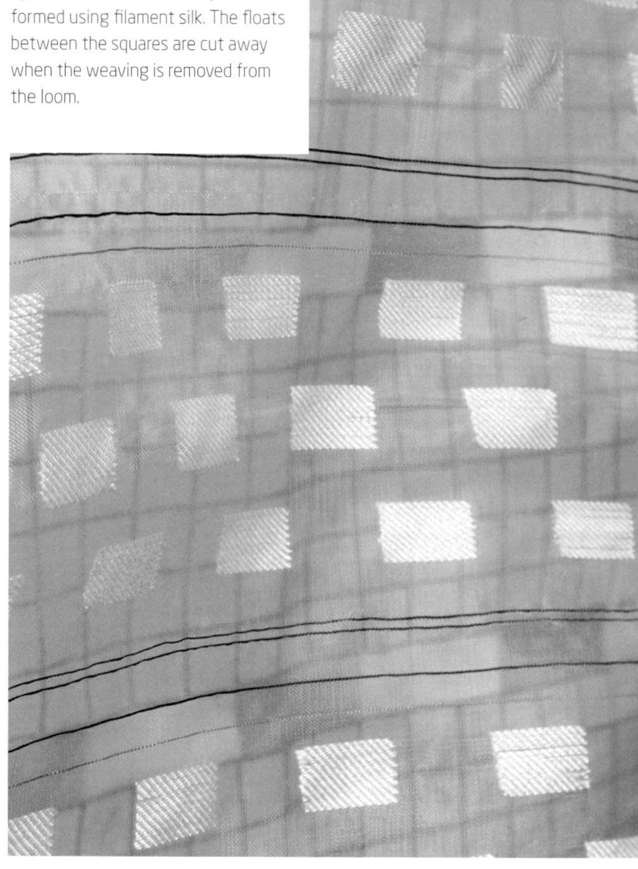

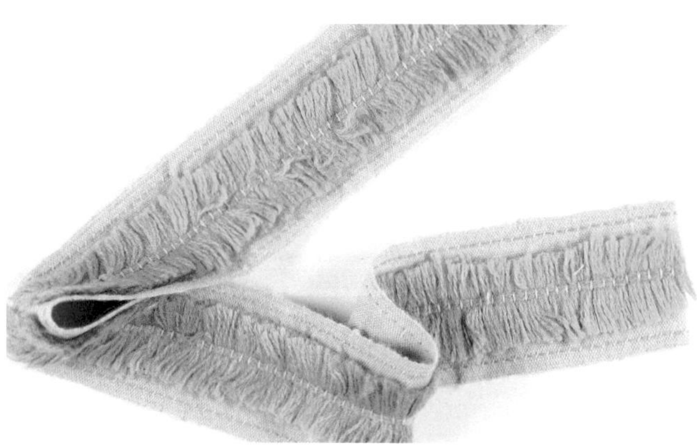

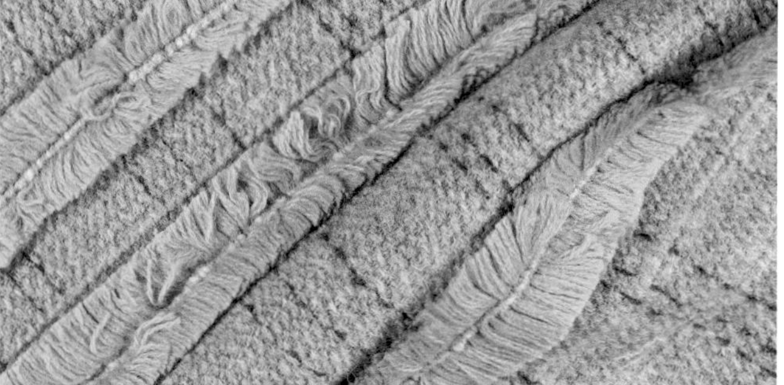

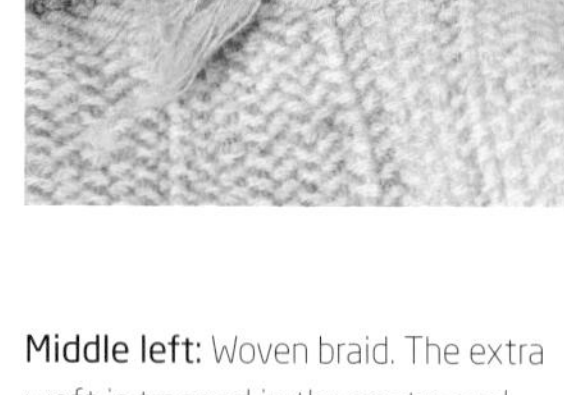

Middle left: Woven braid. The extra weft is trapped in the centre and trimmed at the edges.

Bottom left: The wool ground is woven as a herringbone. The extra weft is also wool with some of the float cut away to leave a vertical fringe.

Middle right: The wool ground is woven as a herringbone. The extra weft is also wool with some of the float cut away to leave blocks of fringes.

2. Point draft

Threading						
4				X		
3			X		X	
2		X				X
1	X					

3. Waved point draft

Threading																													
4				X											X	X										X			
3			X		X	X								X			X	X	X					X	X		X		
2		X					X	X	X				X							X	X		X					X	X
1	X									X	X	X										X							

Lifting plan examples: extra-weft threading plans 2 and 3

F						G						H						I						J			
			0											0				0								0	0
	X		X						X				X			X			X		X					X	X
0	0	0							0					0				0								0	
X		X						X	X						X	X		X		X				X			X
0	0							0	0				0								0					0	
	X		X				X	X						X	X				X		X			X	X		
0							0	0	0				0			0				0	0					0	0
X		X				X	X						X	X		0		X		X					X	X	
			0			0	0	0					0							0	0			0	0		
	X		X			X			X				X			X			X		X			X			X
0							0	0	0				0								0				0		
X		X						X	X						X	X		X		X						X	X
0	0							0	0				0					0							0		
	X		X				X	X					X	X					X		X				X	X	
0	0	0							0				0					0						0	0		
X		X				X	X					X	X					X		X				X	X		
1	2	3	4			1	2	3	4			1	2	3	4			1	2	3	4			1	2	3	4

Lifting plan examples: extra-weft threading plans 2 and 3

K						L						M						N			
							X		X												
						X		X													
						O	O	O													
							X		X												
						O	O	O													
						X		X													
			O			O	O						O	O							
X			X				X		X			X			X			X			X
			O			O	O						O	O				O			
		X	X			X		X						X	X					X	X
		O	O			O							O	O							O
	X	X					X		X				X	X					X	X	
		O	O			O						O	O							O	
X	X					X		X				X	X					X	X		
	O	O	O						O			O	O						O		
X			X				X		X			X			X			X			X
	O	O	O						O			O	O					O			
		X	X			X		X						X	X					X	X
O	O	O				O						O									O
	X	X					X		X				X	X					X	X	
O	O	O				O						O									O
X	X					X		X				X	X					X	X		
O	O					O	O					O							O		
X			X				X		X			X			X			X			X
O	O					O	O								O					O	
		X	X			X		X						X	X					X	X
O						O	O	O							O						O
	X	X					X		X				X	X					X	X	
O						O	O	O							O			O			
X	X					X		X				X	X					X	X		
1	2	3	4			1	2	3	4			1	2	3	4			1	2	3	4

Plan F: Positive diamond – plain ground.
Plan G: Negative diamond – 2 x 2 twill ground.
Plan H: Geometric – 2 x 2 twill ground.
Plan I: Geometric – plain ground.
Plan J: Chequerboard – 2 x 2 herringbone ground.
Plan K: Chevron – 2 x 2 ground.
Plan L: Extended diamond – plain ground.
Plan M: Triangle – 2 x 2 twill ground.
Plan N: All-over diamond – 2 x 2 twill ground.

Extra-weft threading examples over 6 shafts

4. Point draft

Threading										
6						X				
5					X		X			
4				X				X		
3			X						X	
2		X								X
1	X									

5. Waved point draft

Threading																														
6									X	X													X							
5								X			X	X										X		X						
4					X	X	X						X								X				X	X	X			
3			X	X										X						X								X	X	
2		X												X	X	X			X											X
1	X																X	X												

LIFTING PLANS FOR THE GROUND CLOTH

As well as plain weave, you can use any of the six-shaft twill or crêpe weaves shown in previous chapters for your ground cloth. Try different combinations to create additional interest and variety in the background of your pattern. Remember that if using twill weaves, the weft will beat down more readily, so use a slightly thicker weft yarn to that in the warp to retain the desired pattern size.

Lifting plan examples: extra-weft threading plans 4 and 5

O									P									Q					
0	0	0	0	0					0	0	0	0										0	0
		X			X				X		X	X		X				X	X				X
0	0	0	0	0					0	0	0											0	0
	X			X						X	X		X	X				X				X	X
0	0	0	0						0	0											0	0	0
X			X						X	X		X	X								X	X	X
0	0	0	0						0	0											0	0	0
		X			X				X		X	X		X					X	X	X		
0	0	0							0										0	0	0		
	X				X					X	X		X	X				X	X	X			
0	0	0							0					0					0	0	0		
X					X				X	X		X	X					X	X	X			
0	0								0					0					0	0	0		
		X			X				X		X	X		X				X	X				X
0	0								0										0	0	0		
	X			X						X	X		X	X				X				X	X
0									0	0								0	0	0			
X			X						X	X		X	X								X	X	X
0									0	0								0	0	0			
		X			X				X		X	X		X						X	X	X	
					0				0	0	0							0	0				
	X			X						X	X		X	X					X	X	X		
					0				0	0	0	0						0	0				
X			X						X	X		X	X					X	X	X			
1	2	3	4	5	6				1	2	3	4	5	6				1	2	3	4	5	6

Plan O: Triangle – 1 x 2 twill ground.
Plan P: Circle – 2 x 1 twill ground.
Plan Q: Triangles and chevrons – 3 x 3 twill ground.

PROPORTIONS OF THE EXTRA-WEFT PATTERNS

To achieve a pleasing shape, the scale of the pattern will be dictated by the number of ends per cm/inch of your warp yarn, and the number of ends in each repeat of the threading. As a general guide, if you want the design to be the same height and width, then the pattern picks in the lifting plan should be equal to the number of ends in each repeat of the threading plan.

For example: a point draft over six shafts has a repeat of ten ends. To achieve a balanced pattern, there should be 20 weft picks – ten to create the ground weave and ten to create the pattern.

DOUBLE EXTRA WEFT

You can introduce additional interest to the figuring by using a second, or even a third, extra weft pick. This results in a slightly heavier cloth, but is very effective in accentuating or contrasting certain areas of a pattern. The examples here show a square within a square, using contrasting colour or texture.

Extra-weft threading example over 6 shafts

6. Block draft

Threading																
6										X		X				
5									X		X					
4						X		X						X		X
3					X		X						X		X	
2		X		X												
1	X		X													

----repeat---- ----repeat---- ----repeat---- ----repeat----

The example shown in Threading plan 6 is a simple block draft. There are several options of achieving different patterns with one, two or three additional extra weft colours. Once you understand the basics you can create your own lifting plans and colour sequences – distorted weft is also an option that could add variety to your designs.

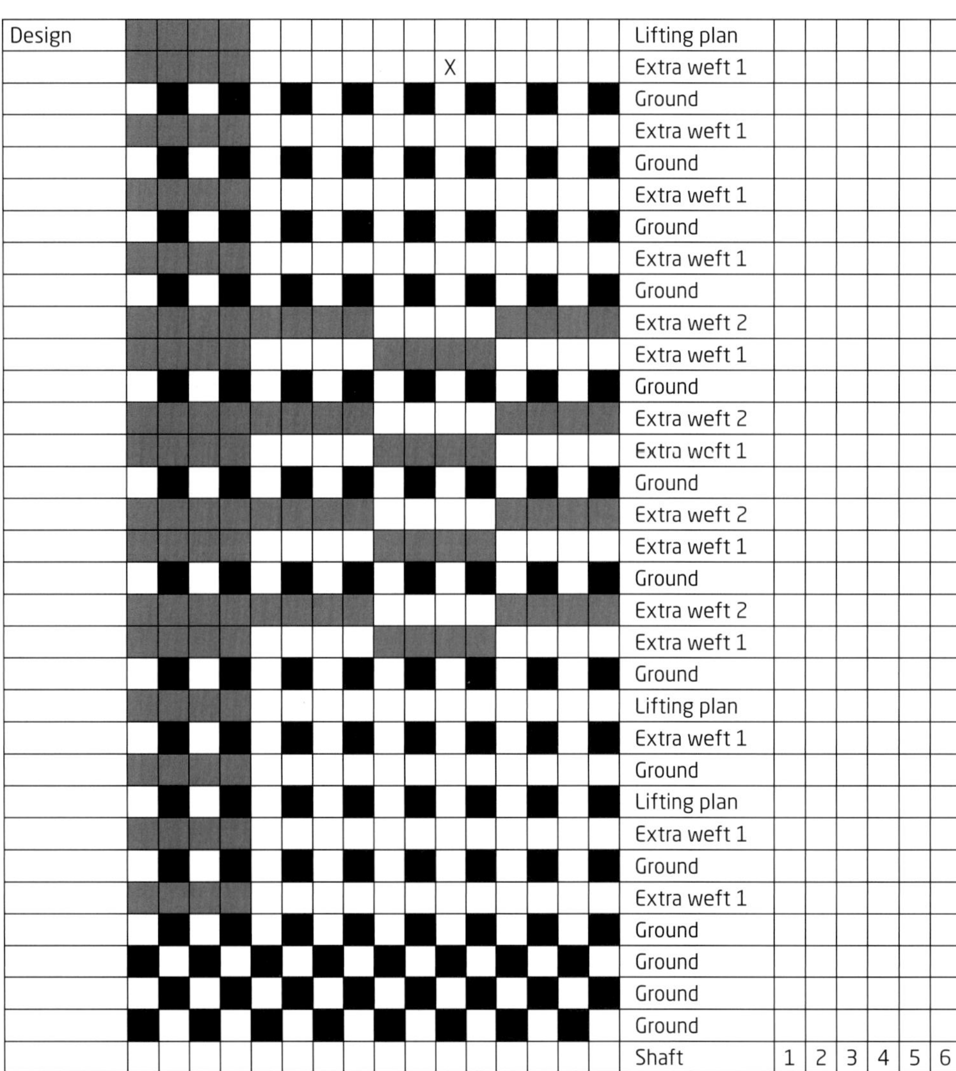

EXTRA WARP AND EXTRA WEFT COMBINED

You can use the extra warp ends in your design to trap extra weft threads to those forming the ground weave. This gives additional surface qualities and the potential to introduce other yarns and colours to your woven fabric collection.

X is the ground warp and O is the extra warp.

Threading plan example over 8 shafts

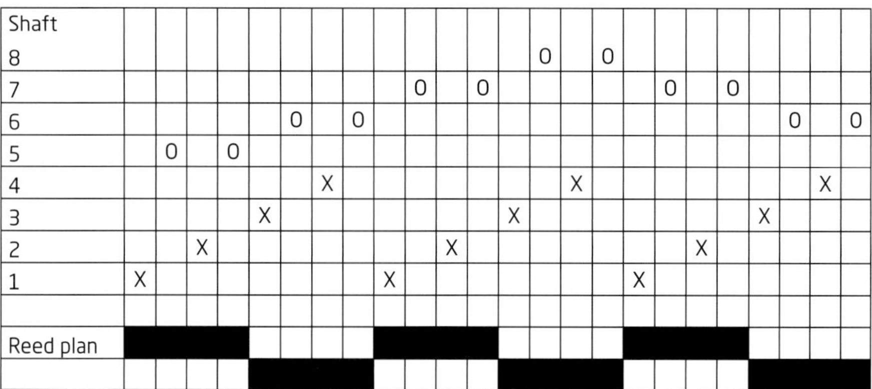

Shaft																								
8														O		O								
7										O		O						O		O				
6						O		O														O		O
5		O		O																				
4							X								X								X	
3					X								X								X			
2			X								X								X					
1	X								X								X							
Reed plan	■	■	■	■					■	■	■	■					■	■	■	■				
					■	■	■	■					■	■	■	■					■	■	■	■

Lifting plan 1: diamond pattern

Lifting plan 2: chequerboard

Extra						O													O	O
Ground	X			X												X				
Extra						O													O	O
Ground			X	X											X					
Extra							O												O	O
Ground		X	X										X							
Extra							O												O	O
Ground	X	X									X									
Extra					O			O											O	O
Ground	X			X												X				
Extra					O			O											O	O
Ground			X	X											X					
Extra							O												O	O
Ground		X	X										X							
Extra							O										O	O		
Ground	X	X									X									
Extra																	O	O		
Ground	X			X												X				
Extra							O										O	O		
Ground			X	X											X					
Extra					O			O									O	O		
Ground		X	X											X						
Extra					O			O									O	O		
Ground	X	X											X							
	1	2	3	4	5	6	7	8					1	2	3	4	5	6	7	8

Two shuttles are used – one for the ground weave and one for the extra weft. The lifts alternate between ground and extra weft. You can use a different colour or thickness or texture for the extra weft, which will give variety and contrast to your collection.

EXAMPLES OF EXTRA WEFT TRAPPED BY EXTRA WARP

Top left: Extra-warp blocks trapping extra-weft floats.

2nd left: Nylon monofilament ground warp and filament silk extra-warp pattern trapping filament silk extra weft.

3rd left: Nylon monofilament ground warp and filament silk extra-warp pattern trapping filament silk extra weft.

Bottom left: Extra-warp threads used to trap ribbon and lurex.

Top right: Viscose cord trapped to give extra-weft floats between the pattern areas.

Bottom right: Viscose floss trapped to give extra-weft floats between the pattern areas.

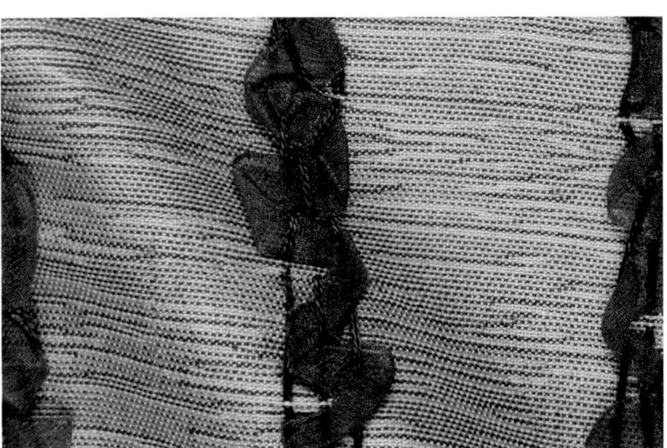

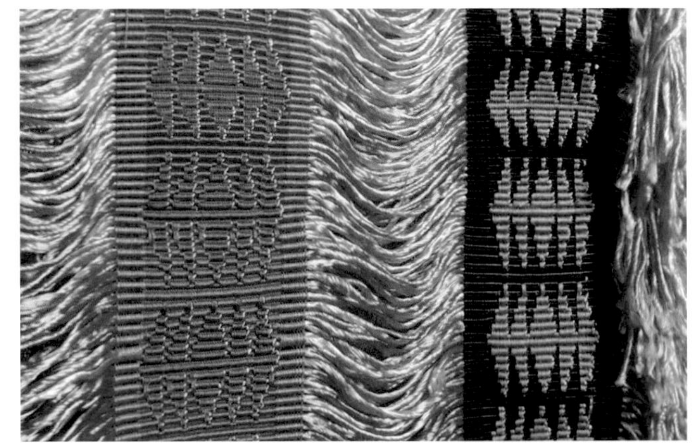

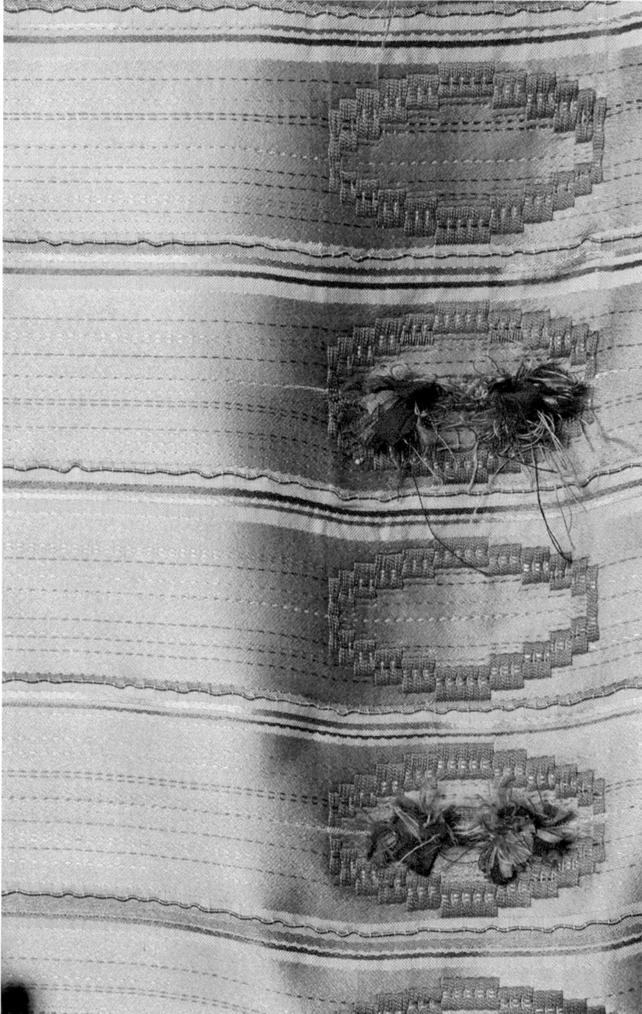

Top left: Satin-weave ground with extra-warp shapes trapping torn fabric strips. (Detail).

Bottom left: Satin-weave ground with extra-warp shapes trapping torn fabric strips.

Top and bottom right: Satin-weave ground with extra-warp shapes trapping torn fabric strips and filament silk.

8
DOUBLE CLOTH

DOUBLE CLOTH

A double cloth is exactly what the name indicates: two layers of fabric woven at the same time, one above the other. It is made using two sets of warp threads and two sets of weft threads, each set being used to produce a layer of cloth. One set forms the face cloth, the other the back cloth, and each requires its own set of shafts. The two layers are joined together when one interchanges with the other – the face cloth is moved behind and is woven on the back, and the back moves up and is woven on the face.

The structure can be woven in as few as four shafts, two shafts allocated for each layer to enable you to use a plain-weave structure for each separate layer. The resulting design is a horizontal double cloth. Each cloth is woven alternately, the first pick weaving the face cloth, and the second pick weaving the back cloth. The fabrics should be stitched together at intervals by interlacing the threads of one fabric with another. When using four shafts, the interchange will be horizontal, resulting in a series of tubes. The more shafts available, the greater the design possibilities. You can create blocks or a chequerboard effect using eight shafts, where the interchange will be vertical as well as horizontal.

Two warp beams are preferable to maintain individual warp tension, one for each cloth, but if the yarn is of the same quality and thickness for each layer, then they can be wound together as one warp and put onto one beam.

The sett of each layer will normally be equal unless yarns of contrasting thickness or texture are used for each warp, or a contrast in density is required, such as a more open effect in one of the layers.

MAKING A STRONGER CLOTH

In all double-cloth fabrics, there is a space created between the two layers. If the finished fabric is to have a functional use, then the interchanges should be frequent, resulting in a stronger cloth. If the interchanges are less frequent, then one layer may hang away from the other, causing a sagging appearance. This can happen when large-scale proportions are used to create the design.

STITCHING THE TWO CLOTHS TOGETHER

If the two layers of fabric are woven independently of each other throughout the design, then one of the following effects will occur when the weaving is removed from the loom.

1. If each layer is woven independently with a separate selvedge and separate shuttle, then the two layers will come apart.

2. If the selvedge has been joined at one side only – using one or two shuttles – then the fabric can be opened out to produce a double-width cloth.

3. If the selvedge has been joined at both sides – using one or two shuttles – then a tube will be created.

'Stitching' the cloths together is achieved by either raising the back cloth to the surface or lowering the face cloth below the back – this is called an 'interchange' of the cloths. When creating more complex patterns, the interchange can happen vertically as well as horizontally.

DESIGN POSSIBILITIES

Double cloth has many applications and is very versatile.

- Contrasting colours can be used in each warp without mixing with or affecting the other. Striped warps can be contrasted against plain-coloured warps, or stripe against stripe.
- Different weft yarns can be used through each layer without affecting the colour or surface of the other.
- Two different textures can be used for each warp, or two contrasting thicknesses.
- 'Blister' or puckering fabrics can be achieved by using yarns with different shrinking properties in each cloth.
- A reversible fabric can be made. Thought should be given to the back of the cloth as well as the front when selecting weft yarns and colours.
- The backing cloth can give stability to a loosely woven face cloth, allowing the characteristics of the yarn to be promoted without the fabric falling apart.
- The spaces created between the two layers can be filled with wadding (batting) to give a quilted effect.

BLISTER OR PUCKERED FABRICS

This is the name given to the resulting effect when two yarns of contrasting stability are used in a double cloth. One of the warps should use a stable yarn such as silk, cotton or linen. The other warp can be a slightly elasticated yarn, an over-spun yarn or a woollen yarn that will shrink when washed. You can use weft yarns of the same quality as the warps to achieve the same effect horizontally.

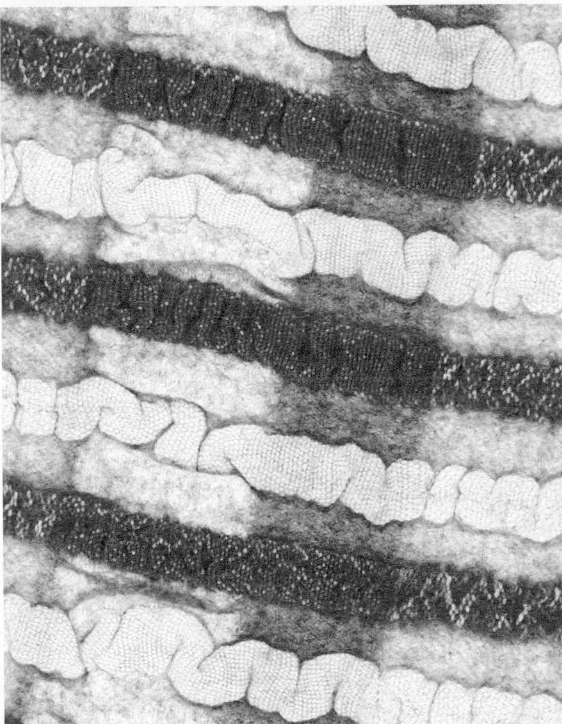

Top left: Double cloth using spun silk for one warp and a high-twist fine worsted yarn for the other, resulting in slight puckering of the silk when washed.

Bottom left: Double-cloth tubes using cotton and wool. The fabric is washed to make the wool felt, causing the cotton tube to pucker.

When the double cloth is removed from the loom, the elasticated yarn will want to return to its normal state, contracting through the warp and weft and resulting in a smaller surface area. The stable layer will remain as it was on the loom, and will be made to 'blister' or 'pucker' by the shrinkage of the unstable yarn.

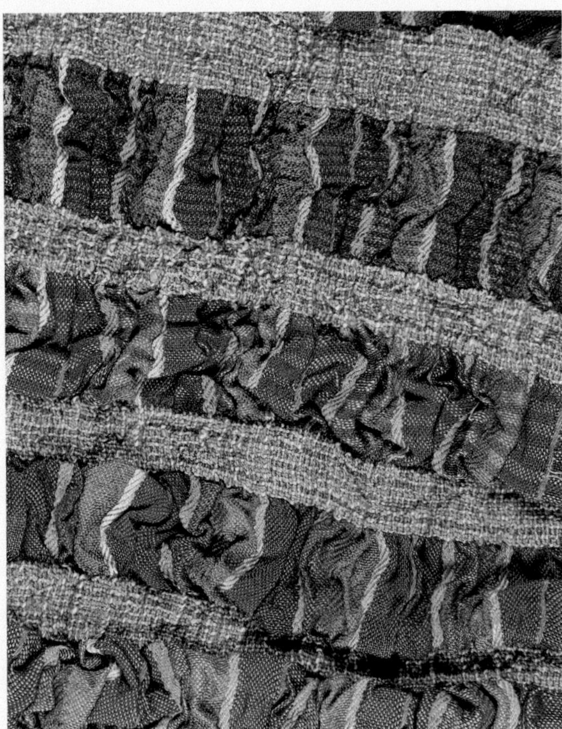

The effect may be rather subtle, depending on the yarns used. Try a gentle hand wash in warm water to encourage the yarn to shrink further. If a woollen yarn has been used, then you will need to give it a more vigorous hand wash for a longer period to achieve the necessary shrinkage.

Top right: The double-cloth tubes are made to pucker when an elastic yarn is used to weave the two cloths together. The warps are spun silk and linen.

Bottom right: The two warps forming this double cloth are silk in one and a cotton lycra for the other. The warps are woven firmly together to stop the elastic from contracting, and woven as a double cloth to allow puckering.

DOUBLE PLAIN INTERCHANGE – WARP YARNS OF EQUAL THICKNESS

The most basic double cloth can be achieved by using four shafts – two for the face cloth and two for the back cloth. A plain-weave structure is used. The ends are threaded alternately. For ease of demonstration in this chapter, the face cloth is black and threaded on shafts 1 and 3. The back cloth is white, and threaded onto shafts 2 and 4.

X = black end, O = white end

Lifting plan 1: face (black) on top

1. Lift shaft 1 and put through a black weft thread.

2. Lift shafts 1 and 3 (face cloth) out of the way, and lift shaft 2 to form a plain weave in the back cloth. Use a white weft yarn.

3. Lift shaft 3 and put through a black weft. This forms the second pick in the plain-weave construction on the face cloth.

4. Lift shafts 1 and 3 (face cloth) out of the way, and lift shaft 4 to form the second pick in the plain-weave structure in the back cloth. Use a white weft yarn.

5. Repeat until the desired proportion is achieved.

6. Interchange the cloths, and follow Lifting plan 2, so that the back cloth weaves on top.

Lifting plan 2: back (white) on top

1. Lift shafts 2 and 4 (back cloth) out of the way, and lift shaft 1 to form the first pick of the plain weave in the face cloth. Use a black weft.

2. Lift shaft 2 and put through a white weft.

3. Lift shafts 2 and 4 (back cloth) out of the way, and lift shaft 3 to form the second pick of the plain-weave construction in the face cloth. Use a black weft.

4. Lift shaft 4 and put through a white weft. This forms the second pick in the plain-weave construction.

5. Repeat until the desired proportion is achieved.

6. Interchange the cloths, returning to Lifting plan 1, so that the face cloth weaves on top.

1. Double cloth on 4 shafts

Threading									Lifting plan 1	X		X	O
4				O				O				X	
3			X				X			X	O	X	
2		O				O				X			
1	X				X				Shaft	1	2	3	4
Reed plan	■	■	■	■									
					■	■	■	■	Lifting plan 2				O
											O	X	O
											O		
											O		O
									Shaft	1	2	3	4

Design

THE REED

When denting the warp yarn you need to remember that there are two warps, one on top of the other and each of the same ends per cm/inch. So if each warp is 14 epcm and and you are using a reed with 70 dents per centimetre, there will be four ends per dent in total – 2 ends per dent for each layer.

If the warp is 32 epi, use a 18's reed at 4epd.

WEFT COLOUR SEQUENCE

In the examples shown here, the face cloth is indicated by an X and black squares and the back cloth with an O and white squares. To achieve a solid black-and-white effect, the weft yarn should follow the same sequence. When the face cloth (black) is being woven, a black weft should be used. When the back cloth (white) is being woven, a white weft should be used. In these examples the odd lifts are weaving the face (black), and the even lifts the back cloth (white).

ORDER OF THE WEFT

When weaving a double cloth it is simpler to keep the weft order the same throughout the design. So if you start by weaving the face cloth first and the back cloth second, keep to this system, even when you make an interchange of layers. You can change the colour or type of yarn at will, but always remember that the order is face, back, face, back throughout the design.

Top: Horizontal tube formed in a basic double cloth using four shafts.

Bottom: Horizontal tube formed in a basic double cloth using four shafts. Shows the face and the back of the design.

DOUBLE PLAIN INTERCHANGE – WARP YARNS OF DIFFERENT THICKNESS

When using yarns of differing thickness the allocation of shafts for each warp needs to be different. Plan 2 shows a face cloth that has finer warp yarn than the back cloth. There are twice as many ends in the face cloth to the back cloth.

X = fine yarn, O = thick yarn

A good way of understanding and visualizing how the double-cloth layers work is to try out the basic structures using strips of paper attached to a piece of card. Use two contrasting colours, one for the face cloth and one for the back cloth. Following Lifting plans 1 and 2, use strips of paper in the same two colours for the weft. Repeat each plan at least twice to see the effect. Once you have mastered this, try the block draft on eight shafts.

It will be simpler for you to put the strips of paper (ends) side by side for the exercise, resulting in a more open appearance, but on the loom, one layer of warp ends will be on top of the other.

2. Double cloth on 4 shafts: contrasting fine and thick warps

Threading									Lifting plan 3				
									Thick weft	X	X		
									Fine weft		X		
									Fine weft	X			
4							O		Thick weft	X	X	O	
3			O						Fine weft		X		
2		X			X				Fine weft	X			
1	X			X					Shafts	1	2	3	4
16's Reed plan	■	■	■						Lifting plan 4				
				■	■	■			Thick weft				O
									Fine weft		X	O	O
									Fine weft	X		O	O
												O	
									Thick weft		X	O	O
									Fine weft	X		O	O
									Fine weft	1	2	3	4

Lifting plan 3: fine warp on top

The weft ratio is 2:1, so the first two picks are weaving the fine (face) cloth as a plain weave. The third pick is weaving the thicker back cloth as plain weave, with the fine face ends being lifted out of the way. Picks four and five are fine, and pick six is thick.

Lifting plan 4: thick warp on top

The lifting plan sequence is the same as in Plan 3 – two fine picks followed by one thick pick.

REED PLAN

When denting the warp yarn in the reed, remember that the ratio is 2:1. The fine yarn is 12epcm and the thicker yarn is 6epcm. Use a reed with 60 dents per cm and put three ends per dent or a reed with 30 dents per 10cm and put 6 ends per dent.

So if the fine yarn is 32 ends per inch and the thicker yarn is 16 ends per inch the total is 48 ends per inch, use either a 16's reed at 3 ends per dent – two fine and one thick per dent.

INTERCHANGING PLAIN-WEAVE BLOCKS

You will need a minimum of eight shafts to achieve a block design, which will give you the opportunity of using horizontal and vertical interchanges. The blocks can be of equal width or they can vary in size. Repeat each block in the threading plan to achieve the desired scale. You can decide on the height of the blocks while weaving.

X = black face ends, O = white back ends

3. Double cloth on 8 shafts: block draft

Threading																
8												O				O
7											X				X	
6										O				O		
5									X				X			
4				O				O								
3			X				X									
2		O				O										
1	X				X											

------------repeat------------ ------------repeat------------

Reed plan																
	■	■	■	■					■	■	■	■				
					■	■	■	■					■	■	■	■

Design A	■	■	■	■	■	■	■	■	■	■	■	■	■	■	■	■		X		X	O	X		X	O
	■	■	■	■	■	■	■	■	■	■	■	■	■	■	■	■				X				X	
	■	■	■	■	■	■	■	■	■	■	■	■	■	■	■	■		X	O	X		X	O	X	
	■	■	■	■	■	■	■	■	■	■	■	■	■	■	■	■		X				X			
	■	■	■	■	■	■	■	■	■	■	■	■	■	■	■	■		1	2	3	4	5	6	7	8
Design B																					O				O
																			O	X	O		O	X	O
																			O				O		
																		X	O		O	X	O		O
																		1	2	3	4	5	6	7	8
Design C	■	■	■	■	■	■	■	■										X		X	O				O
	■	■	■	■	■	■	■	■												X			O	X	O
	■	■	■	■	■	■	■	■										X	O	X			O		
	■	■	■	■	■	■	■	■										X				X	O		O
	■	■	■	■	■	■	■	■										1	2	3	4	5	6	7	8
Design D									■	■	■	■	■	■	■	■					O	X		X	O
									■	■	■	■	■	■	■	■			O	X	O			X	
									■	■	■	■	■	■	■	■			O			X	O	X	
									■	■	■	■	■	■	■	■		X	O		O	X			
									■	■	■	■	■	■	■	■		1	2	3	4	5	6	7	8

Design A: Face on top. Horizontal black band.
Design B: Back on top. Horizontal white band.
Design C: Face on top shafts 1–4 (black). Back on top shafts 5–8 (white).
Design D: Back on top shafts 1–4 (white). Face on top shafts 5–8 (black).

To form horizontal tubes, you need to alternate between Designs A and B.
To form vertical tubes, weave either Design C or D continuously.
To form pockets, you need to alternate between Designs C and D.

EXAMPLES OF PLAIN-WEAVE DOUBLE CLOTH

Plain-weave double cloth in cotton forming vertical tubes. Shows the back (striped warp) and face (plain warp).

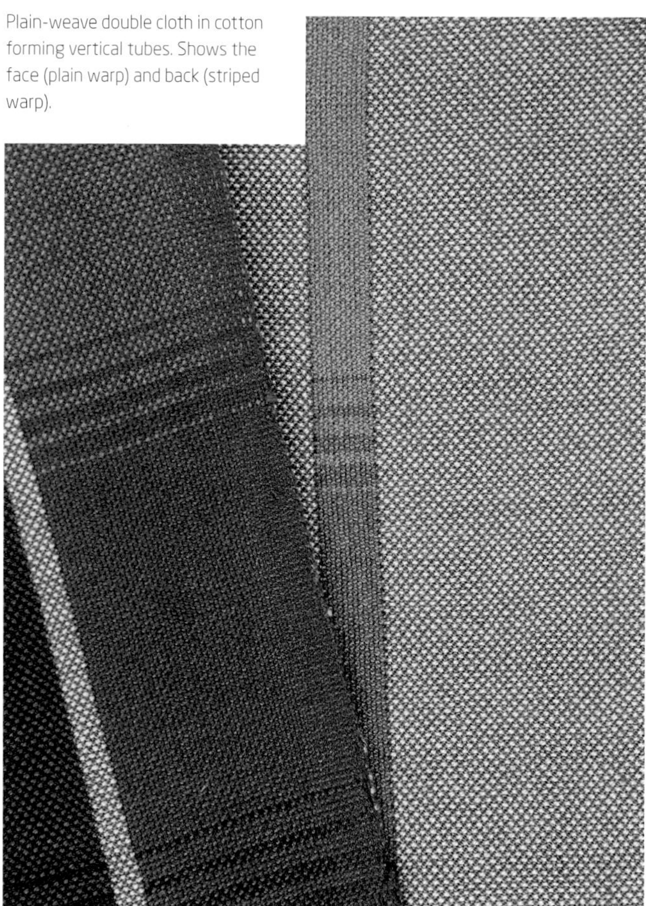

Plain-weave double cloth in cotton forming vertical tubes. Shows the face (plain warp) and back (striped warp).

Plain-weave double cloth in cotton forming blocks. The face warp is green and the back warp is grey. Shows the face cloth.

Plain-weave double cloth in cotton forming blocks. The face warp is green and the back warp is grey. Shows the back cloth.

Plain-weave double cloth forming blocks and horizontal tubes. The face warp is green and the back warp is grey. Shows the face cloth.

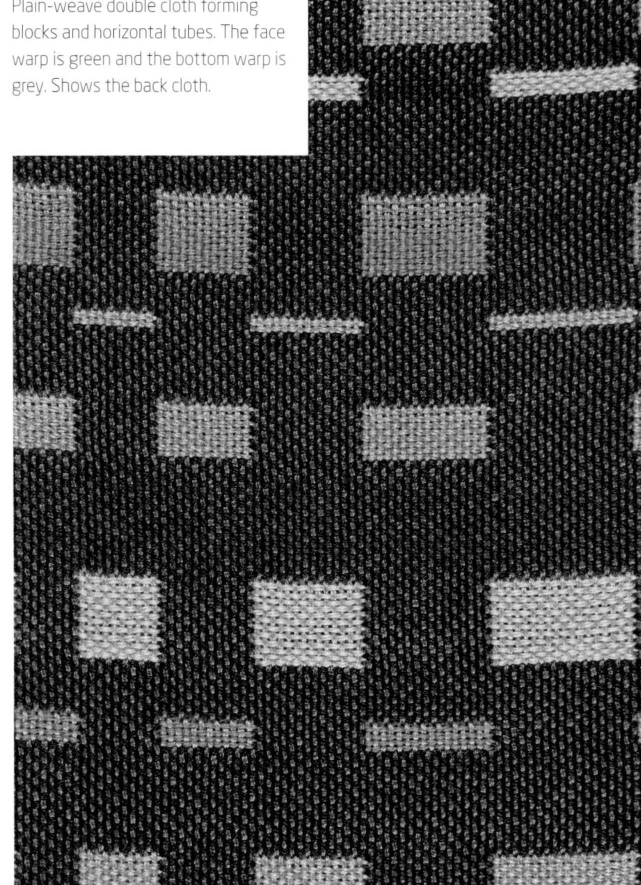
Plain-weave double cloth forming blocks and horizontal tubes. The face warp is green and the bottom warp is grey. Shows the back cloth.

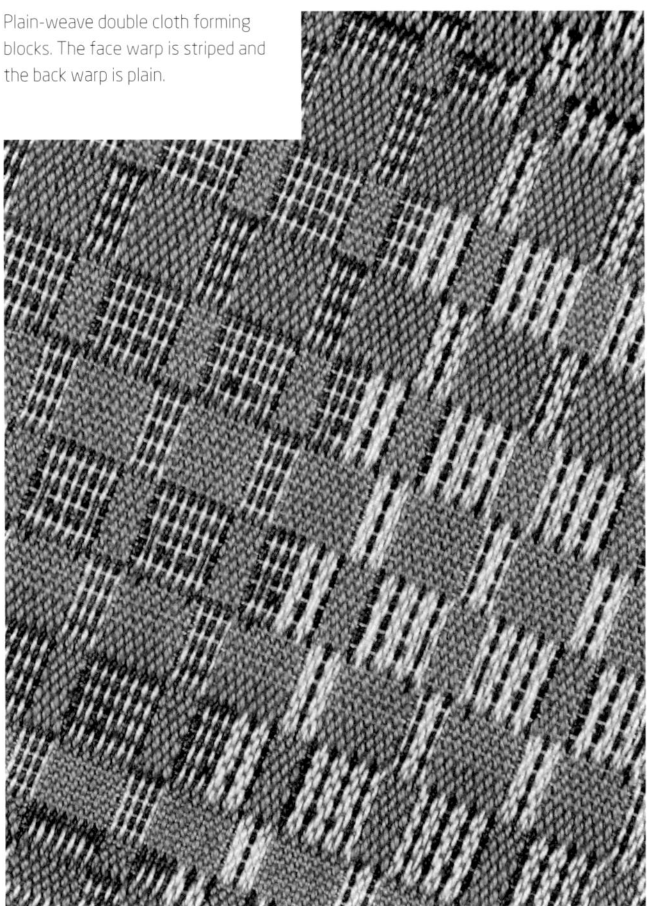
Plain-weave double cloth forming blocks. The face warp is striped and the back warp is plain.

PADDING OR QUILTING EFFECT

You can create padded sections in the double cloth by introducing wadding (batting) to the horizontal or vertical tubes, or to the pockets created when weaving block double cloths. The term 'pocket' in this context applies to the space created by the horizontal and vertical interchanges in a block double cloth.

- Weave a section of double cloth to the desired proportion.
- Lift all shafts corresponding to the layer that is on the top, i.e:

Design A will be shafts 1, 3, 5 and 7,
Design B will be shafts 2, 4, 6 and 8,
Design C will be shafts 1, 3, 6 and 8,
Design D will be shafts 2, 4, 5 and 7.

- With the required shafts raised, insert the wadding material.
- Lower the shafts and change to the next lifting plan in the pattern.

DOUBLE CLOTH WITH SINGLE-CLOTH WEAVES

Contrasting an area of woven single cloth against an area of double cloth will give further design potential to the warp.

Using Threading plan 3 (double cloth on eight shafts: block draft), it is possible to weave a single cloth instead of a double cloth, either across the total width of the fabric, or in blocks. The single-cloth weave will be a considerably denser fabric than the double cloth because there are twice the normal ends per cm/inch being used.

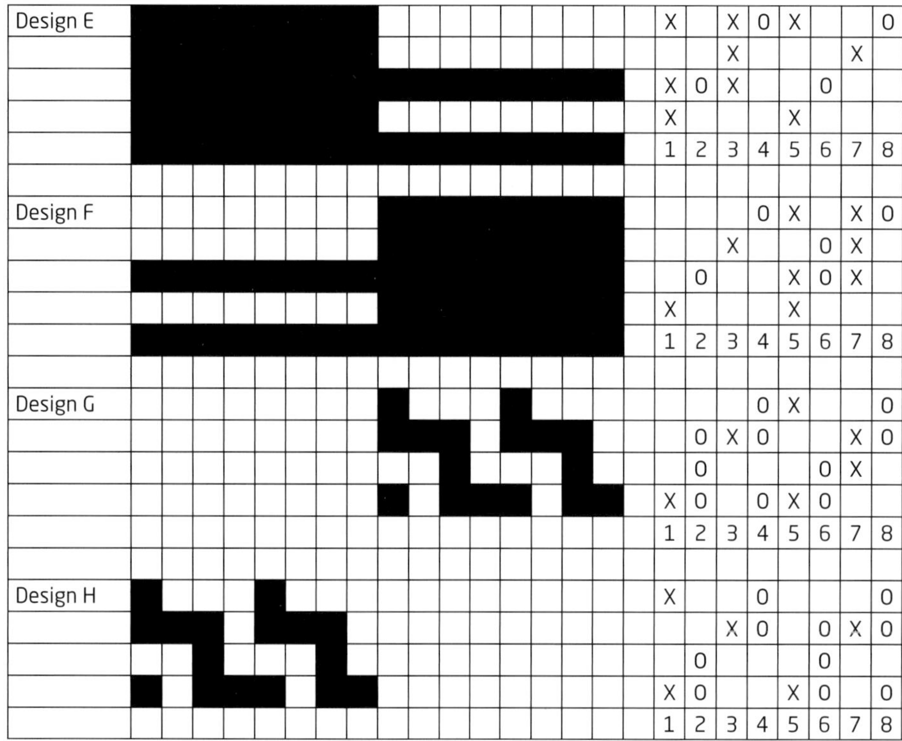

Design E: Shafts 1–4, double cloth face on top (black). Shafts 5–8, 1 x 3 twill.
Design F: Shafts 1–4, 1 x 3 twill. Shafts 5–8, double cloth face on top (black).
Design G: Shafts 1–4, double cloth back on top (white). Shafts 5–8, 2 x 2 twill.
Design H: Shafts 1–4, 2 x 2 twill. Shafts 5–8, double cloth back on top (white).

WEFT COLOUR PATTERNS

In Lifting plans E, F, G and H, if you continue to use alternating black and white weft colours, then a colour and weave effect will appear in the single cloth blocks rather than an apparent twill line.

CREATING PATTERNS USING DOUBLE CLOTH

Weaving fabric using the double-cloth structure can result in very complex designs and compositions by using squares and oblongs of different proportions and colour combinations. There is also the potential to create pattern – the more shafts available, the more intricate this can be.

You need to remember that each layer will use its own set of shafts: if you have 12 shafts available, you will need to allocate six for each cloth; with 16 shafts there will be eight shafts for each cloth and so on.

X = black face ends, O = white back ends

Double cloth on twelve shafts: Point draft

Threading																				
12												O								
11											X									
10										O				O						
9									X				X							
8								O								O				
7							X								X					
6						O												O		
5					X												X			
4				O																O
3			X																X	
2		O																		
1	X																			

--------------------------------------repeat--------------------------------------

Reed plan	■	■	■	■					■	■	■	■					■	■	■	■
					■	■	■	■					■	■	■	■				

THREADING PLAN

When using a double-cloth point draft, each pair of ends works as a unit, i.e. in Plan 6: 1 and 2 will work as a unit, then 3 and 4, 5 and 6, 7 and 8, 9 and 10, and finishing with 11 and 12. When you reverse the threading plan you go to the unit on shafts 9 and 10. If you go directly to shaft 11 for the reverse, there will be two ends.

Lifting plan				0				0			X	0								
Design I		0	X	0		0	X	0		0	X									
		0				0			X	0	X									
		0		0	X	0		0	X											
				0			X	0	X		X	0								
		0	X	0		0	X				X									
		0			X	0	X		X	0	X									
	X	0		0	X				X											
			X	0	X		X	0	X		X	0								
		0	X				X				X									
	X	0	X		X	0	X		X	0	X									
	X				X				X											
			X	0	X		X	0	X		X	0								
		0	X				X				X									
		0			X	0	X		X	0	X									
	X	0		0	X				X											
				0			X	0	X		X	0								
		0	X	0		0	X				X									
		0				0			X	0	X									
	X	0		0	X	0		0	X											
				0				0			X	0								
		0	X	0		0	X	0		0	X									
		0				0				0										
	X	0		0	X	0		0	X	0		0								
Shaft	1	2	3	4	5	6	7	8	9	10	11	12								

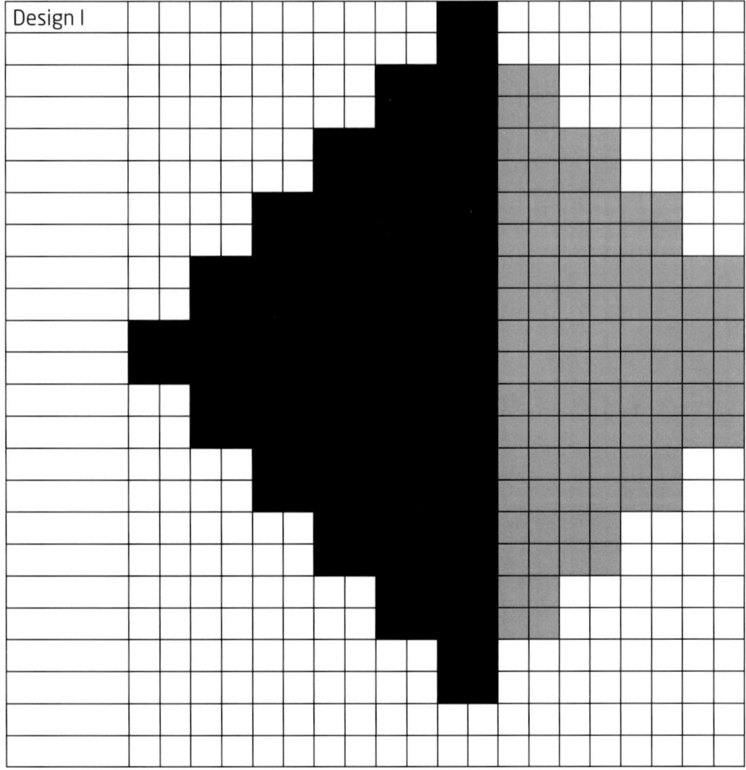

DESIGN SCALE

When weaving double-cloth fabrics the scale of the design will be determined by the thickness of the yarn and by the number of times each pattern unit is repeated.

In block drafts, it is a simple procedure to repeat each unit as many times as you need to achieve the desired scale for the design requirements. The thickness of yarn – ends per cm/inch – is taken into account in the planning, and does not limit the size of the block.

With more complex patterning over point drafts, the thickness of the yarn will determine the scale – fine yarn will give a small-scale pattern, and as the thickness of the yarn increases, the larger the pattern will be.

For example: Plan 4 (12-shaft point draft). 10 ends per cloth per repeat.

- Yarn is 16epc per cloth (40epi) = 0.6cm (¼in)
- Yarn is 8epc per cloth (20epi) = 1.3cm (½in)
- Yarn is 4epc per cloth (10epi) = 2.5cm (1in)

Design I: Forms a diamond pattern. When repeated there will be a black diamond formed by the face cloth, and a white diamond formed by the white back cloth.

Lifting plan	X		X	O				O			X	O								
Design J			X			O	X	O		O	X									
	X	O				O			X	O	X									
	X			O	X	O			X											
				O			X		X		X	O								
		O	X	O		O	X				X									
		O			X	O	X		X	O										
	X	O		O	X				X			O								
			X	O	X		X	O				O								
		O	X				X			O	X	O								
	X	O	X		X	O				O										
	X				X			O	X	O		O								
			X	O	X		X	O				O								
		O	X				X			O	X	O								
		O			X	O	X		X	O										
	X	O		O	X				X			O								
				O			X	O	X		X	O								
		O	X	O		O	X				X									
	X	O				O			X	O	X									
	X			O	X	O		O	X											
	X		X	O				O			X	O								
			X			O	X	O		O	X									
	X	O	X		X	O				O										
	X				X			O	X	O		O								
Shaft	1	2	3	4	5	6	7	8	9	10	11	12								

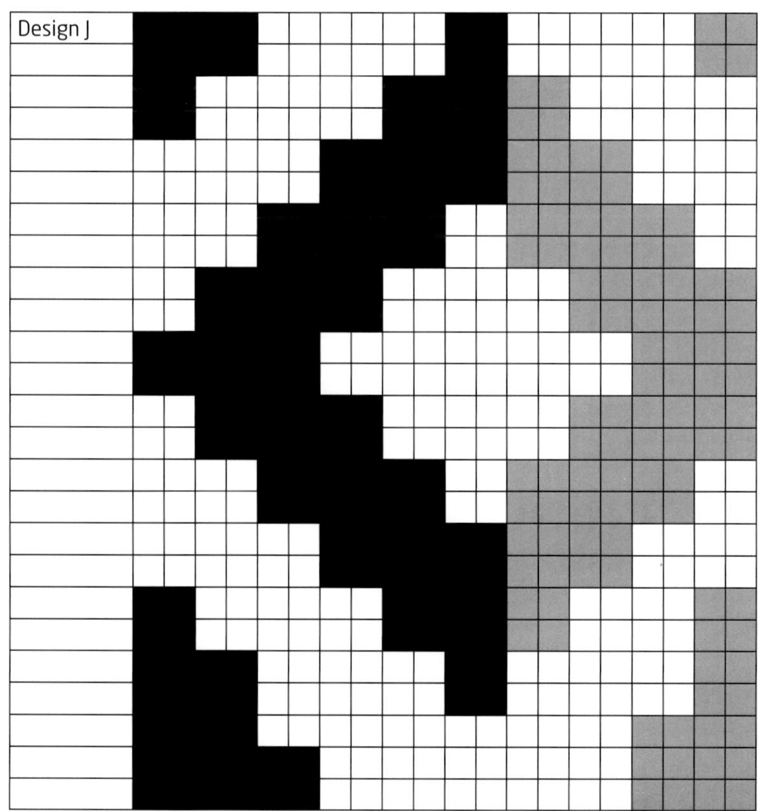

Design J: Forms a diamond pattern. There is a white back-cloth centre to the black face-cloth diamond, and a black face-cloth centre to the white back-cloth diamond.

EXAMPLES OF PATTERNED DOUBLE CLOTH

Teresa Georgallis bag using complex double cloth.

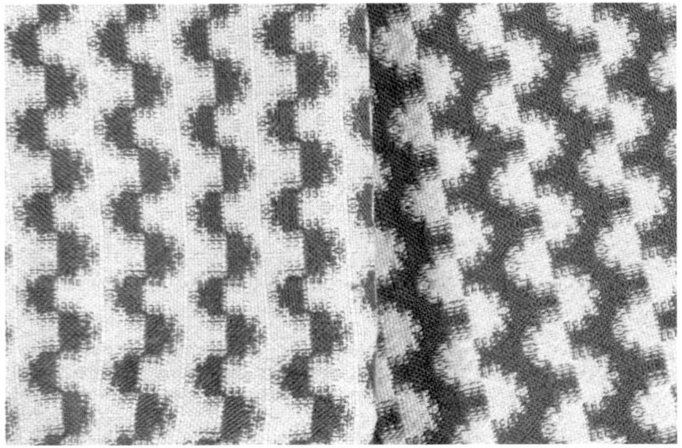

Plain-weave double cloth using a point draft/threading plan and forming a decorative stripe pattern on a reversible fabric. Shows the face and back of the cloth.

Plain-weave double cloth using a point draft/threading plan and forming a spot pattern on a reversible fabric. Shows the face and back of the cloth.

Plain-weave double cloth using a point draft/threading plan forming a pattern on a reversible fabric. The face warp is black and the back warp is striped. Shows face and back of the fabric.

Plain-weave double cloth using a point draft/threading plan forming a pattern on a reversible fabric. The face warp is black and the back warp is striped. Shows the face of the fabric.

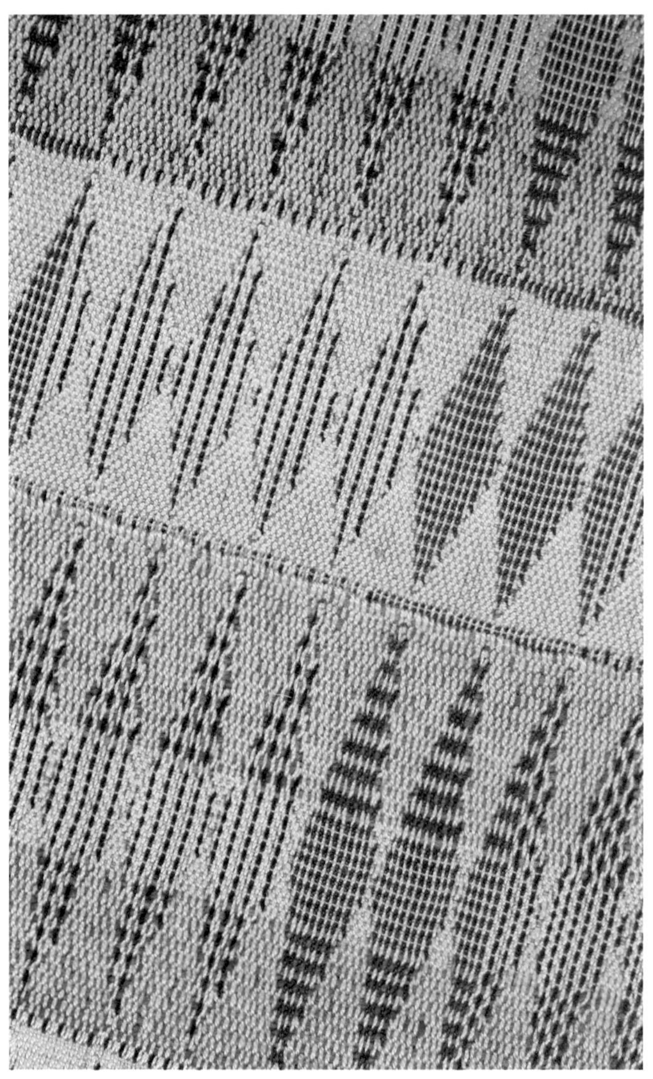

Plain-weave double cloth using a point draft/threading plan forming a diamond pattern. The face warp is striped and the back warp is plain.

COMPLEX LIFTING PLANS

Both layers of the double cloth will be woven as a plain weave. In the example used, the threading plan is a point draft over 12 shafts. The face cloth is threaded on the odd-numbered shafts and the back cloth on the even-numbered shafts.

STEP 1

Draw the threading plan on point paper and then draw out the pattern using one square for each section of the design. Only draw half the pattern, as the shape will naturally mirror itself horizontally when you weave it. So for the lifting plan you only need to draw half of the design. Draw the full design vertically.

If you are using 12 shafts, there will be six shafts allocated to the face and six shafts for the back cloth, so your diagram should use six squares across – one square per unit of two ends. The height of the diagram depends on the pattern – for a regular diamond it will be 12 squares high.

STEP 2

Fill in the squares to indicate which is the face cloth and which is the back cloth forming the pattern or shape. In this example, the dark squares indicate the face cloth, and the white squares indicate the back cloth.

STEP 3

To make the lifting plan simpler to write, extend the drawing so that a square is used for each warp end and weft pick – it will be twice the size of the original. Row 1 will weave the face cloth and row 2 the back cloth, row 3 the face cloth and row 4 the back cloth, and so on until the pattern ends on row 24.

STEP 4

Follow the first row of squares horizontally in the extended drawing at Step 3. The first pick weaves the face cloth. The face cloth is threaded on shafts 1, 3, 5, 7, 9 and 11. To create a plain weave in the face cloth, for the first pick you need to raise shafts 1, 5 and 9 using an X on the first row of the lifting plan.

STEP 5

Lift the back cloth ends that appear on the surface of the design in the first row of the pattern. The back cloth is threaded on the even-numbered shafts, and indicated by the white squares. In the first row, put an O where any back cloth ends will be woven on the surface. In the example used, you need to raise shafts 6, 8 and 10.

STEP 6

Go to the second row. The second pick weaves the back cloth. The back cloth is threaded on shafts 2, 4, 6, 8, 10 and 12. To create a plain weave in the back cloth, for the first pick you need to raise shafts 2, 6 and 10 using an O on the second row of the lifting plan.

STEP 7

Lift the face cloth ends that appear on the surface of the cloth in the second row of the pattern. The face cloth is on odd shafts and indicated by the dark squares. In the example used, you need to lift shafts 1, 3 and 11 using an X on the second row of the lifting plan.

STEP 8

Row 3 weaves the second row of the face cloth. To create a plain weave in the face cloth, lift the alternate odd shafts – 3, 7 and 11 – indicated using an 'X'. In the same row, indicate with an O the back cloth ends that appear on the surface of the design in the third row of the pattern – 4, 6 and 8.

Row 4 weaves the second row of the back cloth. To create a plain weave in the back cloth, lift the alternate even shafts 4, 8 and 12 indicated using an O. In the same row, indicate with an X the face cloth ends that appear on the surface of the design in the fourth row of the pattern – 1, 9 and 11.

Continue through each row of the pattern in the same way until you have completed the lifting plan.

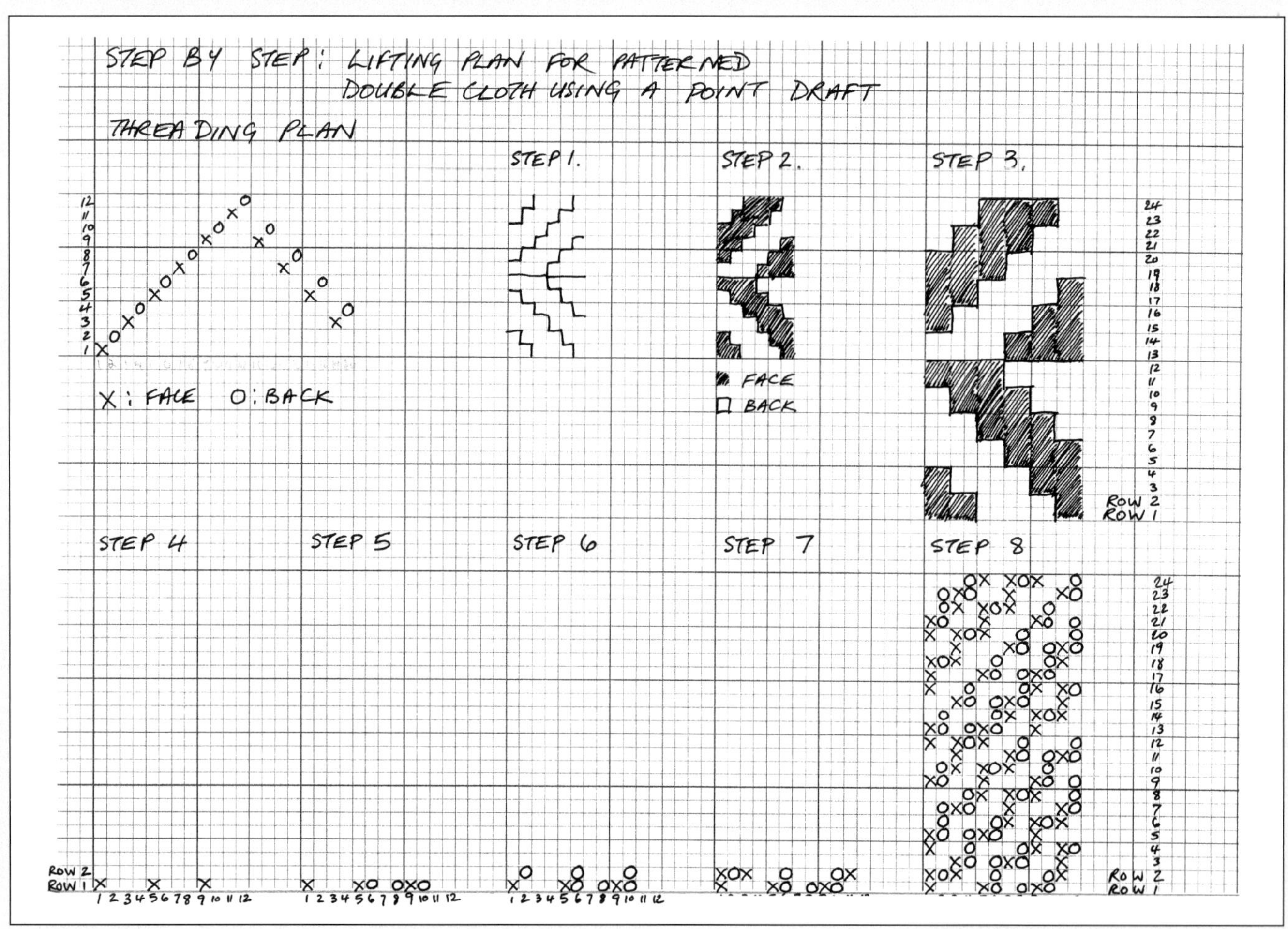

BLOCK POINT DRAFT

This type of draft will give you the option of achieving complex block patterning arrangements, as well as simple pattern designs. Each unit of four ends (two in each layer) can be repeated as many times as you wish and will depend on the thickness of yarn being used and the scale of the pattern required. The more times that each block is repeated, the pattern shape becomes more stepped in appearance when woven.

X = black face ends, O = white back ends

Threading																								
16																O								
15															X									
14														O										
13													X											
12												O								O				
11											X								X					
10										O								O						
9									X								X							
8								O																O
7							X																X	
6						O																O		
5					X																X			
4				O																				
3			X																					
2		O																						
1	X																							

----repeat---- ----repeat---- ----repeat---- ----repeat---- ----repeat---- ----repeat----

Reed plan	■	■	■	■					■	■	■	■					■	■	■	■				
					■	■	■	■					■	■	■	■					■	■	■	■

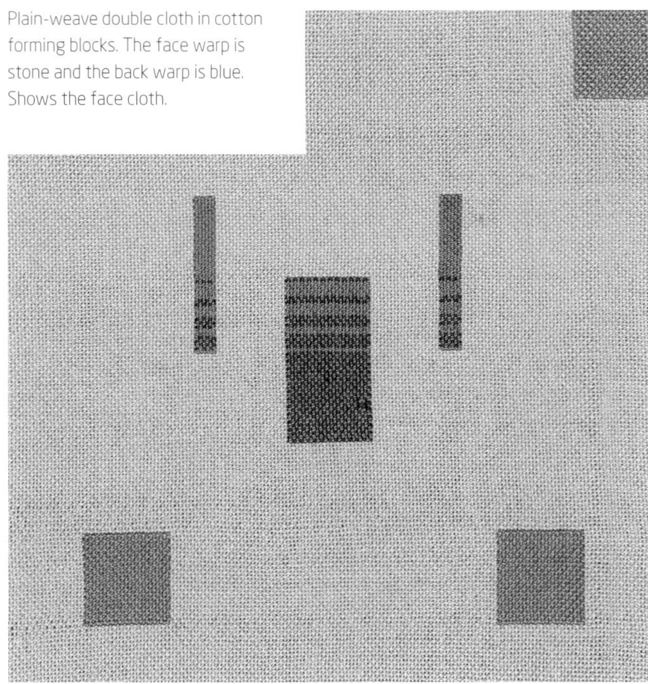

Plain-weave double cloth in cotton forming blocks. The face warp is stone and the back warp is blue. Shows the face cloth.

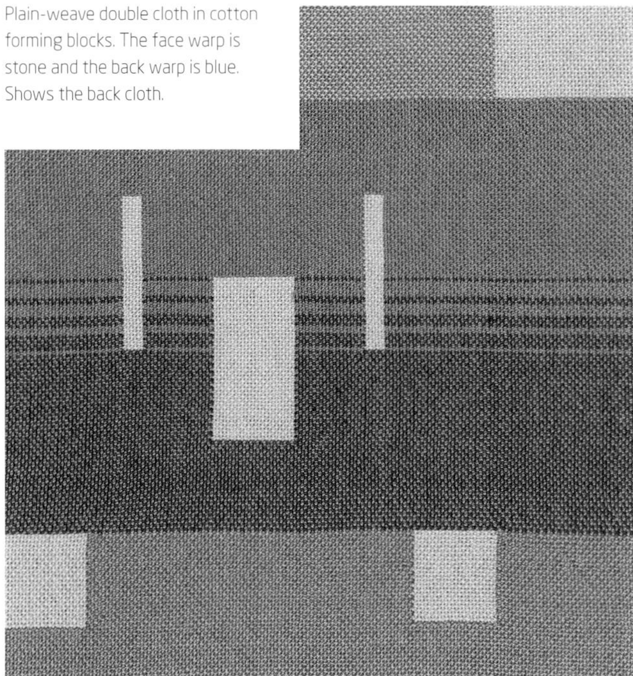

Plain-weave double cloth in cotton forming blocks. The face warp is stone and the back warp is blue. Shows the back cloth.

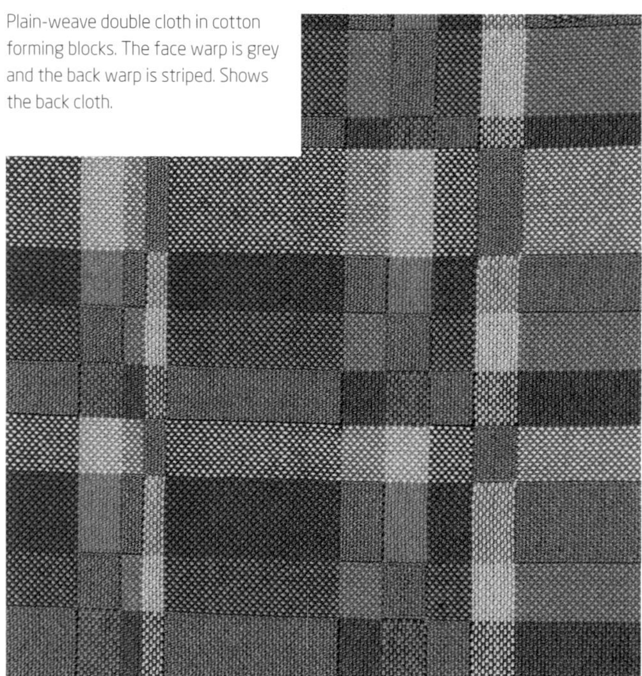

Plain-weave double cloth in cotton forming blocks. The face warp is grey and the back warp is striped. Shows the back cloth.

Plain-weave double cloth in cotton forming blocks. The face warp is grey and the back warp is striped. Shows the face cloth.

Lifting plan																
Design K				O	X		X	O				O	X		X	O
		O	X	O			X			O	X	O			X	
		O			X	O	X			O			X	O	X	
17-20	X	O		O	X				X	O		O	X			
	X		X	O				O	X		X	O				O
			X			O	X	O			X			O	X	O
	X	O	X			O			X	O	X			O		
13-16	X				X	O		O	X				X	O		O
	X		X	O	X		X	O				O	X		X	O
			X				X			O	X	O				
	X	O	X		X	O	X			O			X	O	X	
9-12	X				X				X	O		O	X			
	X		X	O	X		X	O	X		X	O				O
			X				X				X			O	X	O
	X	O	X		X	O	X		X	O	X			O		
5-8	X				X				X				X	O		O
				O	X		X	O	X		X	O	X		X	O
		O	X	O			X				X				X	
		O			X	O	X		X	O	X		X	O	X	
1-4	X	O		O	X				X				X			

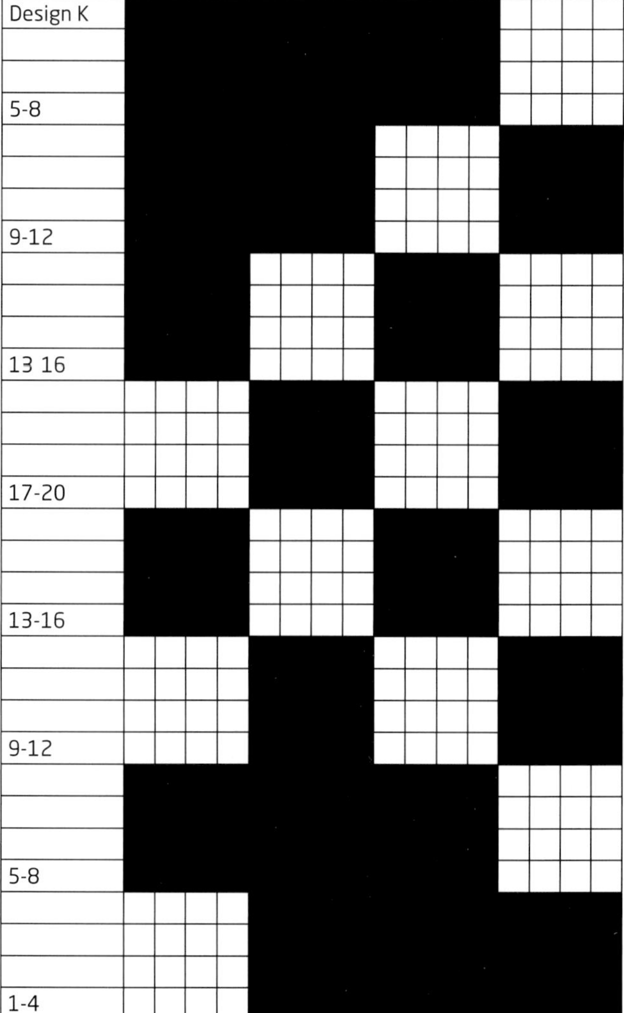

Lifting plan																
Design L	X		X	O	X		X	O	X		X	O				O
			X				X				X			O	X	O
	X	O	X		X	O	X		X	O	X			O		
29-32	X				X				X				X	O		O
	X		X	O	X		X	O				O				O
			X				X			O	X	O		O	X	O
	X	O	X		X	O	X			O				O		
25-38	X				X				X	O		O	X	O		O
	X		X	O	X		X	O				O	X		X	O
			X				X			O	X	O			X	
	X	O	X		X	O	X			O			X	O	X	
21-24	X				X				X	O		O	X			
	X		X	O				O				O	X		X	O
			X			O	X	O		O	X	O			X	
	X	O	X			O				O			X	O	X	
17-20	X				X	O		O	X	O		O	X			
	X		X	O				O	X		X	O	X		X	O
			X			O	X	O			X				X	
	X	O	X			O			X	O	X		X	O	X	
13-16	X				X	O		O	X				X			
				O				O	X		X	O	X		X	O
		O	X	O		O	X	O			X				X	
		O				O			X	O	X		X	O	X	
9-12	X	O		O	X	O		O	X				X			
				O	X		X	O	X		X	O	X		X	O
		O	X	O			X				X				X	
		O			X	O	X		X	O	X		X	O	X	
5-8	X	O		O	X				X				X			
				O	X		X	O	X		X	O				O
		O	X	O			X				X			O	X	O
		O			X	O	X		X	O	X			O		
1-4	X	O		O	X				X				X	O		O

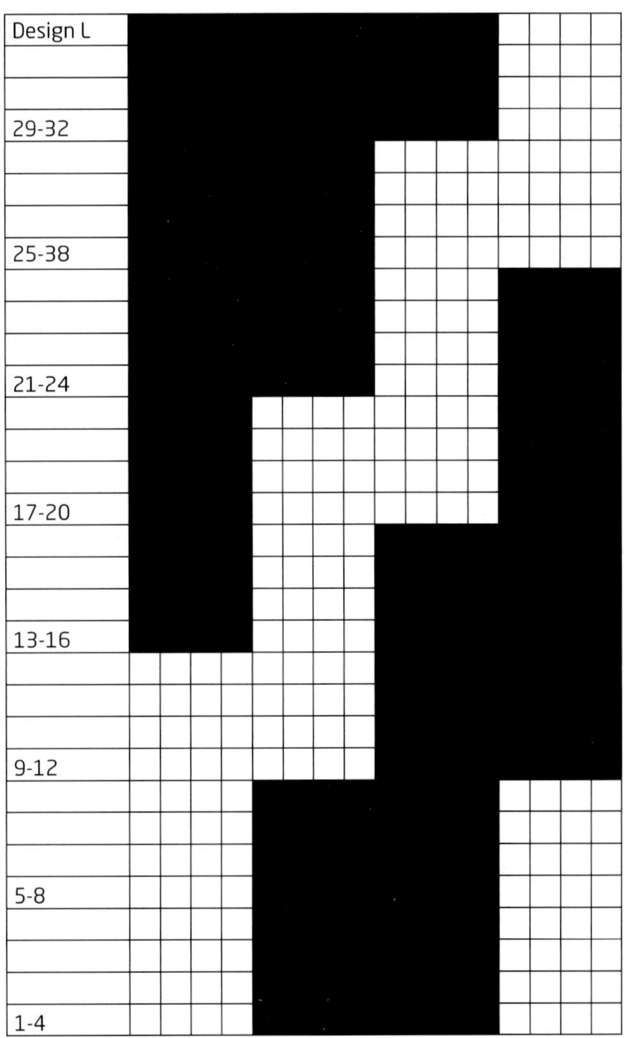

Plain-weave double cloth in cotton forming blocks and horizontal tubes. The face warp is stone and the back warp is blue.

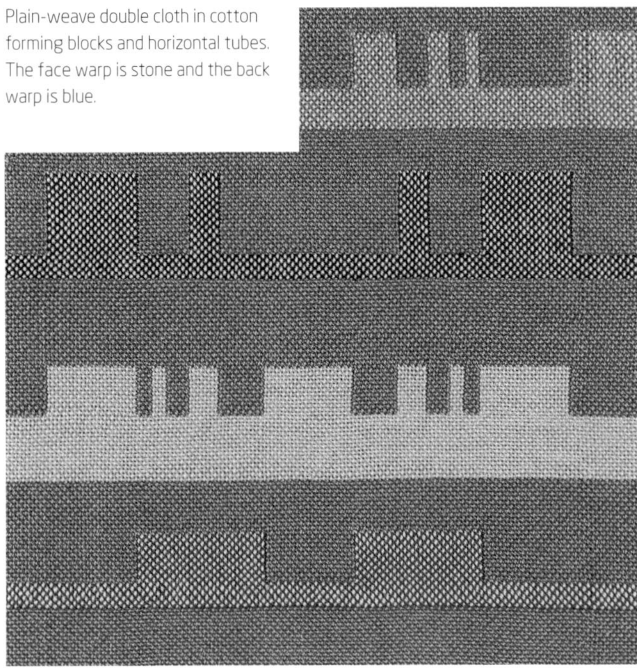

PLEATS

Horizontal pleats can be woven into your fabric. As with the double-cloth structure, two warps are necessary – one to form the pleat and one to form the ground cloth that will hold the pleat in place. Each warp must be wound onto separate beams; this is because the warp that you use to form the pleat will be woven independently of the ground cloth, and the tension relaxed to make the pleat. In theory, since each warp is tensioned independently of the other, pleats can be created using either warp.

However, if you plan your design so that only one of the warps will be used for pleating, then the pleat warp should be at least 50 to 75 per cent longer than the ground warp. This is because you will be weaving considerably more of the pleat warp. The additional length depends on how often you will be producing pleats, and how big they are. If you intend to use either warp for pleating to create contrast, then calculate the lengths accordingly.

The height of a pleat is restricted by practical considerations. There needs to be sufficient room to pass the shuttle through the open **shed** when weaving the pleat, and the sley (batten) needs to be able to reach the fell (edge) of the cloth when the finished pleat is pulled back.

You can weave a pleat using as few as four shafts, with each cloth allocated its own two shafts. However if you have more shafts at your disposal you can use a variety of structures to form the pleat, such as twills or satin.

Multiple small pleats have been woven repeatedly through the design to create surface movement.

TENSION

When the pleat has been formed, the tension on the pleat warp is naturally quite loose until it has been firmly woven into the ground cloth. Use the following steps to ensure that no mistakes are created during the weaving.

- After folding the pleat, hold it in place with the sley while lifting the shafts for the first row of plain weave to join the two warps together.
- Push back the sley as near to the shafts as it will go.
- Insert the first weft pick in the sequence.
- Beat firmly into place with the sley.
- Until there are sufficient picks to keep the pleat in place, when you change to the next pattern row in the lifting plan there is a tendency for the pleat to pull out. Hold the pleat in place with the sley and change to the next row of plain weave.
- Beat down firmly before you introduce the next weft pick.
- Push the sley back to the shafts and insert the second pick in the sequence.
- Repeat for a minimum of eight picks so that the pleat is held firmly in place.
- Tighten the tension on the pleat warp if necessary.
- If the pleat pulls out then you have not woven the cloths together sufficiently before returning the tension.

When using a very smooth, slippery yarn, such as a nylon or silk monofilament, then you will usually need to use more picks to hold the pleat in place.

STEP 1

Start by weaving the two warps together firmly – usually a plain-weave structure is used, and four to eight picks should be sufficient. Weave the pleat warp independently of the ground warp to twice the height required for the finished pleat.

STEP 2

The ground warp is not woven at this stage, and will be floating underneath the pleat.

STEP 3

Ensuring that no shafts are raised, release the tension on the pleat warp sufficient to allow the cloth to be pulled back to the fell (where the two warps were woven together in step 1) with the reed.

The woven cloth will be folded in half to form the pleat.

STEP 4

Weave the two cloths together using a plain-weave structure. You will find that for the first three to four picks, the pleat warp will still be a little slack, so make sure that you push the reed back as near to the shafts as possible to allow the shuttle to pass over or under the slack ends as you weave.

STEP 5

You will need to beat down the weft firmly to hold the pleat in place.

At least eight picks should be woven to ensure that the pleat is held firmly in place.

When you have woven the two cloths together sufficiently to hold the pleat, check the tension on the pleat warp and adjust it if necessary – it may still be a little slack from loosening it to form the pleat. Either weave the warps together to form a greater distance between the pleats, or begin the next pleat.

PLEATS ON FOUR SHAFTS

Two shafts are allocated for each warp. X is one warp (odds), and O is the second warp (evens).

Shaft									Lifting plan 1		O		O
4				O				O		X		X	
3			X				X				O		O
2		O				O				X		X	
1	X				X				Shaft	1	2	3	4
Reed plan	■	■	■	■									
					■	■	■	■	Lifting plan 2			X	
									Pleat on odd shafts	X			
												X	
										X			
									Shaft	1	2	2	3
									Lifting plan 3				O
									Pleat on even shafts		O		
													O
											O		
										1	2	3	4

Lifting plan sequence for pleat:

1. Use Plan 1 to join the two cloths together.

2. Use either Plan 2 or 3 to weave the pleat.

3. When the pleat is the required length, slacken the tension on the warp on which you have produced the pleat.

4. Pull back the pleat and weave the cloths together using Plan 1. Use at least eight weft picks.

5. Continue to weave the ground together or begin another pleat using either Plan 2 or 3.

Lifting plan 4	X		X	O	Lifting plan 5				O
			X				O	X	O
	X	O	X				O		
	X					X	O		O
	1	2	3	4		1	2	3	4

Pleated fabric using nylon monofilament, coloured wire and reeds.

EXAMPLES OF SIMPLE PLEAT FABRICS

Double warp forming pleats. The stone/natural-coloured warp is on four shafts and the black and white stripe on two shafts. The stone warp has been pleated.

The stone warp has been pleated. A 1 x 3 weft-faced twill weave has been used in the pleats to create a stronger colour contrast. Pictured with the yarn wrap.

The stone warp has been pleated. A 1 x 3 weft-faced twill weave has been used in the pleats to create a stronger colour contrast. Pictured with yarn wrap and inspirational work.

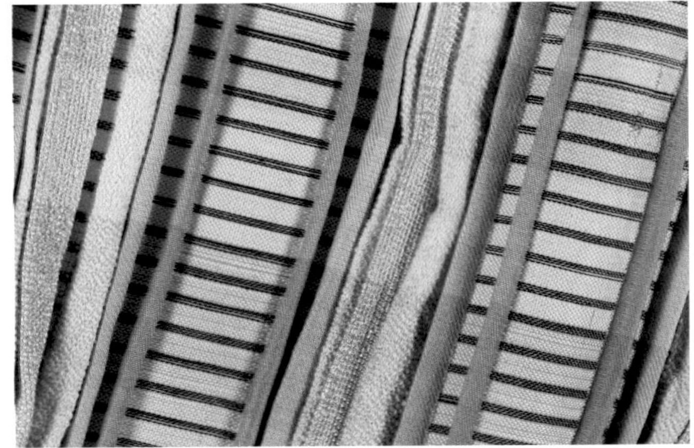

The stone warp has been pleated. Textured yarns have been used in some pleats to add contrast to the surface quality.

Double cloth using threading plan 1:

Using Threading plan 1, you can also create a horizontal double cloth to give more variety to your fabric compositions. The double-cloth structure can be used between pleats – after the pleat is held in place using Lifting plan 1 – or can be used throughout the composition to give variety to your collection of designs.

1. Lifting plan 4 will weave the warp on the odd shafts on the top, and the warp on the even shafts on the back.

2. Lifting plan 5 will weave the warp on the even shafts on the top, and the warp on the odd shafts on the back.

3. Alternate between the two plans for horizontal tubes.

Horizontal raised tube using threading plan 1:

Rather than making a sharp pleat where the start and finish of the pleat meet when the tension is released, or a flat double cloth, it is also possible to make a raised tube on the surface of the fabric.

1. Use Lifting plan 1 to weave the cloths together.

2. Use Plan 4 to create a double-cloth section – the back cloth will form the base of the tube.

3. Use Plan 2 to weave the cloth threaded on the odd shafts independently of the cloth on the even shafts.

4. When a sufficient amount has been woven, slacken the tension of the warp on the odd shafts.

5. Draw the weaving to the edge of the cloth and use Lifting plan 1 to combine the two cloths together. Use at least eight picks to hold the raised tube in place.

6. When you have woven the two cloths together sufficiently to hold the raised tube, check the tension on the slackened warp and adjust the tension if necessary – it may still be a little slack from loosening it to form the tunnel.

7. For a raised tube using the warp on the even shafts, use Lifting plan 5 to form the base of the tunnel and Lifting plan 3 to form the additional weaving.

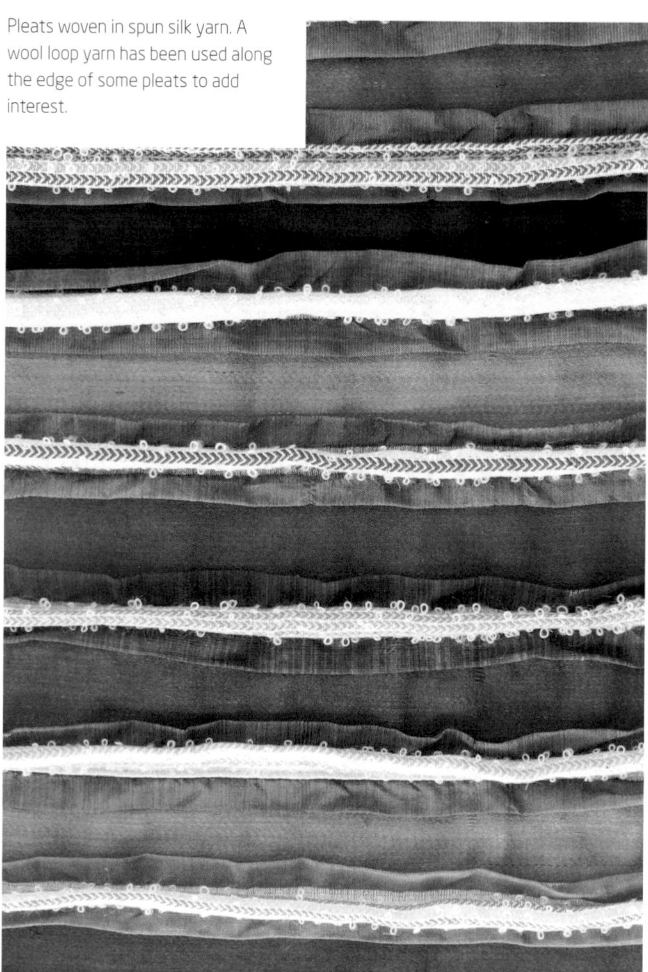

Pleats woven in spun silk yarn. A wool loop yarn has been used along the edge of some pleats to add interest.

Both the ground warp and the pleat warp are in cotton. The pleats have been stitched together in a repeat pattern to give a smocked effect.

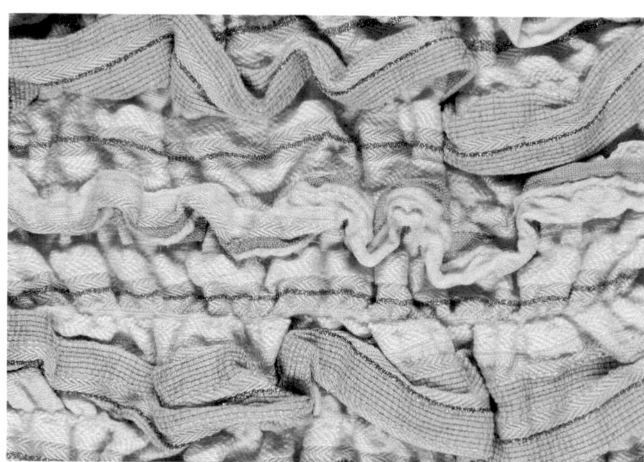

Design options when weaving pleats

- Weave half the pleat in one colour, and the remainder in a contrast colour. When the pleat is folded it will have a different colour on each side.
- Use a feature yarn such as a thick or textured yarn at the halfway stage of weaving the pleat to give a fancy edge when the pleat is folded in half.
- Stitch the pleats together after weaving to give a smocked effect, or a waved effect. This will show the contrasting colours or textures on either side of the pleat, and will reveal the ground-weave sections where the pleat is held in place.
- Combine different proportions/sizes of pleat to suggest movement. Begin with small pleats of 0.6cm (¼in) and gradually increase the scale of each pleat.
- Use a weft/warp-faced twill or a satin weave to give a more lustrous quality to the pleat.
- Use a double-cloth structure to add interest in the ground weave.
- If you have used more than four shafts for your pleat cloth, you can combine weaves such as twill, plain weave or satin in horizontal bands across the pleat, which will give additional surface and colour interest.
- No two pleats need use the same colour or yarn in the weft.
- Use an elastic yarn in the weft when weaving the two cloths together, immediately before and after weaving the pleat. This will allow the pleat to contract horizontally and form a ruffle. This effect is evident only when the weaving is removed from the loom.

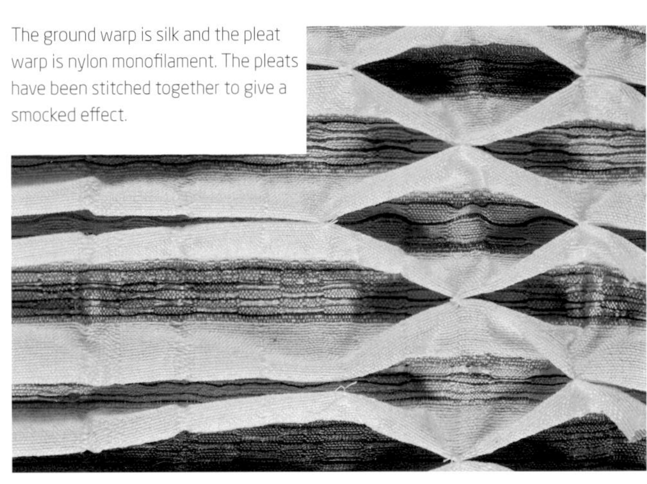
The ground warp is silk and the pleat warp is nylon monofilament. The pleats have been stitched together to give a smocked effect.

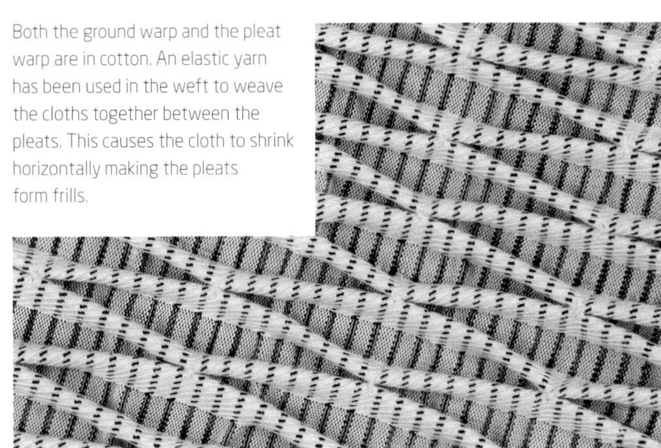
Both the ground warp and the pleat warp are in cotton. An elastic yarn has been used in the weft to weave the cloths together between the pleats. This causes the cloth to shrink horizontally making the pleats form frills.

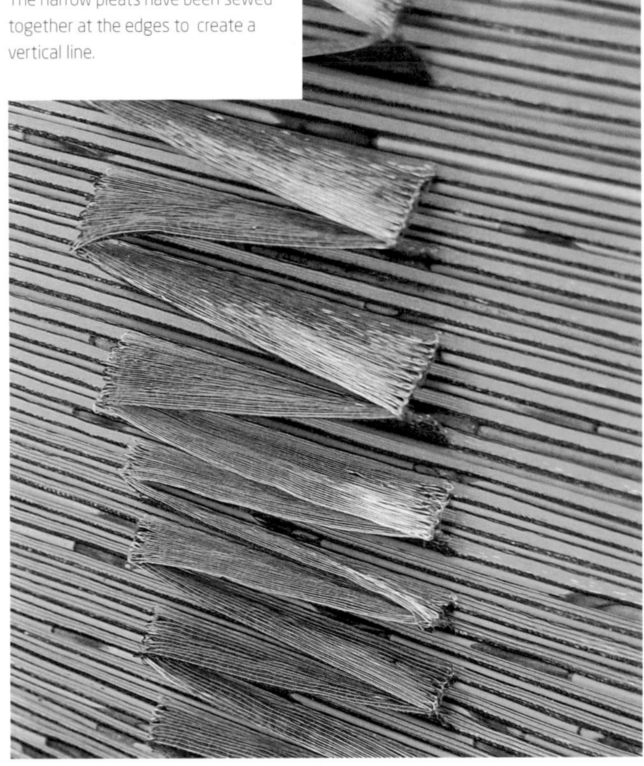
The narrow pleats have been sewed together at the edges to create a vertical line.

NARROW BAND PLEATS

Rather than weaving pleats that cover the whole width of the weaving, it is possible to create a pleat that is narrower than the ground cloth as a feature of your design. Only the narrow section of additional warp will be pleated – the ground is there to hold it in place. You can have one, two, three or more narrow sections of pleat warp. If you do have multiple sections of individual bands of pleats, the warp threads will all be wound onto the same beam. All of the bands will have to be pleated at the same time to avoid problems with the tension. If you want the bands to pleat at different times in the design, then you will need to allocate a beam for each pleat section so that the tension can be relaxed independently for each band.

The ground warp is nylon monofilament with spun silk for each of the two pleat warps. Each of the pleat warps needs to be tensioned independently to allow pleats to be made at different times.

The ground warp and the additional pleat warps are in cotton. A variety of yarns have been used in the pleats to add interest to the surface quality.

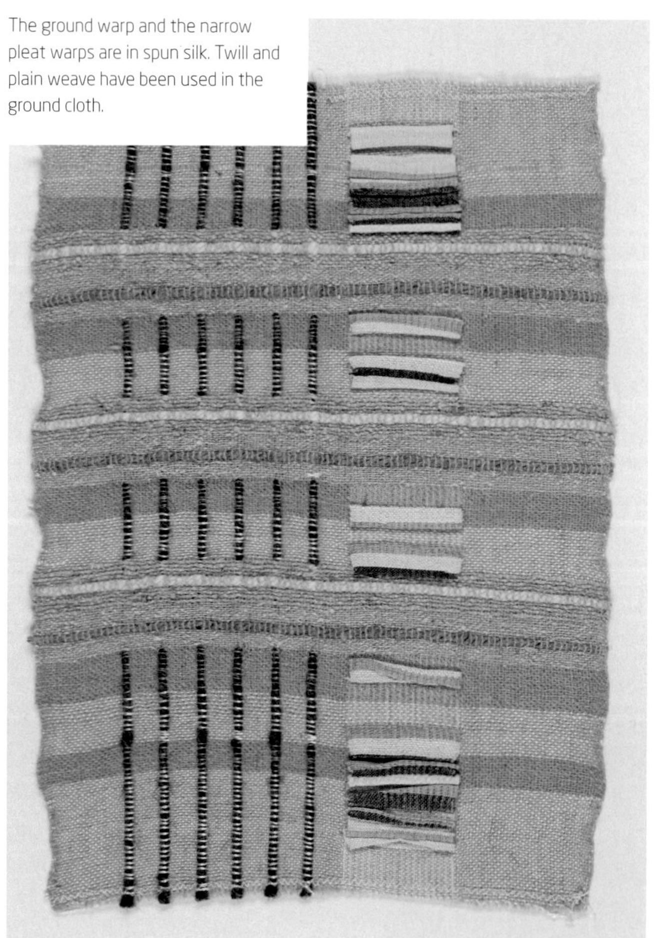

The ground warp and the narrow pleat warps are in spun silk. Twill and plain weave have been used in the ground cloth.

The ground warp is nylon monofilament with spun silk for each of the two pleat warps. Nylon monofilament has been used in the weft to form the pleats; one shuttle has been used for both narrow strips, allowing the nylon to form floats between the pleat warps.

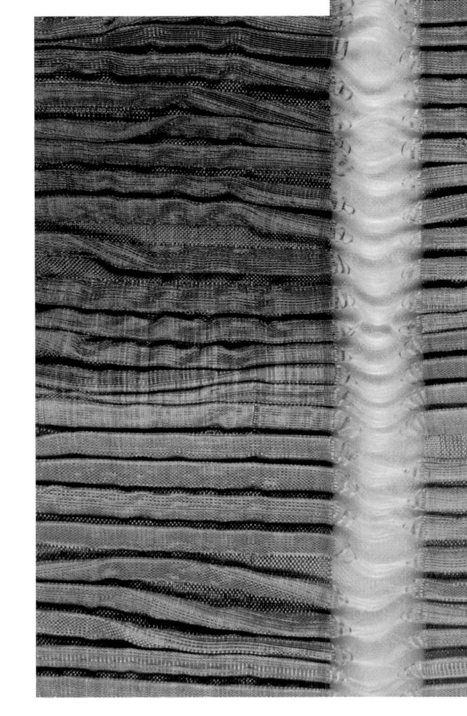

The ground warp and the narrow pleat warp are in spun silk. A variety of twill and plain weave has been used to form the pleats and the ground cloth.

The ground warp and the narrow pleat warps are in spun silk. Twill and plain weave have been used in the ground cloth.

Two shafts are allocated for each warp. X is the ground warp on shafts 1 and 2, and O is the narrower section of pleat warp on shafts 3 and 4.

Shaft																
4								O				O				
3						O				O						
2		X		X			X				X			X		X
1	X		X		X				X				X		X	

----repeat---- -----------repeat----------- ----repeat----

Reed plan	■	■			■	■	■	■					■	■		
			■	■					■	■	■	■			■	■

Lifting plan 1		X		O	Lifting plan 2				O
	X		O					O	
		X		O					O
	X		O					O	
	1	2	3	4		1	2	3	4
Lifting plan 3				O	Lifting plan 4	X	X		O
		X	O	O			X		
			O			X	X	O	
	X		O	O		X			
	1	2	3	4		1	2	3	4
Lifting plan 5	X	X		O					
	X	X	O						
	X	X		O					
	X	X	O						
	1	2	3	4					

Lifting plan sequence for pleat:

1. Use Lifting plan 1 to join the ground and narrow band together.

2. Use Lifting plan 2 to weave the pleat.

3. When the pleat is the required length, slacken the tension on the warp you have produced the pleat on.

4. Pull back the pleat and weave the cloths together using Plan 1. Use at least eight weft picks.

5. Continue to weave the ground and band together or begin another pleat using Plan 2.

USING SEPARATE SHUTTLES

Use two separate shuttles when weaving the narrow pleat, double cloth or tunnel: one to weave the ground and one to weave the pleat. If you have multiple sections of warp making several pleats, then a separate shuttle (or bobbin) will be used for each, otherwise the weft will float in the spaces between each section. If you want the weft to float between each pleat as a design feature, then just use one shuttle across all of the pleat sections.

DOUBLE CLOTH USING THREADING PLAN 2:

You can produce a double cloth in the section where the narrow band is threaded. The narrow band can either lie flat on top of the ground weave, or it can be slightly raised to make a small woven tunnel.

Use two separate shuttles for each of the double cloth alternatives – one to weave the ground and one to weave the narrow section.

Double-cloth sequence A: layers on the surface only

1. Use Lifting plan 1 to weave the cloths together.

2. Use Lifting plan 3 to weave the double cloth with the narrow warp section on top.

3. When the double-cloth section is the required scale, use two picks (or more if required) of Lifting plan 1 to weave the two cloths together.

Double cloth sequence B: layers on the surface and the back

1. Use Lifting plan 3 to weave a double cloth with the narrow warp section on top.

2. When you have woven the double cloth to the required scale, use Lifting plan 4 to weave the ground cloth on the top and the narrow warp section at the back.

3. Alternate between the two lifting plans as required.

Double cloth sequence C: raised tube on the front

1. Use Lifting plan 1 to weave the cloths together.

2. Use Lifting plan 3 to weave a double cloth with the narrow warp section on top.

3. Use Lifting plan 2 to weave the narrow warp section independently of the ground warp.

4. When a sufficient amount has been woven, slacken the tension of the narrow warp section.

5. Draw the narrow warp section of weaving to the edge of the cloth and use lift 1 to combine the two cloths together. Use at least eight picks to hold the raised tube in place.

6. When you have woven the two cloths together sufficiently to hold the raised tube, check the tension on the slackened warp and adjust the tension if necessary – it may still be a little slack from loosening it to form the raised tube.

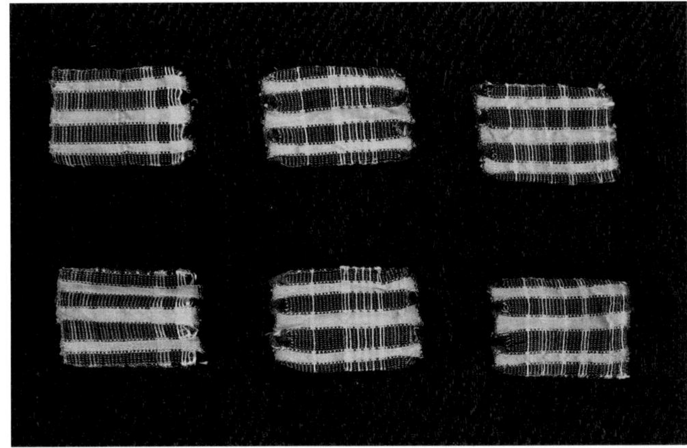

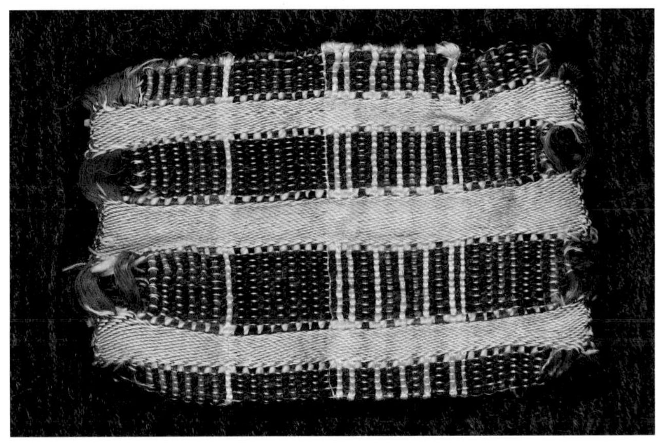

Top: The ground warp is wool, while filament silk is used for the pleat warps. Rather than form a pleat in the usual way, the pleat has not been pulled forward, and the wool floats in the ground have relaxed and shrunk after washing. This has formed a tunnel effect in the silk warps.

Middle: Detail of the wool ground warp and filament silk top layer.

Bottom: All-over placement of the wool ground warp and filament silk top layer.

Double cloth sequence D: raised tube on the back

1. Use Lifting plan 1 to weave the cloths together.

2. Use Lifting plan 4 to weave the ground cloth on top and the narrow warp section at the back.

3. Use Lifting plan 5 to weave the narrow warp section independently at the back of the cloth.

4. When a sufficient amount has been woven, slacken the tension of the narrow warp section.

5. Draw the narrow warp section of weaving to the edge of the cloth and use Lifting plan 1 to combine the two cloths together. Use at least eight picks to hold the raised tube in place.

6. When you have woven the two cloths together sufficiently to hold the raised tunnel, check the tension on the slackened warp and adjust the tension if necessary – it may still be a little slack from loosening it to form the raised tube.

Cotton ground warp with wool twist yarn in the weft. The additional top warp is in nylon monofilament.

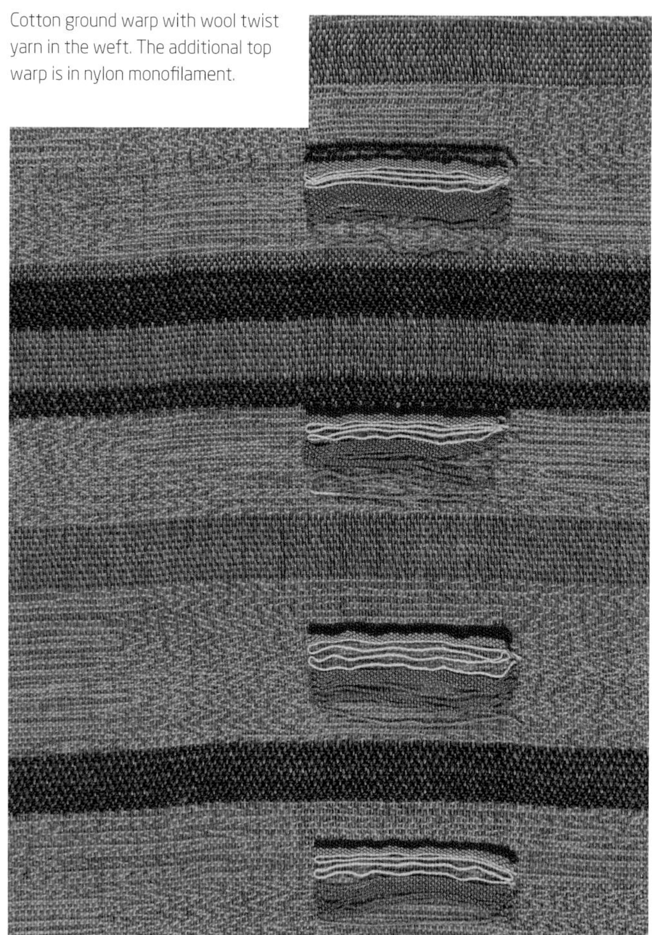

Both the ground warp and narrow top warp are in cotton. The ground is woven as a colour and weave and the top layer in contrasting colours.

The ground warp is cotton and the narrow band is nylon monofilament.

PLEATED FABRIC ON EIGHT SHAFTS

If six shafts are allocated for the pleat warp, and two for the ground cloth, then twill weaves or satin can be used to give additional design features.

Two shafts are allocated for each warp. X is the ground cloth on shafts 1 and 2, and O is the pleat warp on shafts 3 to 8.

Threading plan 3

Shaft												
8												O
7										O		
6								O				
5						O						
4				O								
3		O										
2			X				X				X	
1	X				X				X			
Reed plan	■	■	■	■					■	■	■	■
					■	■	■	■				

Lifting plan 1: Weaves both cloths together. Lifting plans 2, 3 and 4 weave the pleat cloth independently of the ground. The method of making the pleat is exactly the same as if you were using four shafts; the difference here is that you have six shafts allocated to the pleat warp, and can make use of many more weave structures to form the pleats.

Lifting plan 2: Weaves the pleat warp as a plain weave.

Lifting plan 3: Weaves the pleat warp as a satin weave.

Lifting plan 4: Weaves the pleat warp as a 3 × 3 twill.

You can use any of the six shaft patterns shown in Chapter 3 to form the pleat. Remember that when plotting out your lifting plan, the ground warp is threaded over shafts 1 and 2, and the pleat warp is threaded over shafts 3 to 8.

Double-cloth layers and raised tubes can also be created using exactly the same process as in the four-shaft woven pleat.

Lifting plan 1		X		O		O		O
	X		O		O		O	
		X		O		O		O
	X		O		O		O	
	1	2	3	4	5	6	7	8

Lifting plan 2				O		O		O
			O		O		O	
				O		O		O
			O		O		O	
	1	2	3	4	5	6	7	8

Lifting plan 3						O		
								O
				O				
							O	
					O			
			O					
	1	2	3	4	5	6	7	8

Lifting plan 4			O	O				O
			O				O	O
						O	O	O
					O	O	O	
				O	O	O		
			O	O	O			
	1	2	3	4	5	6	7	8

Lifting plans: double cloth and raised tubes

Lifting Plan 5	X	X		0		0		0	Lifting Plan 6				0		0		0
		X									X	0	0	0	0	0	0
	X	X	0		0		0					0		0		0	
	X									X		0	0	0	0	0	0
	1	2	3	4	5	6	7	8		1	2	3	4	5	6	7	8
Lifting plan 7						0			Lifting plan 8			0	0				0
								0				0				0	0
		X	0	0	0	0	0	0			X	0	0	0	0	0	0
				0											0	0	0
							0							0	0	0	
	X		0	0	0	0	0	0		X		0	0	0	0	0	0
					0								0	0	0		
			0									0	0	0			
		X	0	0	0	0	0	0			X	0	0	0	0	0	0
						0						0	0				0
								0				0				0	0
	X		0	0	0	0	0	0		X		0	0	0	0	0	0
				0											0	0	0
							0							0	0	0	
		X	0	0	0	0	0	0			X	0	0	0	0	0	0
					0								0	0	0		
			0									0	0	0			
	X		0	0	0	0	0	0		X							
	1	2	3	4	5	6	7	8		1	2	3	4	5	6	7	8

Lifting plan 5: Double cloth in plain weave. The ground warp is on the top and the pleat warp on the back.

Lifting plan 6: Double cloth in plain weave. The ground warp is on the back and the pleat warp is on the top.

Lifting plan 7: Double cloth with the pleat warp on top. The ground warp is woven as a plain weave on the back. The pleat warp is woven as a satin on the top. Because the plain-weave structure is a closer and tighter weave than the satin weave, you will use one pick for the ground warp, followed by two picks for the pleat warp. If you weave the cloths at equal rates the structure of the pleat warp will be open in appearance and the weft yarn will not be held firmly and will tend to slip out of place.

Lifting plan 8: Double cloth with pleat warp on top. The ground warp is woven as a plain weave on the back. The pleat warp is woven on the top as a 3 × 3 twill. As with Plan 7, the weft ratio is 1:2, one pick for the ground warp followed by two picks for the pleat warp to compensate for a more open weave.

Top: The pattern woven into the ground has been echoed in the pleats. Both the ground and pleat warp are cotton.

Bottom: Both the ground and pleat warp are spun silk. The ground is woven in a twill weave and the pleats are made using a distorted weft structure.

POCKETS

It is possible to weave pockets with side openings as part of the cloth design. In basic terms, a pocket is a tube that is closed on one side. A minimum of six shafts are needed to produce the structure. Two warps are required – one to form the ground cloth, and the other to make the pocket, or pockets. Each warp should be wound onto a separate beam.

In Threading plan 4, four shafts are used for the ground cloth – 1, 2, 3 and 4, indicated by an X. The ground warp on shafts 3 and 4 will be used to close the pocket on one side. The pocket warp O is on shafts 5 and 6.

Woven pocket using wool yarn.

Threading plan 4

Shaft																				
6								O								O				
5						O								O						
4										X		X								
3									X		X									
2		X		X			X								X			X		X
1	X		X		X								X				X		X	

----repeat---- ----repeat---- ----repeat---- ----repeat---- ----repeat----

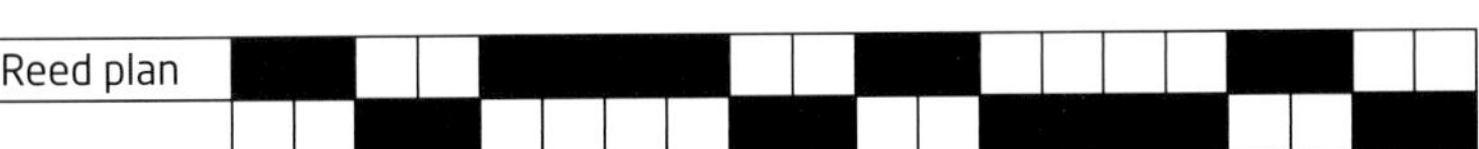

Reed plan

Lifting plan 1		X		X		O	Lifting plan 2				X		O
1	X		X		O				X		X	O	O
2		X		X		O				X		O	
3	X		X		O			X		X		O	O
4	1	2	3	4	5	6		1	2	3	4	5	6

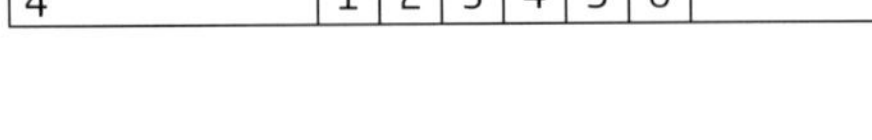

HOW TO WEAVE THE POCKETS

There will be two pockets formed using Threading plan 4 – one that has a left-hand opening, and one that has a right-hand opening. You will need to use two separate shuttles when weaving Lifting plan 2 – one for the ground weave pick and one for the pocket.

1. Use Lifting plan 1 to weave the ground and the pocket cloth together.

2. Use Lifting plan 2 to form the pockets. The first pick in the pattern weaves the ground, and the second pick weaves the pocket. Shafts 3 and 4 are used when weaving each cloth. This traps the weft when weaving the pocket warp, and closes the pockets down one side. The left-hand pocket will be closed on the right edge, and the right-hand pocket will be closed on the left edge.

3. Use Lifting plan 1 to weave the cloths together and close the pocket.

STRENGTHEN THE EDGES

When making pockets, remember that they are individual cloths in their own right, and will need strengthening at the edge to keep them neat. To make the edges denser, when threading the yarn for the pocket section, put two ends of warp yarn through the first six heddles at the start (shafts 5 and 6). If you are mirroring the pocket as in Threading plan 4, put two ends of yarn through the last six heddles to finish the pocket.

RIBBONS

You can weave a narrow band on top of a ground cloth, running vertically down the weave on top of the ground warp. If it is stitched to the ground down its centre, it will give the impression of a superimposed ribbon. The effect is greatly enhanced if there is a contrast in surface between the two warps. Use a fine, shiny yarn such as silk or viscose for the narrow warp, and a coarse or matt yarn such as linen, wool or cotton for the ground warp.

You will need a minimum of six shafts to achieve the effect. The warp ends used to stitch the ribbon to the ground cloth will need to be allocated their own two shafts, as will the ribbon warp and the ground warp.

The ground warp and the stitching ends will be wound onto one beam, and the narrow ribbon warp will be wound onto a second beam.

The ground warp is on shafts 1 to 4 and is indicated with an X. The threads on shafts 3 and 4 are used to stitch the ribbon warp to the ground. The threads on shafts 5 and 6 form the ribbon and are indicated with an O.

Threading plan 5

Shaft																										
6							O			O			O			O			O			O				
5						O			O			O			O			O			O					
4														X												
3											X															
2		X		X				X												X				X		X
1	X		X		X												X						X		X	

----repeat---- --------repeat-------- ----------repeat----------

Reed plan	■	■			■	■	■	■	■	■							■	■	■	■	■	■			■	■
			■	■							■	■	■	■	■	■							■	■		

Lifting plan 1				X		O
				X		
		X		X	O	O
			X			O
			X		O	
	X		X		O	O
	1	2	3	4	5	6

In Threading plan 5, because the warp yarn is finer than the narrow ribbon band, there are twice as many ends to the cm/inch to the ground warp. So if the ground warp is 10epc (24epi), the ribbon warp will be 40epc (48epi).

You can have any number of ribbon warps across the width of the ground cloth. When weaving the fabric you will need a separate shuttle for each ribbon warp, and one for the ground. If the ribbon warps are very narrow, a bobbin for each will be easier to handle.

HOW TO WEAVE THE RIBBON

Because the warp yarn used for the ribbons is finer than the ground yarn, you will need to weave one pick of ground to two picks of ribbon.

- The first pick in the lifting plan will weave the ground cloth.
- The second and third picks weave the ribbon. Shaft 3 is lifted for both picks.
- Pick four in the lifting plan weaves the ground cloth.
- The fifth and sixth picks weave the ribbon. Shaft 4 is lifted for both picks.

WORKING ON THE EDGES

As for pockets, remember that narrow band pleats or ribbons are individual cloths in their own right, and will need strengthening at the edges to keep them neat.

To make the edges denser, when threading the yarn for the narrow band or ribbon section, put two ends of warp yarn through the first six heddles at the start (shafts 5 and 6), and two ends of warp yarn through the last six heddles at the finish of the ribbon.

Alternatively, you could make a feature of the edges by using a textured or thicker yarn in the first and last two heddles when threading the narrow band or ribbon warp.

You will still be able to weave pleats, double cloths and raised tubes using the threading plan for the ribbons. The warp on shafts 5 and 6 will form the pleats or raised tubes, and the warp on shafts 1 to 4 will form the ground. Make the ribbon warp (or warps) longer than the ground warp to allow for the extra length used if you are intending to experiment with the additional structures.

TROUBLESHOOTING

WARP WINDING

Retaining the cross

When you have wound the warp to the correct number of ends, retain the cross created while winding the warp. This is so you can record the sequence in which the ends are wound and will be needed when you spread the warp in the raddle, and when you thread the ends through the shafts. Before removing the warp from the warping mill, use a length of strong yarn, about 30cm (12in), to retain the cross at the top and bottom of the mill. On the left-hand side of the cross, thread one end of the strong yarn from the front to the back, then, bring it back to the front on the right- hand side of the cross. Tie the two ends firmly together. When you begin to spread your warp in the raddle, the strong yarn is replaced by two 'cross sticks', which are secured to each other at either end. Leave a gap of approximately 5cm (2in) between the sticks to allow you to count the threads efficiently. The cross sticks should be kept in the warp throughout the weaving process.

Avoiding knots in the warp yarn

If a knot appears in the yarn when you are winding the warp, it is best to remove it at the warp making stage.Take the yarn back to the posts at the start or finish of the warping mill – whichever is closest. Cut out the length of yarn including the knot and re-tie the ends. By tying the knot at the start or finish the length of warp, you will avoid the knot showing in your weaving, and prevent it from possibly causing an obstruction in the reed whilst weaving.

SPREADING THE WARP IN THE RADDLE

Correcting a warp winding mistake

If, when you dent your warp ends in the raddle, you find that you have miscounted and missed out a thread or a number of threads, then it is easy to add the missed ends at this stage in this way: tie a new thread to the beam in the place it is missing from; pass it through the raddle in the correct dent and through the cross sticks, and take it to the full length of the warp; repeat the procedure for each missing end.

If the mistake is not noticed until you are threading the warp, then you can replace individual ends in this way: wind a quantity of the missing warp yarn onto a bobbin; thread the end through the cross sticks and through the eye of the heddle in the usual way; with the bobbin at the back of the loom, place a dress makers pin through the yarn on the bobbin, and wrap the warp end around to secure it; attach a small weight to the end to put it under the same tension as the rest of the warp.

DENTING THE WARP IN THE REED

Creating a firm edge to the weaving

Your hands and shuttle are in constant contact with the outer warp ends as you weave, which will weaken them and can cause breakages. To help prevent this, you can double dent the edges. Double denting adds density to the yarn and strengthens the edges. When planning your warp, so that you do not lose width from your warp, you can add additional threads in the same type and colour at the start and finish of the warp winding.

THREADING THE WARP

Dealing with unused heddles

There are usually additional heddles on the shafts that you will not use in your threading plan. If your loom has metal heddles, to avoid the unused ones at the side of the weaving rubbing and weakening the warp ends, tie them back to the side of each shaft with a strong yarn.

Correcting missing a shaft in the threading sequence

If the sequence is shaft 1, 2, 3 then 4, for example, you may accidentally miss shaft 4 from the second repeat: 1, 2, 3, 4. 1, 2, 3. 1, 2, 3, 4. This will mean that two ends will lift at the same time – on shaft 3 at the end of the second repeat and shaft 1 at the beginning of the third repeat.

Make a replacement heddle on shaft 4 in the position it was missed in the repeat, using a strong smooth yarn such as a 2/3 cotton. Wind a quantity of the missing warp yarn onto a bobbin. Thread the end through the cross sticks and the yarn heddle and then through the reed. This will result in there being an extra end in the dent, which will show as a dense line in the weaving. To prevent this, you can re-dent the warp for a perfect finish.

Correcting threading consecutive ends on the same shaft

If the sequence is shaft 1, 2, 3 then 4, for example, you may accidentally thread two ends on shaft 2 and missed shaft 3 in the second repeat: 1, 2, 3, 4. 1, 2, 2, 4. 1, 2, 3, 4. When you weave there will be two ends lifting at the same time. Make a replacement heddle on shaft 3 in the position it was missed in the repeat,using a strong smooth yarn such as a 2/3 cotton. Pull out the end from the threading mistake on shaft 2 – tie on additional yarn if the end is too short to re-thread and tie on.Thread through the eye of the yarn heddle and re-dent.Tie the end to the front stick attached to the beam.

DENTING MISTAKES

Correcting missing a dent or putting too many ends through a dent

This will show as an open line through the weaving if you have missed a dent, or as a dense line if you have put too many ends in one dent.

You will need to re-dent from the place that you made the mistake. If the mistake is to the right of the centre, then pull out the warp ends to the right and re-dent from left to right. If the mistake is to the left of the centre, then pull out the warp ends to the left and re-dent from right to left.

Correcting crossed ends in the reed

As you are denting, you may by mistake take two ends in the wrong sequence, crossing them over the other threads. It will be obvious as you begin weaving as they will interfere with an open clear shed. The crossed ends will either be lifted at the wrong time, or will cause other threads to lift at the wrong time. The shuttle will not be able to pass through the shed cleanly and could break warp ends as you weave, or the weft will not cross the end correctly and show up as a mistake in the weaving. Locate the denting mistake and pull out the twisted threads from the reed. Re-dent in the correct order and re-tie to the stick attached to the beam.

PROBLEMS WITH THE WARP

Dealing with loose ends

If after tying on there are a few loose ends that are not weaving in to the cloth correctly, locate the loose end and with a dress makers pin pull the slack back to the woven cloth. Pin into the cloth horizontally.

Dealing with broken ends

A warp thread may break for several reasons: a slack tension where the end is not raised sufficiently causing the shuttle to cut through it; a weak place in the yarn; a mistake in the denting causing the shuttle to hit and cut through the warp end. If you experience broken ends remember that they should be repaired immediately to prevent the broken end causing further damage by twisting itself around other warp threads, restricting other ends from lifting sufficiently for the shuttle to pass through, leading to more broken threads. Always use the same type and colour of yarn for the repair.

To repair a break in front of the heddle: pull the broken end attached to the weaving through the reed to the fell of the cloth; tie on a mending end securely to the broken warp end; trim the knot and re-dent through the reed; pin a dress makers pin through the cloth horizontally – following the weft – directly in front of the repaired end; wrap the mended end around the pin in a figure of eight to secure it and then continue to weave.

To repair a break in behind the heddle: pull the broken end attached to the weaving through the reed to the fell of the cloth; if the breakage occurs behind the heddle, trace the end back to the place it sits in the cross sticks; tie on a mending ensuring that it is long enough to attach to the front of the weaving; trim the knot and thread the repaired end through the empty heddle and through the reed; wrap the mended end around the pin in a figure of eight to secure it and then continue to weave.

When the fabric is removed from the loom, remove the pin and darn both ends through to the back of the cloth and trim.

PROBLEMS IN THE WEFT

Tensioning the weft

If you pull the weft yarn too tightly it will cause the weaving to become narrower than the planned width. The ends at the edge of the cloth will rub against the metal wire in the reed and break. But, if there is not sufficient tension in the weft, then loops will appear at the edge of the weaving.

Feel the tension of the weft yarn by holding your thumb over the eye of the shuttle – the eye should be facing you. When you feel a light tension in the yarn, place the pick with the baton to the fell of the cloth. If there is still a loop of yarn at the edge, gently pull the excess through before you change to the next lift.

Tying in the weft
keep the edges neat and avoid dangling threads at the edge of the cloth – when you begin to weave, or when the bobbin runs out or you want to introduce a new yarn or colour – you can bind the weft into the weaving.

When starting to weave, with your first pick, leave about 2.5cm (1in) of weft yarn at the side of the warp. When you open the shed for your second pick, weave in ½" (1.5cm) and pull the excess through to the back of the weaving. Pass the shuttle across the width of the open shed. Change sheds and continue to weave.

When introducing a new bobbin, you will need to tie in the end of the last pick. At the end of a bobbin, leave a length of yarn free at the edge of the cloth. With a new full bobbin in the shuttle, open the shed for the next lift in the pattern. Weave in the end from the spent bobbin – about 1.5cm (½ in) is sufficient – and pull the remainder through to the back of the cloth.Through the same shed, pass the shuttle with the new bobbin from the opposite side to where the last bobbin ran out, leaving about 2.5cm (1in) of yarn at the edge. Change sheds and weave in the loose thread left from the first pick of the new bobbin for about 1.5cm (½in). Pass the shuttle through the same shed and continue to weave.

GLOSSARY

Back cloth: weaving that forms the reverse of a double-cloth construction.

Batten: or 'sley' or 'beater'. It holds the reed and is used to position the weft yarn when weaving.

Beam: roller on which the warp yarn is wound at the back of the loom, and the woven cloth at the front of the loom.

Beater: *see* 'batten'.

Beating-up: action of the reed as it positions each pick of weft to the fell of the cloth.

Bedford cord: weave structure with clearly defined vertical ribs.

Block draft: term used when a number of shafts are nominated for a group of ends, and a second, third or fourth set of shafts are nominated to further groups of ends.

Bobbin: tube or spool that holds the weft yarn for use in a boat or roller shuttle.

Brighton honeycomb: similar in appearance to the honeycomb structure, but is created using a straight. The texture of the weave in a Brighton honeycomb is less regular than that in the traditional honeycomb.

Corduroy: cut-pile fabric usually formed of a straight line of floats that are cut when the cloth is removed from the loom (this may happen on the loom in industry).

Cramming and spacing: when the density of the yarn in the reed is varied. For a dense fabric, the ends per cm/inch are increased from the norm (crammed), and for a light, open fabric the ends per cm/inch are reduced (spaced).

Cross: or 'lease' Crossing of the warp yarn between the warp posts during winding to keep the ends in order when threading.

Cross sticks: or 'lease sticks'. Used to retain the cross or lease created when winding the warp.

Cutting line: the warp threads that divide the ribs in Bedford cord and corduroy structures.

Dent: space between each metal intersection in the reed. The spaces in the raddle are also called dents.

Denting: or 'sleying'. Action of pulling the warp threads through the reed.

Denting plan: required if a feature such as spacing and cramming in the warp is used. The plan shows the number of warp ends in each dent.

Draft: 1) or 'threading plan', or in American English the 'draw-in'. Indicates which warp end is threaded on to which shaft and in what order. 2) American-English term for the instructions of the threading, lifting and weave plan, as well as the treadle tie-up and treadling sequence.

Draw-down: or 'weave plan'. Drawing of the weave structure usually produced on point paper.

Dressing the loom: setting up the loom for weaving. This includes spreading the warp onto the beam, threading, denting (sleying) and tying on the warp.

End: individual warp thread.

End and end: warp sequence that has either two colours or two types of yarn alternating.

EPCM and EPI: ends per cm or inch.

Face cloth: front of a double-cloth construction.

Fell: edge of the cloth that is nearest to the reed.

Float: warp or weft threads that pass over two or more threads of the opposite set.

Float: cloth fault. Caused either by mistakes in the threading plan, reed plan or lifting plan, or poor warp tensioning.

Floats: collection of threads sitting on the surface of a ground cloth that are pinned down at prescribed intervals to create a shape or pattern.

Gauze: open, lacy weave such as mock leno.

Ground cloth: firmly woven cloth that acts as a base for figures and shapes formed by additional warp or weft threads.

Ground ends: warp threads used for the ground warp when creating an extra warp or weft patterned fabric.Heddle: or 'heald'. Made of metal or cord with an eye in the centre through which a single warp end is threaded. They are suspended on the shafts.

Honeycomb weave: or 'waffle weave'. Formed by arranging warp and weft floats in a diamond. A course of plain weave outlining the diamond formation pins down the floats.

Hopsack weave: or 'basket weave'. Based on an extension of plain weave where, rather than one thread, two or more threads are used as one unit.

Interchange: when weaving a double cloth, it is when one cloth interchanges with the other so that the face cloth is woven on the back, and the back is woven on the face.

Lifting plan: or 'peg plan' for a dobby loom, or 'treadle plan' with tie-up for a treadle loom. Shows which shafts to lift and in what order.

Medallion: round or oval shape formed when weaving a distorted weft structure.

Mock leno: weave structure that results in a slightly perforated cloth, giving a lacy effect.

Pick: individual weft thread.

Pick and pick: weft sequence that has either two colours or two types of yarn alternating.

Plain weave: or 'tabby'. It is the simplest of the weave structures. The plain-weave construction is uniform and is based on a repeat unit of two warp ends and two weft picks crossing over and under each other in alternate order.

Point draft: threading plan that reverses at the point it reaches the last shaft being used in the sequence. On six shafts the order is shaft 1, 2, 3, 4, 5, 6, 5, 4, 3, 2.

Point paper: or 'graph paper'. Squared paper used to plan out the weave.

PPCM or PPI: picks per cm or inch.

Raddle: or 'spreader'. Resembles a large comb with 'dents' of equal size, divided by metal bars or wooden rods. The warp threads are divided evenly into the dents.

Railroading: used to describe a fabric that is designed through the weft and turned through 90 degrees when taken from the loom. A horizontal stripe will become a vertical stripe when the woven fabric is railroaded.

Reed: comb that has metal intersections, and is used to divide the warp yarn evenly across the front of the loom. It is housed in the sley and beats the weft yarn to the fell of the cloth.

Reed hook: flat hook used to pull the warp ends through the reed when denting.

Reed plan: indicates how many warp threads are passed through each dent in the reed.

Repeat: when an identical sequence is reproduced more than once consecutively.

Sateen weave: structure formed by breaking the twill order. These fabrics typically have an unbroken cloth surface, with a preponderance of weft picks covering the warp threads.

Satin weave: structure formed by breaking the twill order. These fabrics typically have an unbroken cloth surface, with a preponderance of warp ends covering the weft threads.

Seersucker: or 'crinkle cloth' has distinctive puckered areas in contrast to stable areas within the finished fabric. The effect is normally formed as vertical stripes.

Selvedge: or 'selvage'. Edge on the left- and right-hand side as the fabric is woven. They are often reinforced with additional warp threads.

Sett: number of ends per cm/inch, which determines the density of the weaving.

Shaft: or 'harness'. Frame on which the heddles are suspended.

Shed: the opening formed by raising or lowering of the shafts when weaving. It is the space through which the shuttle passes.

Shuttle: used to carry the bobbin on which the weft yarn is wound, and passes through the raised warp threads when weaving. The most common type of shuttle is a boat or roller shuttle. A stick shuttle is used for thicker yarns.

Sley: *see* 'batten'.

Sleying: *see* 'denting'.

Spreader: *see* 'raddle'.

Straight draft: where the warp ends are threaded consecutively on each shaft i.e. 1, 2, 3, 4, 1, 2, 3, 4 and so on.

Threading: or 'drawing in' or 'entering'. Threading the warp ends through the heddle eyes.

Threading plan: *see* 'draft'.

Tie-up: order in which the pedals or treadles are tied to the shafts.

Tram: single thread of loosely twisted silk – usually only 2–5 turns per inch (2.5cm).

Twill line: diagonal line formed when weaving a twill structure.

Twill weave: fabric with diagonal lines across the fabric formed by the structure.

Wadding end: thick warp end trapped between the ground cloth and weft floats, which add definition to a Bedford cord structure.

Wadding pick: thick weft pick trapped between the ground cloth and additional warp floats, which add definition to a horizontal or wavy Bedford cord structure.

Warp: lengthways threads of a cloth that run through the loom, individually called ends.

Warp-faced cloth: fabric that has a preponderance of warp threads on the surface of the cloth.

Warping board: board or frame with pegs to wind the warp to the desired length.

Warping mill: cylindrical frame. The warp yarn is wrapped around the mill in a spiral to the desired length.

Warping plan: shows how many ends are needed to make the warp and in what order to achieve the required width and design of the cloth.

Weave plan: *see* 'draw-down'.

Weft: the series of threads that pass horizontally from selvedge to selvedge between the warp threads, individually called picks.

Weft plan: shows how many picks of each colour/type of yarn are used in the weft of the design.

Weft-faced cloth: fabric that has a preponderance of weft threads on the surface of the cloth.

Yarn wrap: way to test yarns, colours and compositions before making the warp, by wrapping the threads around a strip of stiff card.

FURTHER READING

BOOKS ON WEAVING

Alderman, Sharon. *Mastering Weave Structures.* Interweave Books, 2008

Bengtsson Bjork, Brigitta and Ignell, Tina. *Simple Weaves.* Trafalgar Square Books

Chandler, Deborah. *Learning to Weave.* Interweave Press Inc., 1995

Dalgaard, Lotte. *Magical Materials to Weave: Blending Traditional and Innovative Yarns.* Trafalgar Square Books, 2012

Davison, Marguerite P. *A Handweavers Pattern Book.*

Dixon, Anne. *The Handweavers Pattern Directory.* A & C Black, 2008

Field, Anne. *Collapse Weave.* A & C Black, 2008

Goerner, Doris. *Part 1: Single Cloth Construction.* WIRA. British Technology Group.

———. *Part 2: Compound Structures.* WIRA. British Technology Group.

Hecht, Ann. *The Art of The Loom: Weaving, Spinning and Dyeing Across the World.* British Museum Press, 2001

Lundell, Laila and Elisabeth Windesjo. *The Big Book of Weaving.* Collins and Brown, 2008

Moore, Jennifer. *The Weavers Studio: Double Weave.* Interweave Press, 2010

Oelsner, G.H. *A Handbook of Weaves.* Dover Publications, 2011

Patrick, Jane. *The Weavers Idea Book: Creative Cloth on a Rigid Heddle Loom.* Interweave Press Inc., 2010

Phillips, Janet. *Designing Woven Fabrics.* Natural Time Out Publications, 2009

Richards, Ann. *Weaving Textiles That Shape Themselves.* The Crow wood Press, 2012

Selby, Margo. *Contemporary Weaving Patterns.* A & C Black, 2011

Sutton, Anne and Diane Sheehan. *Ideas in Weaving.* Hutchinson

Sutton, Anne. *The Structure of Weaving.* Hutchinson

Watson, William. *Advanced Textile Design.* Woodhead Publishing

———. *Textile Design and Colour.* Woodhead Publishing

Wilson, Susan: *Weave Classic Crackle and More.* Schiffer Publishing, 2011

BOOKS ON TEXTILES

Braddock Clarke, Sarah E. and Marie O'Mahoney. *Techno Textiles 2: Revolutionary Fabrics for Fashion and Design.* Thames and Hudson.

Braddock, Sarah E. and Marie O'Mahoney. *Techno Textiles.* Thames and Hudson

Clarke, Simon. *Textile Design.* Laurence King, 2011

Colchester, Chloe. *Textiles Today: A Global Survey of Trends and Traditions.*

Cole, Drusilla. *Textiles Now.* Laurence King, 2008

Gillow, John and Bryan Sentence. *World Textiles: A Visual Guide to Traditional Techniques.* Thames and Hudson, 2005

Hallett, Clive and Amanda Johnston. *Fabric for Fashion: The Swatch Book.* Laurence King, 2010

———. *Fabric for Fashion.* Laurence King, 2010

Hemmings, Jessica. *Warp and Weft: Woven Textiles in Fashion*, Art and Interiors. Bloomsbury, 2013

McCarty, Cara and Matilda McQuaid. *Structure and Surface: Contemporary Japanese Textiles.* The Museum of Modern Art.

Nuno. *Boro Boro.* Nuno Nuno Books

———. *Fuwa Fuwa.* Nuno Nuno Books

———. *Kira Kira.* Nuno Nuno Books

Quinn, Bradley. *Textile Designers at the Cutting Edge.* Laurence King, 2009

———: *Textile Visionaries: Innovation and Sustainability in Textile Design.* Laurence King, 2013

Wilson, Janet. *Classic and Modern Fabrics: The Complete Illustrated Source Book.* Thames and Hudson, 2010

BOOKS ON DESIGN

Cole, Drusilla. *The Pattern Source Book: A Century of Surface Design.* Laurence King, 2009

Martin, Raymond. *The Trend Forecaster's Handbook.* Laurence King, 2010

Smith, Paul. *You Can Find Inspiration in Everything.* Thames & Hudson, 2003

Steed, Josephine and Frances Stevenson. *Basics Textile Design 01: Sourcing Ideas: Researching Colour, Surface, Structure, Texture and Pattern.* AVA Publishing, 2012

INDEX

Italics refer to images

PICTURE CREDITS

4 Katie Foster; 5 Rachel Wallis; 6 'Sails' collection, Angharad McClaren; 7t Jonathan Saunders/Getty Images; 7b Willow/Mahlia Kent; 8 Ellen Hayward; 11–21, 25 photographs by Alan Duncan; 28 t Linda Hartshorn; 28 b 'Tabby' project, Asa Parsons; 29 t Nozipho Mathe; 29 b Rachel Wallis; 30 t Imogen Beoghton-Dykes; 30ml, b Fiona Sutherland; 30 mr Jenny Gordon; 31 t Katie Foster; 31 b Georgina Woolridge; 32 tl Emma Birtwistle; 32 br Sarah May Johnson; 33 t Sarah May Johnson; 33 m, b Ayse Simsek; 34 Mandy Lee; 36 b Rachel Wallis; photography by Alan Duncan; 38 t Laura Montandon; 38 b Samantha Ingle; 39 Lucie Fellows; 40 Mandy Lee; 42 Rebecca Caldwell; 44 Hanna Bowen; 46 Sarah May Johnson; 47 Hanna Bowen; 48 tl Emma Birtwistle; 48 tr Sarah Deamer; 48 mr Ellen Simpson; 48 bl, br, 49 Emma Burt; 50 Hanna Bowen; 52 t Mandy Lee; 52 b Katie Hale; 53 Emma Burt; 56 Elizabeth Hudson; 58 Anna Birtwistle; 60 tl, tr, bl Sarah May Johnson; 60 br Lucie Fellows; 61 tl, ml, bl Nicola Adams; 61 tr Lucie Fellows; 61 br Olivia Sammons; 62 tl, r Chelsey Jones; 62 bl Jaymini Bedia; 65tl, ml Jan Shenton; 65 tr, bl Chelsey Jones; 65 br Jennifer Gregory; 66 Jodie Hatton; 67 tl, tr Jennifer Gregory; 67 b Emma Birtwistle; 68 t Sarah Deamer; 68 b Jaymini Bedia; 69 l Ellie Hawkins; 69 tr, br Emma Burt; 71 Sarah Deamer; 72 Kirsty Morris; 74 Helen Foot; 75–6, 78–9 Kirsty Morris; 80, 82, 84–90 Jan Shenton; 93 Jaymini Bedia; 94 tl Georgina Woolridge; 94 bl, r Lindsey Smith; 95 l, br Katie Foster; 95 tr Fiona Deans; 96 tl Jenny Craddock; 96 tr Fiona Deans; 96 br Jan Shenton; 97 Emma Birtwistle; 99 Jaymini Bedia; 101 Jan Shenton; 102 Kirby Harris; 104 tl Emma Birtwistle; 104 tr Jenny Craddock; 104 bl Ketsarin Goodwin; 104 br Jaymini Bedia; 105 tl, br Emma Burt; 105 tr Jaymini Bedia; 108 Alice Pointon; 109 tl Charlotte Harris; 109 tr Ellie Hawkins; 109 bl Alice Pointon; 109 br, 110 tr, tl Kirby Harris; 110 b Jenny Craddock; 112 unknown; 113 photographs by Alan Duncan; 114 tl, tr Georgina Woolridge; 114 bl Jaymini Bedia; 114 br Ellie Hawkins; 115 tl Samantha Ingle; 115 bl Ellie Hawkins; 115 r Sarah Deamer; 116 unknown; 118 t Jennifer Gregory; 118 bl Anna Champeny (www.annachampeney.com); 118 br Jodie Hatton; 121 tl Jennifer Gregory; 121 tr Rebecca Caldwell; 121 bl Sarah May Johnson; 121 br Jodie Hatton; 126 Victoria Martoccia; 127 Jan Shenton; 129 Jennifer Gregory; 132–3 Megan Chamberlin; 135 Anna Champeney (www.annachampeney.com); 138 Jan Bowman; 139 Jan Shenton; 140 Katie Hale; 141 Charlotte Hoad; 146 Elizabeth Owen; 149 unknown; 150 Elizabeth Owen; 154 'Rhythm and Sequence', Teresa Georgallis 157 t Jenny Craddock; 157 m, b Katie Hale; 158–9 Sarah Deamer; 160 tl Katie Hale; 160 tr Amy Lee; 160 ml, mr Ellie Hawkins; 160 b Alice Pointon; 161 tl Lily Tennant; 161 tr, m, b Jan Shenton; 165 t Rebecca Caldwell; 165 bl Imogen Beighton-Dykes; 165 br Olivia Sammons; 166 tl Ellie Hawkins; 166 tr Chelsey Jones; 166 bl Nozipho Mathe; 166 br Nicola Adams; 167 t Jan Shenton; 167 b Nicola Adams; 168 Jan Shenton; 171 t, bl Sarah Stones; 171 br Jaymini Bedia; 173 Ellen Hayward; 174 t Anna English; 174 m, b Jennifer Gregory; 180 tl Nozipho Mathe; 180 tr, br Laura Winstone; 180 m Jan Shenton; 180 bl Alice Kennedy ; 181 Lauren Balding; 182 Annah Legg; 185 tl, tr Jan Shenton, 185 bl Jodie Hatton; 185 br Emma Burt; 187 Jan Shenton; 190, 191 t Annah Legg; 191 b Lisa Devonshire; 196 t Teresa Georgallis; 196 b Fiona Deans; 197 tl, bl Sarah Lynn; 197 r Lisa Devonshire; 199–201 Annah Legg; 202 'Twilight', Laura Thomas; 203 photographs by Alan Duncan; 204 'Tropical Fusion', Jan Bowman; 205 Rachel Wallis; 206 t Emily Whitesmith; 206 b Charlotte Hoad; 207 t Emily Whitesmith; 207 m Charlotte Hoad; 207 b 'Oriental Dawn', Jan Bowman; 208 t Sarah May Johnson; 208 bl Abigail Cooper; 208 br Chelsey Jones; 209 tl, bl, br Emma Burt; 209 tr Sarah May Johnson; 211 Lucie Fellows; 212 t Anna Warren; 212 bl Lisa Devonshire; 212 br Laura Montadon; 214 t Lisa Devonshire; 214 b Ellen Simpson; 215–216 Jan Shenton.

Unless otherwise indicated, all photographs by Alan Duncan, the author or the fabric designer.

All line drawings by Lily Tennant

ACKNOWLEDGEMENTS

A very big thank you to Lily for her drawings, to Alan for photographing the designs, and to all of the incredibly talented designers who generously allowed their work to be included in the book. The woven designs illustrated throughout are stunning examples that will, I am sure, inspire others to weave. Thanks also to Anne Townley and Sophie Wise for their support throughout the writing of this book.